COURTS IN CONFLICT

Courts in Conflict

INTERPRETING THE LAYERS OF JUSTICE IN POST-GENOCIDE RWANDA

Nicola Palmer

OXFORD
UNIVERSITY PRESS

OXFORD
UNIVERSITY PRESS

Oxford University Press is a department of the University of Oxford. It furthers the University's objective of excellence in research, scholarship, and education by publishing worldwide. Oxford is a registered trade mark of Oxford University Press in the UK and certain other countries.

Published in the United States of America by Oxford University Press
198 Madison Avenue, New York, NY 10016, United States of America.

First issued as an Oxford University Press paperback, 2019
ISBN 978-0-19-094189-5

Library of Congress Cataloging-in-Publication Data
Palmer, Nicola Frances, 1983- author.
Courts in conflict : interpreting the layers of justice in post-genocide Rwanda / Nicola Palmer.
pages cm
Includes bibliographical references and index.
ISBN 978-0-19-939819-5 ((hardback) : alk. paper)
1. Transitional justice—Rwanda. 2. Gacaca justice system—Rwanda. 3. Restorative justice—Rwanda.
4. Genocide—Rwanda. 5. Postwar reconstruction—Rwanda. I. Title.
KTD157.7.P35 2015
345.67571'0122—dc23

2014038581

Contents

Acknowledgments

THIS BOOK WAS made possible thanks to the remarkable generosity of many people and institutions. Thank you to the Rhodes Trust and the Vice-Chancellor's Fund at the University of Oxford without whose generous financial support I would not have been able to complete this research. In addition, my research in Rwanda was made possible thanks to the support of the Queen's College and the Faculty of Law at the University of Oxford, along with the American Society of International Law, the Economic and Social Research Council (ESRC), and the human rights organization, Redress.

For her intellectual guidance and full engagement with my work, I would like to acknowledge and wholeheartedly thank Liora Lazarus. For their valuable comments and insightful questions, thank you to my D.Phil examiners Kieran McEvoy and Ian Loader. Thank you too Blake Ratcliff, Alden Domizio, and the rest of the editorial staff at Oxford University Press (OUP) and the three anonymous reviewers who offered valuable feedback on the initial manuscript. In addition, the support and mentorship offered by Jonny Steinberg, Carolyn Hoyle, Peter Robinson, Jeremy Horder, and Larry Kaufmann has been invaluable: thank you. To my current colleagues at King's College London (KCL), a special thanks to Prabha Kotiswaran, Ben Bowling, Genevra Richardson, and Cian Murphy. Thank you too for the support offered by my two Deans, Timothy Endicott at the University of Oxford and David Caron at KCL.

For their insights and deep commitment to Rwanda, I remain hugely grateful to Nyanja Nzabamwita, Dick Prudence Munyashuli, Irenee Bugingo, Ngabo Kayijuka, and Valence Rukesha. I have learned an enormous amount from you all. I am also grateful for the assistance and insights offered by Lars Waldorf, Denis Bikesha, Everard O'Donnell, Richard Karegyesa, and Inneke Onsea.

While at Oxford, the intellectual community provided by Oxford Transitional Justice Research (OTJR) was both energizing and supportive, with particular thanks to Briony Jones, Julia Paulson, Par Engstrom, Teddy Harrison, James Upcher, and Emily Braid. For the opportunity to present this work in multiple forums, I would like to acknowledge, among others, the organizers of both the African Studies and OTJR Seminar Series at the University of Oxford, the Law and Society Association Annual meeting in San Francisco (2011), and The Legacy of the International Criminal Tribunal for Rwanda Conference hosted at University of Johannesburg in South Africa (2013). For their involvement since the start of the project, thank you Hannah Clayton, Alinda Vemeer, and Lucie Lambert. For their wisdom and stability in my early days in Oxford, I would like to acknowledge and thank Sindiso Mnisi Weeks, Salih Soloman, Makuena Leboela, and Hannah Tonkin. In addition, for the warmth of the Rhodes Scholar community, I would like to thank many people, with special mention of Miles Jackson and Rebecca Brubaker.

For much of the early writing, it was the unfailing support of the many residents of Western Road that made it seem possible. Thank you to Kate Orkin, Kirsty Bobrow, Janet Jobson, Joe Raimondo, Jane Reddick, Rich Armstrong, Neil Kruger, and Ryan Goss. To my family and friends, including those back in South Africa, thank you for still believing in me all these years later. Special thanks to my brother Richard Palmer, my grandparents, June and John Eller; all of my cousins; and my close friends Debbie Matthee, Ross Esson and Lucy O'Keeffe.

To my parents, Tally and Tony Palmer, thank you for the reading of countless numbers of drafts and for your unwavering love and support.

Finally, to Phil, with all my love, for being my partner on every step of this journey—thank you.

Map of Rwanda

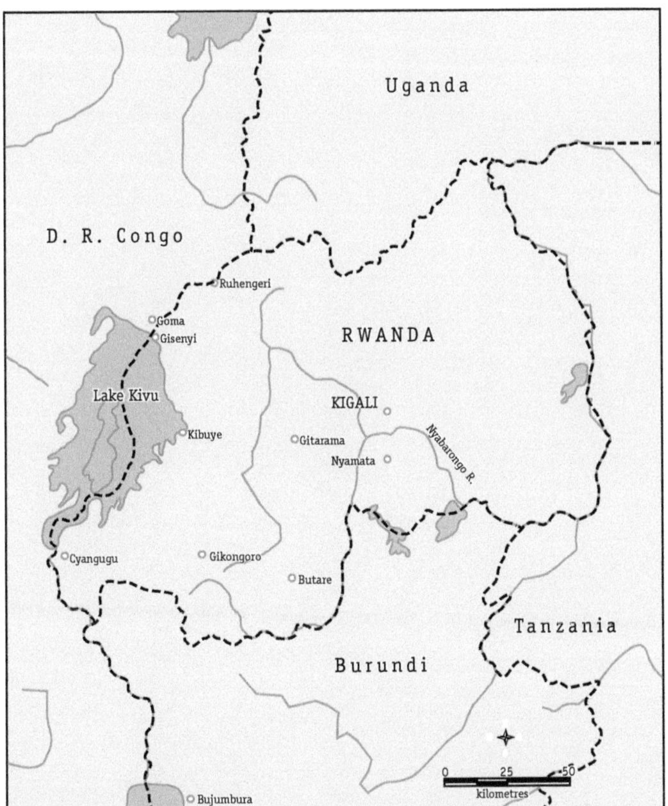

The research site in the Northern Province was located outside the town of Ruhengeri, and the site in the Western Province was outside the town of Kibuye.

Abbreviations

AI	Amnesty International
APROSOMA	Association pour la Promotion Sociale de la Masse
ASF	Avocats Sans Frontières
ASP	Assembly of State Parties
CDR	Coalition pour la Defence de la République
CUREC	Central University Research Ethics Committee
DCHR	Danish Centre for Human Rights
FAR	Forces Armées Rwandaises
HRW	Human Rights Watch
ICC	International Criminal Court
ICG	International Crisis Group
ICRC	International Committee of the Red Cross
ICTR	International Criminal Tribunal for Rwanda
ICTY	International Criminal Tribunal for the former Yugoslavia
IRC	International Rescue Committee
IRDP	Institute for Research and Dialogue for Peace
MDR	Mouvement Démocratique Républicain
MRND	Mouvement Révolutionnaire pour le Développement
MSM	Mouvement Social Muhutu
NGO	Non-governmental Organization
NURC	National Unity and Reconciliation Commission
OTP	Office of the Prosecutor
PARMEHUTU	Parti du Mouvement de l'Emancipation des Bahutu
PL	Parti Libéral

PSD	Parti Social Démocrate
PRI	Penal Reform International
RDF	Rwandan Defence Forces
RPF	Rwandan Patriotic Front
RTLM	Radio-Télévision Libre des Mille Collines
TRC	Truth and Reconciliation Commission
UN	United Nations
UNAMIR	United Nations Assistance Mission in Rwanda
UNSC	United Nations Security Council

Introduction

THIS RESEARCH BEGAN in a prison: a small concrete room in Ruhengeri, Northern Rwanda. Eugène, the man sitting at the interview table, was accused of participating in a massacre in the Ruhengeri High Court building on April 7, 1994. He was arrested in 1998, along with thousands of other Rwandans suspected of participating in the genocide. By 2006, eight years of incarceration had brought him into contact with a broad range of local, national, and international transitional justice processes set up in response to the crimes committed during the genocide and Rwandan civil war that ran from 1990 to 1994. He was charged under the 1996 domestic legislation outlawing the crime of genocide,[1] and his case was initially intended to go before the Special Chamber of the Rwandan Supreme Court. By 2004, he had appeared as a witness before the United Nations International Criminal Tribunal for Rwanda (ICTR),[2] established to try the most senior accused, and more recently, he had given evidence before a localized *gacaca* court.[3]

[1] Organic Law No. 08/96 of August 30, 1996 on the Organization of Prosecutions for Offences Constituting the Crime of Genocide or Crimes against Humanity Committed since October 1, 1990.

[2] United Nations Security Council Resolution 955 (8 November 1994) Statute of the International Criminal Tribunal for Rwanda UN Doc S/INF/50.

[3] *Gacaca* is a state-implemented but locally administrated transitional justice process that draws its name and some of its procedural aspects from a traditional Rwandan process of dispute resolution. Organic Law No. 40/2000 of 26/01/2001 Setting Up *Gacaca* Jurisdictions and Organizing Prosecutions for Offences Constituting the Crime of Genocide or Crimes against Humanity Committed between 1 October 1990 and 31 December 1994, Official Gazette of the Republic of Rwanda, March 2001 (*Gacaca* Law 2001). This initial legislation has been amended on five occasions. As discussed in Chapter 4, the most notable amendments occurred in 2004 and 2008.

These international-, national-, and community-level justice processes have operated concurrently in Rwanda, trying people accused of varying degrees of participation in the genocide. In written law the courts are complementary: they do not raise jurisdictional challenges to one another, and they purport to pursue similar objectives. Although often examined in isolation,[4] as Eugene's experience attests, overlap and engagement among these different layers of post-genocide justice has been impossible to avoid and is necessary to analyze.

The points of interaction among ICTR, the national courts, and *gacaca* are notable. All three courts address international crimes committed during a single conflict. In addition, there is considerable potential for movement of cases between the legal jurisdictions. Article 8 of the ICTR Statute acknowledges the concurrent jurisdiction of international and domestic prosecutions for serious violations of international humanitarian law.[5] Within this tiered judicial structure, the primacy of the ICTR means that it may formally request the national courts to defer to its competence.[6] However, as part of the ICTR's completion strategy under Rule 11 *bis* of its Rules of Evidence and Procedure, a designated Trial Chamber is empowered to transfer cases already before the ICTR "to competent national jurisdictions, as appropriate, including Rwanda."[7] Similarly, legislation in Rwanda has enabled the movement of cases from the national courts to *gacaca*.[8] Furthermore, the case law developed in one arena has been applied in another, and evidence raised in one court has been introduced and relied upon in the decisions handed down in the other jurisdictions, with 70 percent of the ICTR Trial Chamber decisions making reference to proceedings that occurred in the *gacaca* courts.[9]

---

[4] The majority of scholarship has looked at either the ICTR or the *gacaca* courts in isolation, while leaving the national courts broadly neglected. Among the limited pieces of comparative work on post-genocide justice, there is a strong orientation toward the ICTR and its international counterparts, the International Criminal Tribunal for the former Yugoslavia (ICTY) and the International Criminal Court (ICC). See Victor Peskin, *International Justice in Rwanda and the Balkans: Virtual Trials and the Struggle for State Cooperation* (Cambridge University Press 2008). Studies that have engaged with the concurrent Rwandan courts have been largely descriptive or have focused on assessing the courts against retributive or restorative notions of justice, addressing each of the courts as atomized legal formations. See Nicholas Jones, *The Courts of Genocide: Politics and the Rule of Law in Rwanda and Arusha* (Routledge-Cavendish 2009); Gerald Gahima, *Transitional Justice in Rwanda: Accountability for Atrocity* (Routledge 2013); Charity Wibabara, *Gacaca Courts versus the International Criminal Tribunal for Rwanda and National Courts* (Nomos 2014). Common across these approaches is a failure to account for the extensive set of interactions among the three courts.

[5] UNSC Res 955 (1994) Statute of the International Criminal Tribunal for Rwanda art 8 s 1.

[6] Ibid. s 2.

[7] UNSC Res 1503 (28 August 2003) UN Doc. S/RES/1503.

[8] Organic Law No. 13/2008 of 19/05/2008, Modifying and Complementing Organic Law No. 16/2004 of 19 June 2004 Establishing the Organisation, Competence and Functioning of the *Gacaca* Courts Charged with Prosecuting and Trying the Perpetrators of the Crimes of Genocide and Other Crimes against Humanity Committed between October 1, 1990 and December 31, 1994, Official Gazette of the Republic of Rwanda, May 2008 (*Gacaca* Law Modified 2008) art 1.

[9] This point of overlap is discussed in detail in Chapter 2 and is based on a review of all the Trial Chamber judgments until January 1, 2014. Official website of the International Criminal Tribunal for Rwanda, http://www.unictr.org, accessed June 20, 2014.

Yet, the points of contact among these three systems of justice extend well beyond the written law. While procedurally distinct, all three of the courts depend heavily on oral testimony and, as seen in Eugéne's case, they often require participation from a common group of witnesses. Most adult Rwandans have participated in at least one of these processes and, in some cases, two or three. The courts intersect through people's lived experience of post-genocide justice. This social reality means that the courts' participants are aware of and make direct comparisons among the courts. The legal concurrence of the three courts, the subject matter overlap, and the potential for transfer of cases among them means that the courts are aware of, examine, and impact upon each other's work.

A situation reminiscent of Lawrence Durrell's *Alexandria Quartet*[10] emerges, with one conflict, three courts, and four distinct groups of participants interpreting the practices of these courts: the lawyers and judges at the ICTR, those working for the Rwandan national courts, the *gacaca* personnel, and, crucially, the individuals over whom the courts have exercised authority. This book explores how these various participants understand the social practices of the three institutions in question. In doing so, it provides a hermeneutic analysis of the legal cultures of the post-genocide courts, drawing attention to the divergence in the objectives of these institutions and the tensions in their practice despite their legal compatibility. Such an interpretive cultural analysis enables a better understanding of the formal and informal interactions among the courts that sheds light on the legitimacy of these criminal justice processes.

Given the clear and unavoidable overlaps among the courts, the question of how concurrent spheres of criminal justice are interpreted, and whether they are able to complement one another, is crucial to the specific Rwandan context. It is also a question of wider application. Lawrence Rosen suggests, "it may be that it is in the law that the contest between a sense of the local and the global will receive some of its most serious testing."[11] He concludes his examination of law as culture with the proposition that "it is still an open question whether international law will simply be the law of the powerful or whether, local practice working around the edges of the formal law will be of the greater import."[12] Regardless, "the changes [between the local and the international] will be reciprocal despite the seemingly incommensurate array of powers"[13] Examining the interactions that have occurred among the ICTR, the national courts, and *gacaca* enables an exploration of the nature of this reciprocity.

---

[10] Lawrence Durrell, *Balthazar (Alexandria Quartet)* (Penguin Books 1958). The *Alexandria Quartet* is a tetralogy of novels that present four perspectives on a single set of events. As Durrell explains in his preface to the second of the four novels, *Balthazar,* the novels aim to explore relativity and the notions of continuum and subject-object relations, as the interpretations of events differ across participants and change over time.

[11] Lawrence Rosen, *Law as Culture: An Invitation* (Princeton University Press 2006).

[12] Ibid. 167–168.

[13] Ibid. 168.

Mapping the current literature on transitional justice and international criminal law highlights the continued and extensive interaction among multiple justice processes established in response to specific instances of extraordinary violence. In this context, Rwanda provides an early example of multilevel judicial responses, a practice that has increasingly arisen through the work of the International Criminal Court (ICC). A brief discussion of these writings prior to laying out the full argument of the book supports the value of pursuing a historically grounded and interpretive approach to examining Rwanda's concurrent post-genocide courts while highlighting the broader relevance of a detailed country-specific study.

I. TOWARD AN INTERPRETIVE APPROACH TO TRANSITIONAL JUSTICE

Transitional justice emerged as a term to explain the exceptional use of law during periods of political change.[14] Mapping the scholarly trajectory of the use of this term makes visible three important trends in the current institutional responses to political violence. First, in addition to the initial communal objectives of political stability, national reconciliation, and democracy, more recently the literature on transitional justice examines the individualized goals of retribution, healing, restoration, and reparation. Second, bolstered by the advent of ICC, there is a growing focus on the nature of the violence itself. What starts to become apparent is that transitional justice increasingly refers to the use of law in response to exceptional violence, rather than the exceptional use of law as a way of consolidating democratic transition. Finally, states are only one player within a much larger transnational network of private actors, civil society groups, and international organizations that have become major drivers for both top-down and bottom-up transitional justice initiatives.

All three of these trends help to explain the increasing use of multiple concurrent or sequenced transitional justice institutions. A series of responses accommodates both a wider set of objectives and the strong drive to include criminal trials as a necessary part of dealing with particular types of extraordinary harm. Proliferating processes, objectives, and actors responding to the same violence increasingly characterize the practice of transitional justice. Inside these wider developments, the Rwandan post-genocide courts are an early example of concurrent transitional justice institutions engaging with one another over an extended period. An examination of what these courts have been understood to achieve enables a better explanation of the interactions among these institutions and moves the scholarship toward an interpretive approach to transitional justice.

While the criminal trials in Nuremberg in the wake of World War II remain a touchstone in the study of transitional justice,[15] the term itself was first invoked in the 1990s at

---

[14] Ruti G. Teitel, *Transitional Justice* (Oxford University Press 2000); Neil J. Kritz, *Transitional Justice: How Emerging Democracies Reckon with Former Regimes* (United States Institute of Peace 1995).

[15] Ruti G. Teitel, "Transitional Justice Genealogy" (2003) 16 Harvard Human Rights Journal 76.

the height of the "third wave" of democratization.[16] As a result, the early fault lines in the scholarship fell on whether criminal trials should be pursued in an effort to re-establish the rule of law[17] or if alternative processes such as truth commissions[18] or conditional amnesties[19] would be better placed to support rule-of-law development and the consolidation of democratic institutions. Notably, across these divides, the objectives of transitional justice were generally conceived at a collective level, associated with creating an overall historical record of abuse,[20] establishing functioning legal institutions,[21] or moving toward stability or national reconciliation.[22]

However, by the mid-2000s there was an increasing recognition of the nonlinear nature of most political transitions,[23] which lent support to the position that these exceptional justice initiatives should be examined within their specific political, social, and historical contexts.[24] Nonetheless, the objectives of transitional justice remained clearly tied to the overarching goal of democratization.[25] While, in practice, criminal trials, truth commissions, memorialization projects, and restorative justice processes were implemented with increasing frequency across the globe.

As the study and operation of transitional justice expanded, the early legalist drive toward criminal trials remained strong despite the absence of a general international legal obligation for a state to prosecute international crimes.[26] This continued move toward

---

16 Samuel P. Huntington, "The Third Wave: Democratization in the Late Twentieth Century" in Neil J. Kritz (ed), *Transitional Justice: How Emerging Democracies Reckon with Former Regimes*, vol 1 (United States Institute of Peace 1991).

17 Diane F. Orentlicher, "Settling Accounts: The Duty to Prosecute Human Rights Violations of a Prior Regime" (1991) 100 The Yale Law Journal 2537; Juan E. Mendez, "Accountability for Past Abuses" (1997) 2 Human Rights Quarterly 255.

18 Carlos S. Nino, "The Duty to Punish Past Abuses of Human Rights Put into Context: The Case of Argentina" (1991) 100 The Yale Law Journal 2619; Priscilla B. Hayner, *Unspeakable Truths: Facing the Challenge of Truth Commissions* (Routledge 2002); Mark Freeman, *Truth Commissions and Procedural Fairness* (Cambridge University Press 2006).

19 Kader Asmal, "Truth, Reconciliation and Justice: The South African Experience in Perspective" (2000) 63 MLR 1.

20 The central role of history was most forcefully argued in Hannah Arendt's criticism of the criminal trial of Adolf Eichamnn in Israel, in Hannah Arendt, *Eichmann in Jerusalem: A Report on the Banality of Evil* (Faber and Faber 1963). The contribution of the courts to a historical record was later identified as one of the broader objectives of transitional justice in Teitel, *Transitional Justice* 73.

21 Jack Snyder and Leslie Vinjamuri, "Trial and Error: Principle and Pragmatism in Strategies of International Justice" (2003) 28 International Security 5.

22 Jeremy Sarkin and Erin Daly, "Too Many Questions, Too Few Answers: Reconciliation in Transitional Societies" (2004) 35 Columbia Human Rights Law Review 661.

23 Thomas Carothers, "The End of the Transition Paradigm" (2002) 13 Journal of Democracy 5; Fionnuala Ní Aoláin and Colm Campbell, "The Paradox of Transition in Conflicted Democracies" (2005) 27 Human Rights Quarterly 172.

24 Teitel, "Transitional Justice Genealogy" 76.

25 David A Crocker, "Transitional Justice and International Civil Society: Toward a Normative Framework" (1998) 5 Constellations 492, 494; Sarkin and Daly, 687; Teitel, *Transitional Justice*, 5.

26 Antonio Cassese, *International Criminal Law* (Oxford University Press 2003), 302.

trials has been described as a "justice cascade"[27] and has been supported by the growing number of ratifications of the Rome Statute of the ICC.[28] Yet in focusing attention on the type of harm that makes a case legally admissible, the practice of the International Criminal Tribunal for the former Yugoslavia (ICTY), the ICTR, the hybrid courts, and more recently the ICC has played a key role in decoupling the use of criminal law from the notion of democratic consolidation. The objectives of these criminal proceedings have moved away from broader claims of democracy and the rule of law toward the more specific retributive, deterrent, or expressive functions ascribed to criminal law.[29]

In addition, the rise of international criminal law has been accompanied by a critical turn in transitional justice scholarship, challenging this dominant legalist stance and arguing, as Kieran McEvoy has, that courts are "but one element of a broader transitional process."[30] This has led to an increasing interest in bottom-up justice initiatives in the wake of political violence often established and supported by nonstate actors.[31] These shifts in the scholarship have resulted in a growing awareness of individual objectives of healing, forgiveness,[32] restoration, and reparation[33] while highlighting disagreements between global and local transitional justice objectives within an environment of diverse actors with multiple interests.[34]

The growing emphasis on pursuing multiple responses to political violence can be understood as one outcome of these general shifts. The concurrent or sequenced use of a

---

[27] Kathryn Sikkink, *The Justice Cascade: How Human Rights Prosecutions Are Changing World Politics* (Norton Series of World Politics ed, WW Norton and Company 2011); Ellen Lutz and Kathryn Sikkink, "The Justice Cascade: The Evolution and Impact of Foreign Human Rights Trials in Latin America" (2001) 2 Chicago Journal of International Law 1.

[28] Created by an international treaty, the ICC is instituted and governed by the Rome Statute. While the large number of ratifications of the Statute and promulgation of enabling domestic legislation certainly strengthens the international legal norm to prosecute these crimes, the Court's authority is consistent with how international criminal law has developed until this point. It derives its power through treaty law and, as was the case with the ICTY and ICTR, through the use of the Security Council's mandate to act in the interests of international of peace and security. While 122 countries are now party to the ICC, this does not establish a general obligation on nonparty states to pursue criminal trials for these violations. William Schabas, *An Introduction to the International Criminal Court* (3rd edn, Cambridge University Press 2007) 60–61.

[29] Rob Cryer et al., *An Introduction to International Criminal Law and Procedure* (2nd edn, Cambridge University Press 2010) 24–30.

[30] Kieran McEvoy, "Beyond Legalism: Towards a Thicker Understanding of Transitional Justice" (2007) 34 Journal of Law and Society 411.

[31] Kieran McEvoy and Lorna McGregor, "Transitional Justice from Below: An Agenda for Research, Policy and Praxis" in Kieran McEvoy and Lorna McGregor (eds), *Transitional Justice from Below: Grassroots Activism and the Struggle for Change* (Hart Publishing 2008).

[32] Phil Clark, *The* Gacaca *Courts, Post-Genocide Justice and Reconciliation in Rwanda: Justice without Lawyers* (Cambridge University Press 2010).

[33] Carla Ferstman, Mariana Goetz, and Allan Stephens (eds), *Reparations for Victims of Genocide, War Crimes and Crimes against Humanity* (Martinus Nijhoff Publishers 2009).

[34] Rosalind Shaw, Lars Waldorf, and Pierre Hazan, *Localizing Transitional Justice: Interventions and Priorities after Mass Violence* (Stanford University Press 2010).

number of justice processes incorporates both a broader set of transitional justice objectives and the clear drive to include criminal trials as a necessary part of responding to specific harms. In line with this thinking, a number of transitional justice scholars[35] and practitioners[36] have advocated for "holistic responses" to gross human rights violations, in which multiple institutions respond to a single set of violations. This is not to say that the scholarship has not been critical of incorporating both bottom-up and top-down justice initiatives, but rather to emphasize that, although there is a clear move toward using multiple justice interventions, there has been only limited engagement with how the processes might influence one another and to what extent they are compatible and mutually reinforcing. An interpretive method, as discussed below, offers one route to explore these interactions.

At the same time, the practice of the ICC and its specific reading of the principle of complementarity have supported these scholarly shifts. According to the Rome Statute of the ICC, the principle of complementarity establishes that a case will not be admissible before the Court if that same case is, or has been, genuinely investigated or prosecuted at the national level.[37] However, in practice, due to the ICC Chamber's narrow reading of what constitutes a case, finding that it must concern the same person and broadly the same conduct,[38] the involvement of the Court has encouraged domestic trials alongside, and in addition to, international prosecutions.

---

35 Scholars adopting very different research methodologies support the arguments in favour of "holism." An interesting example is to read the argument for a "transitional justice balance" among trials, truth commissions, and amnesties developed through a global database alongside the theoretical argument of taking a "thicker" reading of accountability in which amnesties can coexist with formal justice processes and complement nonjudicial enforcement mechanism such as truth commissions or restorative justice processes. See Tricia D. Olsen, Leigh A. Payne, and Andrew G. Reiter, *Transitional Justice in Balance: Comparing Processes, Weighing Efficiency* (U.S. Institute of Peace Press 2010) and Louise Mallinder and Kieran McEvoy, "Rethinking Amnesties: Atrocity, Accountability and Impunity in Post-conflict Societies" (2011) 6 Contemporary Social Science: Journal of the Academy of Social Science 107. In addition, scholars who are leading the critical discussions on international criminal law have recommended the use of multiple concurrent processes as a means of responding to some of the weaknesses in the purely legalistic response to atrocity. See M. Drumbl, *Atrocity, Punishment, and International Law* (Cambridge University Press, 2007).

36 Influential civil society actors such as the International Center for Transitional Justice (ICTJ) advocate the use of multiple justice processes in countries ranging from Tunisia to Colombia. See International Center for Transitional Justice (Vision and Mission Statement) http://ictj.org/about/vision-and-mission, accessed September 25, 2012.

37 Rome Statute of the International Criminal Court (adopted July 17, 1998, entered into force July 1, 2002) 37 ILM 1002. This admissibility rule is laid out in article 17; however, insofar as "complementarity" refers to the broader division of labor between national jurisdictions and the ICC, it is included in many articles of the Statute, including articles 1, 17, 18, 19, 20, 89(4), 90, 93(10), and 94.

38 *Prosecutor v William Samoei Ruto and Joshua Arap Sang,* (Judgment on the appeal of the Republic of Kenya against the decision of Pre-Trial Chamber II of 30 May 2011 entitled "Decision on the Application by the Government of Kenya Challenging the Admissibility of the Case Pursuant to Article 19(2)(b)) ICC-01/09-01/11, A Ch (30 August 2011): para. 47. According to the most recent admissibility decisions of the Court, "substantially the same conduct" is understood to comprise specific factual incidents in which

The practical effect of this approach is seen most recently in Libya where the case brought against Saif Al-Islam Gaddafi was held to be admissible at the international level because the conduct covered in the national proceeding against him were not sufficiently similar to the ICC's case against him.[39] Meanwhile, the case against his co-accused Abdullah Al-Senussi was found to address sufficiently similar conduct, leaving it within the domestic jurisdiction.[40] As a result, concurrent cases relating to overlapping factual incidents are expected to proceed at both the national and international level. Following a similar move toward concurrent proceedings, in Uganda, Thomas Kwoyelo, a middle-level rebel in the Lord's Resistance Army (LRA) was tried in a domestic war crimes chamber while the cases against the senior LRA leaders remain within the jurisdiction of the ICC.[41]

These developments in both transitional justice research and the practice of international criminal law highlight the increasing prevalence of a plurality of legal process, actors, and objectives and the limited examination of the interactions among these "plural forms of ordering"[42] that participate in the same social field. Turning to Rwanda, the question of which transitional justice objectives were given priority in the aftermath of the genocide and how multiple post-genocide criminal courts have operated in an overlapping social sphere are two distinct research questions that come out of this literature. An interpretive examination of these questions enables a deeply interconnected set of answers. To this end, this research pursues what Clifford Geertz describes as "an elaborate venture in . . . thick description."[43] As Geertz articulates in the familiar motif of the wink, it is through culture that the action of a wink, the physical closing of one eyelid, is ascribed meaning. In adopting an interpretive approach to transitional justice,

---

there is sufficient overlap with regard to particularly violent events and those that are significantly representative of the accused overall conduct. *Prosecutor v Saif Al-Islam Gaddafi* (Judgment on the appeal of Libya against the decision of Pre-Trial Chamber I of 31 May 2013 entitled "Decision on the Admissibility of the Case against Saif Al-Islam Gaddafi") ICC-01/11-01/11 A Ch, (21 May 2014) para 72 and *Prosecutor v Abdullah Al-Senussi* (Judgment on the Appeal of Mr. Abdullah Al-Senussi against the decision of Pre-Trial Chamber I of 11 October 2013 entitled, "Decision on the Admissibility of the Case against Abdullah Al-Senussi"), ICC-01/11-01/11-57, A Ch, (24 July 2014) para 75.

39 *Prosecutor v Saif Al-Islam Gaddafi* (Judgment on the appeal of Libya against the decision of Pre-Trial Chamber I of 31 May 2013 entitled "Decision on the Admissibility of the Case against Saif Al-Islam Gaddafi") ICC-01/11-01/11 A Ch, para 72.

40 Following the Chambers reasoning on the same person/same conduct test, it then went on to find that, in line with the second stage of a complementarity assessment, Libya was neither "unwilling nor unable" to genuinely undertake the trial.

41 For a detailed discussion of the relationship between this domestic trial and the ICC, see Sarah M.H. Nouwen, *Complementarity in the Line of Fire: The Catalysing Effect of the International Criminal Court in Uganda and Sudan* (Cambridge University Press 2013).

42 Sally Engle Merry, "Legal Pluralism" (1988) 22 Law & Social Review 869, 873.

43 Clifford Geertz, "Thick Description: Toward an Interpretive Theory of Culture" in Clifford Geertz (ed), *The Interpretation of Cultures: Selected Essays* (Fontana Press 1993) 6.

the question addressed in this book is: How, if at all, are the practices of Rwanda's post-genocide courts being understood?

The research reflected over the next six chapters provides a description of how transitional justice has been "produced, perceived and interpreted"[44] by judicial actors inside Rwanda's three post-genocide courts and within the country more broadly. The description of the ICTR, the national courts, and *gacaca* unravels the "socially established structures of meaning"[45] that render the legal practice of these courts intelligible. This interpretive endeavor is pursued through the collection of empirical data and, in doing so, allows for an "in-context" evaluation of the legitimacy of Rwandan transitional justice processes. Grounded qualitative research with the judges, lawyers, and citizens subject to the authority of the three post-genocide courts allows for the identification of patterns in how legal rules are used and regarded by officials and participants and how these views map onto or differ from the objectives attributed to transitional justice processes in the literature more generally.

How the judges and lawyers understand the courts' actions illuminates the legal cultures of these institutions. Such cultures are made up of the collection of ideas and training, practical experience, institutional wisdom, and professional common sense through which the judges and lawyers understand their work. Drawing on Geertz, David Garland argues that the aim of such an enquiry is to "uncover the structures of social action and the webs of cultural meaning"[46] within an institution in order to provide the proper descriptive basis for normative judgments. A detailed account of the cultures of the post-genocide courts enables a critical examination of the formal and informal interactions that have occurred among these different sites of justice, illuminating the means through which the courts have endeavored to establish their legitimacy.

This introduction lays out the argument of book and then discusses the methods used to pursue interpretive research into Rwanda's post-genocide courts. The book is structured as follows: Chapter 1 begins by situating the violence of the Rwandan genocide and the legal responses to it within a longer historical account of the development of the state, the role and use of ethnicity in political violence, and the exercise of power at the international, national, and local levels. In doing so, the chapter takes seriously the increasing scholarly and practical focus on the exceptional nature of political violence and draws attention to both the continuities and shifts in social control in Rwanda. It is argued that the construction of the Rwandan state in the nineteenth and twentieth centuries led to a small elite holding increasingly centralized power. The ethnic identities of Hutu and Tutsi provided a means of consolidating and contesting this power,

[44] Ibid. 7.

[45] Ibid. 12–13.

[46] David Garland, *Punishment and Modern Society: A Study in Social Theory* (Oxford University Press 1990) 10.

culminating in the extreme violence of the 1994 genocide. Rwanda is a highly centralized state; however, the state has not been as strong at its margins as it is described at the center. An analysis of the connection between local and centralized power is necessary to explain the spread and variation of the genocidal violence, and the implementation of state responses to that violence.

Chapters 2, 3, and 4 provide a thick contextual analysis of the practice of Rwanda's post-genocide courts during the transitional period following the 1994 violence. Detailed qualitative research inside the ICTR, the national courts, and *gacaca* shows that the mandate and initial objectives of these concurrent courts have both shaped and been shaped by their practice. The process is dialectic. What emerges in practice is that the three courts, despite being complementary in law, have been understood to pursue very distinct objectives. These objectives are far narrower than those initially espoused in the courts' founding documents or envisaged in the established literature on transitional justice. In part, the judges and lawyers explain this narrowing in what the courts have been understood to achieve in terms of a number of practical constraints on their work. However, in line with an interpretive approach to this empirical work, their ascription of meaning also illuminates the wider cultural context in which the decisions and activities of the courts have been situated.

As laid out in Chapter 2, the ICTR has been principally concerned with the development of international criminal case law. Chapter 3 shows that the national courts purport to have focused on internal legal reform, while Chapter 4 describes how personnel inside *gacaca* view their central contribution as having been toward obtaining a better local understanding of the conflict. It is arguable that, in this reading, the three courts could still complement one another, with the ICTR contributing to a global legal order, the national courts to the development of domestic judicial capacity, and *gacaca* to providing a local mechanism of truth-telling and accountability. However, the empirical data from within each court indicates that how one process is internally justified affects how the others are viewed and understood by the personnel working inside that particular post-genocide court. How the judges and lawyers understand their own work elucidates aspects of each institution's legal culture. It is within this specific legal culture that the work of the other courts is assessed. For example, the ICTR asserts its contribution to international criminal case law and, consistent with this understanding, criticizes the other two courts for their failure to conform to and develop such law. Similarly, within *gacaca*, the work of the ICTR and the national courts is understood in line with what the local courts themselves purport to have achieved. Actors within *gacaca,* seeing local "truth" and accountability as their central objectives, criticize the ICTR and the national courts for their failure to contribute to local understandings of why neighbors killed neighbors. Hence, how one process is justified affects how the others are viewed, understood, and engaged in practical terms.

The cumulative impact of the different institutional interpretations of transitional justice is that the courts have competed with one another. At points of formal interaction, such as the transfer of cases between two jurisdictions, each court has prioritized its own understood contributions to transitional justice, leading to both misunderstandings and direct competition. At points of informal interaction, such as those experienced by a group of Rwandan prisoners subject to the authority of more than one of the courts, all three transitional justice processes are critically compared.

The empirical analysis laid out in Chapters 2, 3, and 4 shows that we cannot assume that concurrent international, national, and local transitional judicial processes will be compatible even if they do not compete jurisdictionally. The ICTR, the Rwandan national courts, and *gacaca* have not dealt with three different conflicts; they have dealt with one conflict through three different mechanisms. Legal compatibility is insufficient to ensure a mutually reinforcing system of criminal justice for international crimes. Consequently, there is a need to foster cultural complementarity among concurrent international, national, and local transitional justice processes.

Chapter 5 explores why distinct legal cultures may have emerged inside the ICTR, the national courts, and *gacaca,* examining to what extent the objectives of the courts have matched the interests of the citizens over whom they have exercised authority. The nature of the transitional period means that the social structures being studied are undergoing substantial change. This change demands that a prime task of the research is the exploration—and sometimes the discovery—of emerging structures that help explain the relevant social behavior.[47] Chapter 5 argues that the distinct meanings ascribed to the work of the courts can usefully be explained as a process of legitimation. David Beetham's theory of legitimacy aids the examination of this social data, highlighting where and how the legitimacy of the three courts has been pursued and eroded.[48]

The legitimacy of the courts underscores the importance of the beliefs and interests, not only of those who hold power, but also those over whom such power is exerted. Among a group of Rwandan citizens, including those currently incarcerated, the practices of one court were routinely used as the basis to criticize the actions of the others, raising challenges for the legitimacy of transitional justice in Rwanda. The participants who were interviewed did not draw clear distinctions between what each court had been trying to achieve. All three of the courts were routinely measured against their ability to provide full information about the conflict, including the determination of individual involvement in the violence. The legitimacy of the ICTR, the national courts, and *gacaca* was strengthened when they were understood to respond to this need.

In summary, this book argues that the culture of transitional legal institutions impacts upon the legitimate exercise of power during transitional periods of rapid social, political, and legal change. An examination of how the actions of the ICTR, the national courts, and *gacaca* have been understood shows that the courts have embarked

---

[47] Barney G. Glaser and Anselm L. Strauss, *The Discovery of Grounded Theory: Strategies for Qualitative Research* (Aldine Pub. 1967) 235.

[48] David Beetham, *The Legitimation of Power* (Peter Jones and Albert Weale eds, MacMillan 1991).

on an active process of legitimizing their authority. However, in endeavoring to establish the legitimacy of their own actions, they simultaneously challenge the actions of the other courts. In order to avoid this competition, there is a need for more effective debate and criticism among the international, national, and local systems that responds to the shared beliefs, and common interests, of the people subject to the courts' authority. This theory of legitimating behavior explains the actions of international, national, and local courts during a transitional period, and is developed through detailed empirical research.

2. INTERPRETATION, EMPIRICAL RESEARCH, AND THE ROLE OF THEORY

To examine how the actions of the post-genocide criminal courts were being interpreted, I conducted qualitative empirical research over multiple periods of immersion at the ICTR and within Rwanda from June to September 2008, February to April 2009, and March to May 2012. Data was collected through semi-structured interviews, focus groups, participant observation, informal discussions, and the analysis of grey material[49] and case law. In total, this book draws on 182 interviews with decision-makers, lawyers, judges, and general participants within the ICTR, the criminal justice sector in Rwanda, and the National Service for Gacaca Jurisdictions (NSGJ).[50]

Before I embarked on this empirical study, my research was guided by a partial framework of what Glaser and Straus call "local concepts."[51] The choice of initial participants and the set of questions were drawn from the literature on transitional justice and international criminal law, academic writings on the Rwandan conflict, and personal experience of the work of the courts.[52] At the broadest level, all initial participants were required to have been involved in the post-genocide transitional justice processes as witnesses, accused, legal professionals, or administrators. I used semi-structured interviews to develop the selection of participants through the research process with the goal of establishing multiple comparison groups.[53] The institutional structures of the courts provided

---

[49] Within this book "grey material" refers to government reports, newspaper clippings, NGO summary reports, and documents that the author collected in Rwanda. These documents cannot be easily found through conventional channels such as publishers and libraries but the author has all original copies on file.

[50] Officially termed the National Service for Gacaca Jurisdictions, the direct translation from the French name Service National des Jurisdictions Gacaca (SNJG), personnel working inside the institution used the term "National Service for Gacaca Courts."

[51] Glaser and Strauss 45.

[52] Before starting this research, I was employed as an entry-level lawyer at the ICTR. Glaser and Strauss provide an interesting reflection on an academic who had worked as a taxi driver for a number of years and then conducted a study of the culture of compensation of taxi drivers. The authors argue that this academic was able to effectively draw on his early practical professional experience as it provided a "springboard for systematic theorizing." Glaser and Straus 252.

[53] Ibid. 47.

initial differentiation, allowing for the selection of individuals whom I expected to have similar opinions and of those whom I expected to have notably different ones.

Inside the ICTR, I conducted forty interviews with personnel across the four branches of the institution, namely Chambers, the Office of the Prosecutor (OTP), the Registry and the Defence Counsel and Detention Management Section (DCDMS). The participants included the current President of the ICTR Chambers, Judge Vagn Joensen; the previous Presidents, Judges Denis Byron and Eric Møse; Prosecutor of the ICTR, Justice Hassan Jallow; the Deputy Prosecutor, Bongani Majola; Acting Head of Prosecutions, Richard Karegyesa; and Senior Defence Counsel, Ben Gumpet. I expected greater commonality among participants within each section, and interviewed ten or more participants in each. As will be discussed in Chapter 2, what was most striking in the coding of this interview data were the similarities throughout these three groups of participants. The common understanding of the contribution of the ICTR to the development of an international legal order was key to illuminating the legal culture of the Tribunal.

Within Rwanda, I adopted an equivalent approach. To better understand the national courts, I drew on twenty-four interviews conducted with Rwandan judges and lawyers. The participants included the then Rwandan Minister of Justice, Tharcisse Karugarama; the former Prosecutor General, Martin Ngoga; the Chief Justice of the Supreme Court, Justice Sam Rugege; and the past and current Heads of the Genocide Tracking Unit, Jean-Bosco Mutangana and Jean-Bosco Siboyintore.[54] In addition, interviews were conducted with High Court and first instance judges, prosecutors, and private lawyers in Kigali, and in two districts in the Northern and Western Provinces.[55] The objective of this site selection was to account for rural and urban divides in the practice of the courts and to include data from areas with dramatically different experiences of the civil war and genocide.[56]

In examining *gacaca,* I interviewed and conducted informal discussions with fifty personnel involved in the local courts, including the Executive Secretary of the NSGJ,

---

[54] Fourteen of these interviews were conducted in conjunction with Phil Clark. In addition, after the initial analysis of the data, the material from four more interviews conducted by Clark in 2010 were added to the coding sheets to further explore the understood contribution of the national courts to the transitional period. I am enormously grateful for his insights and deep engagement with post-conflict justice in Rwanda, and the joint interviewing provided very rich research material. The footnotes will indicate when the interviews were jointly conducted.

[55] In 2004 Rwanda reorganized its administrative units. In terms of the 1994 administrative structure, the first rural district is located in Ruhengeri at the foothills of the Virunga National Park and the second is in Kibuye, located on the western border of Rwanda on Lake Kivu.

[56] The names of the districts have been removed to ensure the anonymity of some of the study's participants. The rural district in the Northern Province experienced early ethnic violence in the 1960s, in 1973, and at the start of the civil war in 1990. There were lower levels of violence there during 1994, but continued conflict in 1997–1998. In contrast, the rural district in the Western Province experienced both extreme genocide violence and high levels of refugee flows across the then-Zairian border.

Domitilla Mukantaganzwa, and Gratien Dusingizimana, Director of the Legal Support Unit.[57] Among these participants, there were two clear groups: first, those in positions of leadership within the NSGJ, along with the legal officers and local coordinators who oversaw the hearings; and second, a group of *inyangamugayo*[58] or *gacaca* judges who carry the weight of the trials at the local level—collecting evidence and judging cases at the trial and appeal stages. As with the national courts, I limited this local examination to the same two districts outside of the city, in the Northern and Western Provinces, supplemented by further comparative work in 2012 in the Southern Province. Coding of these tiers indicated important differences between how *gacaca* is being understood centrally and implemented locally. Throughout the research period, the social data was collected broadly. In addition to formal interviews and focus groups, I took detailed notes following informal discussions with a number of participants, and I attended nineteen *gacaca* hearings, the proceedings of which were simultaneously translated into English and transcribed by a Rwandan colleague. All of this material was analyzed and provides the empirical basis of this study.

The interviews were conducted with the express consent of the participants, following either a verbal or written explanation of the aims and structure of the research, as approved by the Central University Research Ethics Committee (CUREC) at the University of Oxford. The use of a recording device differed across participants. At the ICTR all interviews were conducted in English, and the majority of them were recorded using a digital device and subsequently transcribed. The interviews with senior national court and *gacaca* officials in Kigali were similarly carried out in English, and the use of a recording device varied according to participants' preferences. In rural areas, interviews were conducted through simultaneous translation between Kinyarwanda and English, and following the participants' expressed consent, I took detailed notes during the interviews.[59]

The words used by the particular participants in this empirical study are key to understanding the social institutions of the ICTR, the national courts and *gacaca*, and the cultural formations that surround the actions of these courts and give them meaning.[60] The concepts used by the interviewees to describe what they are trying to achieve "both reflect and constitute culture."[61] In initially placing the judicial actors at the center of the analysis, as has been most recently pursued by R.A. Wilson in his work on the role of history in international criminal trials, we "get the sense of law as a dynamic and, in some ways, even contingent process, shaped by rules and core principles . . . but also

[57] Seven of these interviews were conducted jointly with Phil Clark.

[58] *Inyangamugayo* is a Kinyarwanda term translating to "persons of integrity." It refers to the laypersons who preside as judges over the *gacaca* hearings. These judges were selected through popular vote in 2001; their role in the process is discussed in more detail in Chapter 4.

[59] The process of translation and its limitations is discussed in more detail in the next subsection.

[60] Engle Merry, 886.

[61] David Nelken, "Using the Concept of Legal Culture" (2004) 29 Australian Journal of Legal Philosophy 1, 10.

refashioned by the changing strategies of the legal actors."[62] What emerged from this interpretive approach is that the objectives of the ICTR, the national courts, and *gacaca* have both shaped, and been shaped by, the practice of the different legal institutions, leading to increased competition despite their legal compatibility.

The analysis of this empirical data was reflexive, in that it occurred while I was conducting the research and after stepping out of the research environment. As Lucia Zedner suggests in discussing a similar approach to criminological research, this allows for both the benefit of immersion in the local context and the possibility of crucial intellectual distancing.[63] I wrote a reflection on this process and its limitations while living in one of the rural research sites, and this gives insights into the practical experience of this interpretive method:

> A net sample; I have waded into this social puddle dragging a net of questions behind me, held together by delicate strings of access to various participants. I have caught in this net interviews, documents, newspaper articles, publications, scrawled words in grubby notepads, recorded words, typed words and images. I drag it back to Oxford to try to sort it out. To identify what the live issues are, to better understand how the system works. There are flaws in this method. The net of questions has holes in it. Information is lost. Some strings of netting are too close together and others too far apart. Something or someone that plays a crucial role in this system may slip through it or may never even pass by. The sampling area is vast. I have to select sites and do repeat samples in pursuit of a better understanding of the justice system in Rwanda. However, a description is not enough—it has to be extrapolated at some point.[64]

This extrapolation took the form of coding the empirical material. Comparing individual accounts of the post-genocide courts' actions enabled the identification of common understandings across the interviews and focus groups. Although commonality is key to identifying recurrent meanings ascribed to the courts' work, this coding was done with an eye not only for the points of agreement but also for those of discord and dissent. In Chapters 2, 3, and 4 a discussion of the broad categories of agreement and an examination of points of difference is undertaken to provide a "thick description" of how particular people, at a particular time, placed their actions "in some sort of comprehensible meaningful framework."[65] This framework structures the legal culture of the ICTR, the Rwandan national courts, and *gacaca*, and provides the interpretive basis to examine and

---

62 R.A. Wilson, *Writing History in International Criminal Trials* (Cambridge University Press 2011) 109.

63 Lucia Zedner, "Comparative Research in Criminal Justice" in Lesley Noaks, Mike Maguire, and Michael Levi (eds), *Contemporary Issues in Criminology* (University of Wales Press 1995) 19.

64 Author's notes, Northern Province, Rwanda, October 28, 2008.

65 Geertz 28.

better explain the interactions that have occurred among the courts, whether through their case law, evidentiary overlap, or transfer of suspects among the jurisdictions.

As Glaser and Straus state,

> comparative analysis requires a multitude of carefully selected cases, but the pressure is *not* on the sociologist to "know the whole field" or to have all the facts "from a careful random sample." His job is not to provide a perfect description of an area, but to develop a theory that accounts for much of the relevant behaviour.[66]

The interview material from the judges and lawyers inside the ICTR, the national courts, and *gacaca* suggested that the narrowing of what transitional justice was understood to achieve was in part a result of different practical constraints on the operation of the three courts. This, however, did not fully account for their relevant behavior.

The three concurrent courts were understood to pursue very different objectives, and such interpretations illuminated the distinct and divergent legal cultures of the concurrent international, national, and local courts. The other courts were critically evaluated in this same cultural context. In their understanding of the processes, the courts' personnel were attempting to establish the legitimate authority of the legal institution. Through the analytical process this legitimating behavior emerged as an area warranting further examination. Additional interviews were conducted with participants over whom the three courts exercised their authority. This extended the study beyond the judges and lawyers, to examine, not only how social meanings of criminal justice are produced, but also how they are circulated and received within Rwanda. This aspect of interpretive research, as Rod Rhodes and Mark Bevir suggests, is in line with bottom-up approaches in the social sciences.[67] It provides an account of the justice processes "from below,"[68] examining the interpretations provided by the prisoners and witnesses who are subject to the authority of the courts. Insights into these informal interactions between the courts creates the foundation for a discussion, in Chapter 5, of how interpretations of post-genocide justice are "reproduced, or disrupted, by—the everyday consciousness and conversations"[69] of the Rwandans who interact with the courts, in different ways, in their everyday lives.

---

[66] Glaser and Strauss 30.

[67] Rod Rhodes and Mark Bevir, "Defending Interpretation" (2006) 5 European Political Science 69.

[68] The idea of transitional justice "from below" has been used to examine grassroots, nonstate efforts to pursue the broad set of objectives of accountability, truth, and reconciliation often associated with transitional justice. However, it has also called for an account of the agency of the "subaltern" or "oppressed" actors in transitional justice processes (McEvoy and McGregor 2–5). In Rwanda, the transitional justice processes have predominantly been state-implemented. This book adopts a notion of transitional justice "from below," to draw attention to how state-initiated transitional justice processes have been understood, experienced, resisted, and at times, co-opted by the participants over which the courts have exercised authority.

[69] Ian Loader and Aogán Mulcahy, *Policing and the Condition of England: Memory, Politics and Culture* (Oxford University Press 2003) 50.

Forty-eight Rwandans who had participated as witnesses or observers in either one or more of their country's transitional justice processes were interviewed. In addition, seventeen participants imprisoned in Rwanda were interviewed, some of whom had been witnesses before the ICTR, and all of whom had been tried by either the national or the *gacaca* courts. The majority of participants came from the same districts in the Northern Province and the Western Province where the courts' participants involved in this study were working. This allowed for a deeper analysis of the informal interactions among the courts that have resulted from individual witnesses and accused persons being subject to the authority of two or more of the post-genocide courts.

In providing this specific account of post-genocide legal institutions, there remains the methodological question of how the particular description is of more general relevance. The second aspect of extrapolation of the empirical data is made possible through the use and deployment of theory. Rather than making Glaser and Straus's larger claim of developing a new theory, following the established writings on sociolegal research, theoretical concepts provide a "basis for classifying and making sense of social data."[70] Reflexively, the social data provides the possibility of illuminating actions not accounted for in the general theory, allowing for incremental developments.[71] In this way Geertz's writings on culture provide a tool for better explaining the interactions among the concurrent courts. How the courts' work is ascribed meaning illuminates a legal culture, and it is within this culture that the work of the concurrent courts is understood. Similarly, Beetham's theory on legitimacy and Rodney Barker's work on the self-legitimating activities of institutions[72] helps to explain why such diverse understandings have emerged and how the courts could have more effectively complemented one another.

The concepts of culture, concurrence, and legitimacy, drawn from theoretical and legal literature, aid in classifying and making sense of interpretations of the courts' work offered by the individuals who have contributed to this practice. These general theories are of broader relevance to examining how the legal cultures of transitional justice institutions are influenced by the active drive for self-legitimation, impacting the courts' ability to complement one another. In doing so, the particular case of Rwanda's post-genocide courts illuminates something that has not been accounted for in the general theory. Both the legal and institutional approach to complementarity in the ICC needs to be infused with a cultural sensitivity. Such sensitivity would take fuller account of the reciprocal relationships among local, national, and international criminal courts and aid in realizing more engaged interpretive approaches to international criminal

[70] Denis J. Galligan, *Law in Modern Society* (Oxford University Press 2007) 11.

[71] Ibid. 12.

[72] Rodney Barker, *Legitimating Identities: The Self-Preservation of Rulers and Subjects* (Cambridge University Press 2001).

law such as Mark Drumbl's notion of adopting a "qualified deference" to domestic proceedings.[73]

3. LIMITATIONS ON THE RESEARCH

Conducting effective qualitative research on post-genocide justice in Rwanda is a delicate contextual process. The Rwandan genocide occurred in an environment of heightened fear, insecurity, and uncertainty.[74] As discussed in detail in Chapter 1, a civil war began in 1990 through insurgencies from the Rwandan Patriotic Front (RPF), an armed force comprising predominantly Tutsi soldiers whose families had fled earlier ethnically motivated violence in Rwanda. Contestation for the control of the Rwandan state was heightened by the advent of multi-party politics, and power was consolidated along ethnic lines, polarizing Hutu and Tutsi identities. On April 6, 1994, President Juvénal Habyarimana's plane was shot down over Kigali. Within hours of the president's death, moderate politicians were executed, roadblocks were set up, and one hundred days of genocidal killing ensued.[75] Targeting mainly Tutsi civilians, at the local level, the violence was characterized by brutal and intimate methods, taking the conflict inside the homes and lives of most Rwandans. The impact of this violent social rupture cannot be underestimated, and the post-genocide environment is both politically sensitive and, at times, tense.

Since the RPF gained control of the country in July 1994, the scholarship on Rwanda has been increasingly polarized. On one side of the debate, the post-genocide state is framed as a model of African development and its leadership as transformative.[76] In this reading, most prominent in the economic literature on the country, there is a focus on Rwanda's rapid economic growth and the remarkable improvements in public services, including healthcare and access to information and communication technology.[77]

---

73 The implications of this research for Drumbl's proposed notion of a "qualified deference" to domestic proceedings are discussed in more detail in the concluding remarks of this book.

74 For a valuable discussion of the role that such fear and uncertainly played in the spread of violence across the country, see Scott Straus, *The Order of Genocide: Race. Power, and War in Rwanda* (Cornell University Press 2006).

75 There is increasingly important and detailed scholarly work on the nature and causes of the genocide discussed in Chapter 1. To examine the current historical consensus on the issues that underpin the prosecutions before the ICTR, see Alison Des Forges, *Leave None to Tell the Story: Genocide in Rwanda* (Human Rights Watch 1999); Linda Melvern, *Conspiracy to Murder: The Rwandan Genocide* (Verso 2004); Gérard Prunier, *The Rwanda Crisis 1959–1994: History of the Genocide* (Hurst 1995); Philip Gourevitch, *We Wish to Inform You That Tomorrow We Will be Killed with Our Families: Stories from Rwanda* (Farrar, Straus & Giroux 1998); and Mahmood Mamdani, *When Victims Become Killers: Colonialism, Nativism and the Genocide in Rwanda* (James Curry 2001).

76 The nature of the Rwandan state is discussed in further detail in Chapter 1. For an initial articulation of this position, see Stephen Kinzer, *A Thousand Hills: Rwanda's Rebirth and the Man Who Dreamed It* (John Wiley 2008).

77 Marco Antonio Hernandez, "Maintaining Momentum with a Special Focus on Rwanda's Pathway out of Poverty" (Edition no. 4. Washington DC; World Bank Group) http://documents.

This research, whether oriented toward policy or academia, is framed by deference to the actions of the state following the tragedy of the genocide. On the other, increasingly dominant, side of the argument, the Rwandan state is understood as authoritarian. Dictated by the RPF elite, its policies often repress the peasant majority.[78] Following from this, researchers have argued that, inside Rwanda, empirical investigation is severely constrained by government pressure and interference.[79] In addition, the generation of knowledge in Rwanda is shaped by the government's construction of events and the self-censorship of the majority of the population.[80]

In Rwanda, gaining access to research participants, canvassing a wide range of opinions, and conducting critical and engaged research in an ethical manner, requires both a constructive engagement with state officials and the ability to undertake independent research. This is undoubtedly possible, but there are limitations that must be acknowledged.

3.1 Obtaining Access and Differing Opinions

My research into the institutions of post-genocide justice required access to senior officials at the ICTR and those inside the Rwandan court and government structures. As with many research contexts, such access depended on the permission of institutional gatekeepers. At the ICTR, the then-Deputy Registrar, Everard O'Donnell, facilitated this access, and in *gacaca,* access was granted by the NSGJ's Executive Secretary, Domitilla Mukantaganzwa. I spent time formulating participant observations inside the ICTR and the NSGJ, and also conducted independent research outside of each of these institutions. The questions that I asked were not reviewed or moderated by any of the gatekeepers, and I was granted full access to the Rwandan prisons during the three research periods.

The first limitation of this study is one of language. Access in Rwanda is about effectively engaging in a cross-cultural dialogue. Although I undertook introductory classes in Kinyarwanda over a period of three months, throughout the research process I remained an outsider to both the language and the country. As a result, I worked very closely with two Rwandan researchers. Both were graduate students with degrees

---

worldbank.org/curated/en/2013/05/17810159/rwanda-economic-update-maintaining-momentum-special-focus-rwandas-pathway-out-poverty, accessed June 10, 2014.

[78] Similarly, for an initial discussion of this position, see Filip Reyntjens, "Rwanda, Ten Years On: From Genocide to Dictatorship" (2004) 103 African Affairs 177.

[79] Susan M. Thomson, '"That Is Not What We Authorised You to Do . . .": Access and Government Interference in Highly Politicised Research Environments' in Chandra Lekha Sriram et al. (eds), *Surviving Field Research: Working in Violent and Difficult Situations* (Routledge 2009).

[80] Bert Ingelaere, "Do We Understand Life after Genocide? Center and Periphery in the Construction of Knowledge in Postgenocide Rwanda" (2010) 53 African Studies Review 41.

in politics and law, respectively, and were in their mid-twenties. They were very much my colleagues in the research endeavor, and I learned an enormous amount from them.

Marie[81] is a politics graduate of mixed Hutu and Tutsi ethnicity, and was in Rwanda at the time of the genocide. She was involved in conducting the majority of the *inyangamugayo* interviews, focus groups, and general participant interviews, particularly within the Rwandan prisons. With a deep contextual understanding of the conflict, Marie and I discussed the initial questions before each semi-structured interview. In part, my foreignness allowed the two of us to delve more deeply into the sensitive issues of justice and governance, and we were able to establish significant rapport with most of the participants. Marie would provide a direct translation for me as I conducted the interviews. Afterward, we would review the responses and how I had recorded them in English. This was an imprecise science, but the discussions allowed for an initial analysis of the data, in line with the reflexive research endeavor. We focused on how the participants had expressed themselves and tried to delve into what their "statements reveal(ed) and conceal(ed) at the same time."[82]

Patrick is a recent law graduate of Tutsi ethnicity who was outside the country at the time of the genocide and attended the *gacaca* hearings with me. He transcribed the hearings while they occurred and facilitated my discussions with the General Assembly participants. These conversations were hugely valuable in gaining a broader insight into how Rwandans view the genocide courts. Following these informal discussions, which were simultaneously translated, with the consent of the participants, I would take detailed notes of the opinions expressed. Again, Patrick and I discussed the interviews and how participants had expressed their understandings of the justice processes. Key informants further assisted in this cross-cultural access, and I had extensive discussions about my methods and findings with researchers at the Institute for Research and Dialogue for Peace (IRDP).

The second constraint on my research related to the environment in which people were willing to express their opinions. During my stay in a town near one of the research sites, I spent my mornings practicing Kinyarwanda with the women in the marketplace. I spoke to the women about their language and their work. One language lesson on words for memory and history was given particular emphasis. Valerie, my teacher, was a well-respected potato trader. She explained to me, "*Kwibuka* is to remember. *Ndi ibuka amateka yanje,* means 'I remember my story.' This is history, *amateka.*" The women around us emphasized the importance of these phrases, but as we continued this discussion they were reluctant to explore the themes further. The market was not the place for talk of history and conflict, Valerie told me. Even in the quieter moments when she and I sat alone behind the potato stall, we did not talk about the war and the genocide.

In contrast, once I was attending a *gacaca* hearing in the same area, sitting next to the women of that same community in a similarly public space, there was a real

81 For the sake of anonymity both of these researchers have been given pseudonyms.

82 Ingelaere 54.

willingness to express opinions, often highly critical, about the conflict, personal and collective history, and transitional justice. Whoever I found myself sitting next to would offer his or her thoughts on *gacaca*, in the breaks between proceedings or during the deliberations of the *inyangamugayo*. As discussed in detail in Chapter 4, it was accepted that *gacaca* was a place where the genocide was talked about, and extensive attendance at the hearings provided a crucial means of research access.

However, not all spaces were as conducive to effective research. In one of the focus groups with the *inyangamugayo*, the *gacaca* coordinator was present, and I was concerned that this affected how the local judges expressed their opinions. I conducted the full focus group, but later that day, I approached a number of the judges in private and conducted additional interviews with them in order to delve further into some of the issues that had come to light in the more general discussion. On another occasion, in the Kigali Central Prison, I requested an interview with a high-profile suspect whose case I had been observing over a period of three weeks. The participant, although she gave her consent to be interviewed, had a very close relationship with the prison staff and, rather than conducting the interview in the designated room, she requested that we speak in the prison warden's office. The warden was present throughout the first half of the interview. My requested interview had provided an opportunity for her to demonstrate to the authorities her strong support for their policies. I conducted the full interview but in analyzing its content, I focused on what it revealed about the power dynamics of providing testimony before the ICTR and pleading guilty before *gacaca*.

Despite these constraints, the diverse and often critical opinions that were offered to me are testimony to the ability to conduct rigorous empirical research on justice and governance in Rwanda. Gathering diverse opinions is central to the research endeavor. As discussed above, a key part of data analysis is reconciling the differing opinions of participants through comparison. Again, direct reference to grounded theory is useful here:

> As everyone knows, different people in different positions may offer as "the facts" very different information about the same subject, and they vary that information considerably when talking to different people. Furthermore, the information itself may be continually changing as the group changes, and different documents on the same subject can be quite contradictory . . . But when different slices of data are submitted to comparative analysis, the result is *not* unbounding relativism. Instead, it is a proportional view of the evidence, since, during comparison, biases of particular people and methods tend to reconcile themselves as the analyst discovers the underlying causes of variation.[83]

[83] Glaser and Strauss 67–68.

In this way, different modes of knowing are explained and integrated theoretically through comparing the diverse opinions of the study participants, looking at explaining both points of commonality and difference. Yet, in a country scarred by genocide, the ability to obtain diverse opinions is dependent on establishing trust. It is at this point that continual and consistently ethical conduct comes to the fore.

3.2 Ethical Research

Access, and more important, continued access, is dependent on ethical conduct throughout the research process. As discussed, all interviews were conducted in line with the research structure submitted and approved by CUREC. However, consent in the Rwandan prison structure is constrained. The prison staff summoned all the prisoners with whom I requested interviews. The participants had little or no scope to resist this summons. Once in the interview, all participants were given the express freedom to discontinue the interview or to decline to respond to a particular question. On occasion this was taken up: one participant, having requested anonymity at the start of the interview, made it clear that he did not want to discuss the ICTR or his involvement with it.[84] Such preferences were respected, and showed that participants could exercise a degree of active consent during this prison-based research.

The three phases of embedded research in Rwanda, the first in 2008, the second in 2009, and the final phase in 2012, meant that it was necessary to maintain strong relationships with participants and to engage in follow-up interviews. Through honestly responding to any questions or concerns raised by participants or potential participants during the research process, I laid the groundwork for a long-term working relationship. The reciprocal nature of the interviews also deepened the exploratory process. During a focus group on *gacaca,* conducted in one of the rural research sites, participants were particularly interested in their opinions being communicated to the judges and lawyers in the concurrent institutions. This further supported the emergent position that there was a need for more direct communication among the local, national, and international transitional justice processes.[85]

Finally, feedback is crucial when evaluating the ethical conduct of the researcher. If the social data has been accurately recorded, and robustly analyzed, and if it fairly reflects how the justice processes have been understood in Rwanda, then the analysis should make sense to the people working in the courts and those subject to the courts' authority. This does not mean that all participants will agree with the findings, which at times seriously challenged the courts' practice, but rather that they should accept as

[84] Interview with prisoners (Participant 3), (Rural District, Northern Province, Rwanda 5 September 2008) notes on file with author.

[85] In response to this particular request from the *gacaca* judges, on April 19, 2011, I returned to Arusha, Tanzania, and presented my findings on the different interpretations of transitional justice in Rwanda to the judges and legal officers of the ICTR.

legitimate the processes of collecting and analyzing the data. Supporting this possibility, the research reflected in this book has been presented and well received in multiple forums in which members of the ICTR, the Rwandan national courts, and senior *gacaca* administrators have been present.

Although the political space in Rwanda is undoubtedly constrained, there is a danger of researchers entering this environment with a set of overly determined assumptions about the factors that will shape the outcomes of their research. In Rwanda, such assumptions include: that the central point of analysis is the Hutu-Tutsi bipolarity,[86] that Rwandans are generally private and silent,[87] and that they will publicly defer to authority exercised from the center.[88] As past research shows, an awareness of these interpretations of the Rwandan social context is crucial. However, a new researcher, entering the research environment operating on the assumption that any of these perspectives is a truism, will severely curtail the exploratory process. It is therefore particularly important to adopt an interpretive methodology that allows for the emergence of social phenomena. As seen in Chapters 2, 3, and 4, the existing scholarship on the subject provides the entry point to the research, but, it is the empirical material read in light of this previous work that guides and determines the book's overall argument on the compatibility of Rwanda's post-genocide courts.

4. CONCLUSION

The next six chapters will provide a "thick description" of how transitional justice processes have been understood in Rwanda. This qualitative work, conducted in line with the discussed methodology, analyzes how the social practices of the ICTR, the national courts, and *gacaca* have been understood during a transitional period. In doing so, this research examines the objectives of transitional justice in practice and contributes to our understanding of the role of legal institutions in establishing legitimate authority during periods of social, political, and legal transition. It leads to clear recommendations on how to strengthen this legitimacy and to better align the objectives of international, national, and local transitional justice processes.

---

[86] Bert Ingelaere, "Changing Lenses and Contextualizing the Rwandan (Post-) Genocide" in F. Reyntjens and S. Marysse (eds), *L'afrique Des Grands Lacs: Annuaire 2005–2006* (L'Harmattan 2006).

[87] Lars Waldorf, "Mass Justice for Mass Atrocity: Rethinking Local Justice as Transitional Justice" (2006) 79 Temple Law Review 88.

[88] Gérard Prunier, *From Genocide to Continental War: The "Congolese" Conflict and the Crisis of Contemporary Africa* (Hurst Publishers 2009).

1 The Rwandan Social Context

1. Introduction

Since 1994, Rwanda has experienced a period of rapid political, social, and legal change. Following the genocide and civil war, law has played a central role in restructuring relations among citizens and between citizens and the state. In part, this has occurred through the incremental establishment of international, national, and local transitional justice processes. To examine the "socially established structures of meaning"[1] that render the actions of these post-genocide courts intelligible, it is important first to identify the particular transitional period under examination. In line with an interpretive approach, this chapter situates all three courts in their shared social and historical context, allowing for an integrated analysis of their practice.

In Rwanda, state power has historically been held in the hands of a few elites, and ethnic identity has emerged and been used as a means of consolidating and contesting this concentrated power. Although influenced by external political factors, Rwandan state actors shape their circumstances in important, albeit constrained, ways, and the society is ordered through both central control and local ties. Yet, the state is not as strong at its margins as it is described at the center. This is seen in the establishment of the Nyiginya Kingdom, its consolidation as Ruanda-Urundi under colonial rule, and

[1] Clifford Geertz, "Thick Description: Toward an Interpretive Theory of Culture" in Clifford Geertz (ed), *The Interpretation of Cultures: Selected Essays* (Fontana Press 1993) 12–13.

through the shifts in political power in 1959, 1973, and finally, in the period leading to and following the 1994 genocide.

The relationship among power in the capital, external players, local state actors, and everyday Rwandans continues to shape the functioning of the post-genocide courts. The local, national, and international criminal justice processes have all operated in a historical context in which ethnicity has been used as a means of consolidating and contesting political power. There is strong state pressure for social conformity; nonetheless, local actors have shown their capacity to strategically align with or resist state objectives. A contextual examination of Rwanda's three tiers of post-genocide justice must first take account of these historical dynamics. Read alongside the general writings on transitional justice, this social and political account highlights strong links among law, ethnicity, and the exercise of state authority, and provides the basis to evaluate the interactions among the courts as a dynamic set of processes that change over time. The result is variability in how these justice processes are both implemented and understood by the different participants involved in the courts' practice.

There is increasingly detailed and important scholarly work on the causes of the Rwandan genocide. The understanding of events has altered significantly since the initial journalistic explanation of the Rwandan violence as an African problem of tribal hatred. In the current dominant historical interpretation, the violence was fueled by nationalism, ethnicity, and propaganda that emerged from the colonial manipulation of traditional understanding of Hutu and Tutsi identity. Specific hardliners were responsible for the genocide that was meticulously planned before the downing of President Juvénal Habyarimana's plane on the evening of April 6, 1994. This planning included the distribution of weapons, militia training, preparatory anti-Tutsi massacres, genocide lists, racist propaganda, and direct and continued incitement of militia to exterminate the Tutsi ethnic minority along with "moderate"[2] Hutu opposition.[3] It is this argument that has underpinned the prosecution of the seventy-four individuals who have appeared before the United Nations International Criminal Tribunal for Rwanda (ICTR).

Although it is important in explaining the actions of the elite in Kigali, Scott Straus argues that this state-centric macro-account of the genocide "eclipses the specific

[2] Nigel Eltringham critiques the use of the term "moderate Hutu," arguing that in delineating this group as those who were killed, it suggests that the surviving Hutu were all involved or complicit in the genocide, leading to the collectivization of guilt in post-genocide Rwanda. See Nigel Eltringham, *Accounting for Horror: Post-Genocide Debates in Rwanda* (Pluto Press 2004) 75–76. A discussion of the use and role of ethnic identity in post-genocide Rwanda is undertaken in Section 4 of this chapter.

[3] Alison Des Forges, *Leave None to Tell the Story: Genocide in Rwanda* (Human Rights Watch 1999), Linda Melvern, *Conspiracy to Murder: The Rwandan Genocide* (Verso 2004), Gérard Prunier, *The Rwanda Crisis 1959–1994: History of the Genocide* (Hurst 1995), Philip Gourevitch, *We Wish to Inform You That Tomorrow We Will Be Killed with Our Families: Stories from Rwanda* (Farrar, Straus & Giroux 1998), and Mahmood Mamdani, *When Victims Become Killers: Colonialism, Nativism and the Genocide in Rwanda* (James Curry 2001).

dynamics that drove the violence."[4] Through an excellent micro-comparative examination of how the violence spread across the country, he argues that

> A more contingent process happened: the call to kill Tutsi emanating from the top became a *de facto* basis for authority. Killing became akin to policy. Local elites claimed power and legitimacy because they had allied with the hardliners. Genocide became the order of the day, one that overwhelmed Hutu opposition, demanded mass compliance, and ultimately took on a life of its own.[5]

Straus's account provides a robust explanation for the spread of violence across Rwanda and helps to explain the regional variation in the experience of the conflict. Rather than focusing exclusively on the actions of the Rwandan state, Straus's grounded research analyzes the processes through which the violence was fomented and spread. It highlights the role of local political opportunism and the importance of specific local ties. In doing so, Straus better explains the role of the state and the individual in the Rwandan genocide. Focusing on the processes through which central decisions in Rwanda took root and were implemented locally helps to explain the causes of the genocide. This focus on the interaction been central state politics and local action is similarly crucial in examining the legal responses to the violence.

To pursue an examination of both the central exercise of power in Rwanda and how it is experienced at the margins of the society, this chapter is structured around three sections. The first takes account of the historiographies of modern Rwanda, supporting the position that those who tell the history influence its content and emphasis. The dominant historical focus on the centralized nature of the Rwandan state has served the interests of those in power while paying insufficient attention to any regional resistance to this power. Rather than a homogenous and centralized polity, the major result of the establishment and expansion of the Rwandan state was that power was secured in the hands of a small elite, and the ethnic identities of Hutu and Tutsi provided a political means of consolidating and contesting this power.

The second section places the genocide within this historical context. In the buildup to and during the civil war from 1990 through to 1994, ethnicity was key to solidifying political power bases. In 1994, this ethnic categorization provided the crucial conflation of civilian and combatant identities that linked national politics to local genocidal violence. As the killing started, the spread of violence was dependent on local political relations, personal ties, and face-to-face mobilization.

Exploring these same themes of state control, local politics, and the role of ethnicity, the final section describes the transitional period following the horrific violence of 1994.

[4] Scott Straus, *The Order of Genocide: Race. Power, and War in Rwanda* (Cornell University Press 2006) 18.

[5] Ibid. 66.

Although there has been an official removal of ethnic identity from political discourse, access to power has remained limited to a small ruling class. In the twenty years following the conflict, criminal justice has been central to current elites' approach to securing power and governing the country. In the Rwandan social and historical context, an analysis of the ICTR, the national courts, and *gacaca* requires an understanding of both the central institutional objectives and the courts' local implementation and interpretation.

2. Ethnicity and the Consolidation of the Rwandan State

The environment in which the Rwandan genocide of 1994 occurred was characterized by heightened distrust, insecurity, and uncertainty in which power was purposefully consolidated along ethnic lines. This was consistent with the historical use of ethnic identity in the country, evident through a brief discussion of the evolution of the Tutsi, Hutu, and Twa identities. The popular distinction among these three ethnic groups turns on means of production. Tutsi are identified as traditionally being pastoralist, Hutu as agriculturalist, and the Twa, a minority group of approximately 2 percent of the population, as being hunters and potters. This understanding of strict ethnic categorization was clearly articulated in the early writings on Rwanda by Western anthropologists.[6] A similar version of ethnic identity was taught in Rwandan schools in the post-independence era and negates any historical understanding of the formation and use of ethnic identity in Rwanda.[7] "Hutu," "Tutsi," and "Twa" emerged as social labels that have gradually taken on an ethnic meaning through the process of state expansion and the political contestation for the control of this state.[8] The political use of ethnic identity and the role, power, and limits of the state in structuring the lives of Rwandans are crucial in understanding how the genocide played out and the context in which the resultant transitional justice processes have operated.

2.1 HISTORIES AND THE STATE

Early articulations of the social label of "Tutsi" centered on cattle ownership, connection to the *mwami*,[9] and later military affiliation.[10] To be Tutsi denoted access to power, but this label was fluid and historically variant. The development of this identity and its counterweight "Hutu" is inextricably linked to the evolution of the Rwandan state. The Nyiginya kingdom was established some time during the seventeenth century under the

---

[6] Jacques J. Maquet, *The Premise of Inequality in Ruanda* (Oxford University Press 1961) 10–14.

[7] Lee Ann Fujii, *Killing Neighbors: Webs of Violence in Rwanda* (Cornell University Press 2009) 108.

[8] Ibid. 45.

[9] *Mwami* is the Kinyarwanda reference to the king.

[10] Jan Vansina, *Antecedents to Modern Rwanda: The Nyiginya Kingdom* (James Curry 2004) 36–37 and 153.

enigmatic conquests of *mwami* Ruganzu Ndori.[11] The territory broadly mapped onto the central provinces of what is the modern state of Rwanda. Although the kingdom has routinely been described as a well-ordered and centralized state,[12] in practice its establishment was hugely contested, and the boundaries of the state fluctuated under the rule of various monarchs.[13] The image of a highly centralized, rigidly stratified, and ancient state was consciously constructed in the recording of Rwandan history in the nineteenth and twentieth centuries.[14] Such a construct served the interests of both the Rwandan elite and a series of non-Rwandan actors, including the initial German colonizers, the Catholic Church, and later, the Belgian administration. These groups, in their own way, exaggerated the continuities and reach of the Rwandan royal court, and later, the colonial state, to preserve a social order that benefited a small minority and enabled increasingly exploitative labor practices.[15]

During the process of state expansion, particularly in the latter half of the nineteenth century, ethnicity helped build cohesion and secure royal power interests. Before the arrival of the German colonialists, the kingdom gained increasing control over land, cattle, and peoples in central Africa under the leadership of *mwami* Kigeri Rwabugiri (ca. 1876–1895).[16] The introduction of a complex network of chiefdoms enabled the king to establish leaders loyal to his royal court in previously autonomous regions.[17] However, there remained local and regional resistance to this central authority[18] and huge contestation within the court that is not reflected in the Nyiginya kingdom's official oral histories of conquest, consolidation, and expansion.

Catherine Newbury suggests that although an identity of "Tutsi" became more rigid under Rwabugiri's chieftains,[19] there was notable regional variation in the use of the term. In Kinyaga in the southwest of the territory, it referred to people directly associated with the royal court.[20] In this reading, prior to the German rule of the Ruanda-Urundi from 1898, Tutsi identity was used as one means to solidify the power of Rwabugiri's court. Jan Vansina argues that the most defining feature of this period was that power was secured

---

[11] Ibid. 44.

[12] The most influential author in this regard is Abbé Alexis Kagame. See Alexis Kagame, *Le code des institutions politiques du Rwanda précolonial* (Belgian Royal Colonial Institute 1952).

[13] For a direct challenge to the dominant interpretations offered by Kagame, see Vansina. According to Vasina's iteration of history, Nori was the first of sixteen monarchs to preside over the state until its final devolution in 1961.

[14] David Newbury and Catherine Newbury, "Bringing the Peasants Back In: Agrarian Themes in the Construction and Corrosion of Statist Historiography in Rwanda" (2000) 105 The American History Review 832, 847–849.

[15] Ibid.

[16] Catherine Newbury, *The Cohesion of Oppression* (Columbia University Press 1988) 38–52.

[17] Ibid. 108.

[18] Fujii 60.

[19] Newbury 11.

[20] Ibid.

in the hands of an elite ruling class. Rwabugiri effectively acquired more personal power, and there was an increase in the strength of the court across the territory as a whole. Rather than indisputable unity of a homogenous society, the political result of this process was greater contestation for this more concentrated power, which deepened regional divides and alliances within the ruling nobility.[21] Ethnic identity became increasingly important in consolidating this power and was reinforced by the colonial administrators' racist support of the supposedly identifiable "Tutsi" group.

Colonial interests accelerated the process of consolidating the state and its growing inequalities. German rule of the Ruanda-Urundi began in 1898, three years after the death of Rwabugiri. Following a palace coup,[22] the new monarch, Yuhi Musinga, effectively allied himself with the military strength of the colonizer. Involvement of German troops secured the monarchy's control in the previously contested regions of the north and northwest of modern day Rwanda[23] and helped to secure Musinga's authority within the court.[24]

Nonetheless, the power of the recently instated chiefdoms was still challenged by local authorities. One of the earliest diary entries of the first missionaries in Rwanda, written in 1903, noted the lack of legitimacy of the court-appointed chiefs in the northwest. As Lee Ann Fujii notes in her discussion of this entry, the local Balera group directly challenged the authority of the newly settled Nduga people, sent to Ruhengeri[25] by the royal court. This resistance to central authority was drawn along clan rather than ethnic lines, as both of these groups would have been "Tutsi" within the current ethnic construct.[26] Newbury provides a similar account of active, although unsuccessful, resistance to court-appointed authorities in the southwest of the country in 1917.[27] At this juncture in Rwandan history, ethnic identity was being drawn on to centralize and secure increasing state power. Nevertheless, there remained both resistance to central authority and powerful alliances along lines other than Hutu and Tutsi identities. These themes are carried through the country's complex histories right up to the interpretations of the *gacaca* courts discussed in Chapter 4, where there emerged clear differences in how the actions of the courts were described by the centrally appointed administrators and those offered by the locally elected *gacaca* judges.

---

21 Vansina 194–195.

22 Ibid. 173. The *coup* removed Rutarindwa who was Rwabugiri's adopted son, who had ascended to the throne prior to Rwabugiri's death.

23 Straus 208, quoting William Roger Louis.

24 David Newbury, "Precolonial Burundi and Rwanda: Local Loyalties, Regional Royalities" (2001) 34 International Journal of African Historical Studies 255, 310–311.

25 In the current Rwandan administrative structure this would have been the Northern Province.

26 Fujii 60. In Rwanda, a person's clan does not indicate the person's ethnicity as all clans included Tutsi, Hutu, and Twa members. See David Newbury, "The Clans of Rwanda: An Historical Hypothesis" (1980) 50 Africa 389.

27 Newbury 128 131.

Although continuities in social structures do carry through to present day Rwanda, the colonial transformation of the ethnic identity and social relations in the country were nonetheless notable. Early colonial ethnographic work on Rwanda records a history of settlement and conquest provided by the ruling Nyiginya clan and told to the new European conquerors. In this telling, the Tutsi pastoralist migrated from the north and introduced cattle-keeping, ironworking, and a structured monarchical state. They ruled over the cultivators and forest dwellers previously living in scattered communities in the kingdom's territory. The hierarchical social relations were structured through a practice of vassalage termed *ubuhake*,[28] which colonial anthropologists interpreted as a clear and rigid social hierarchy. However, as Newbury writes in her critique of Jacques J. Maquet, "the main school of ethnographic thought on Rwanda in colonial times did more to legitimize royalty than royalty itself."[29] She argues that there were multiple types of patron-client relations that varied across regions and over time. *Umuheto* referred to an early practice by which individuals connected to the royal court would, in exchange for limited rights over the animals, protect a particular kinship group's cattle from being claimed by the *mwami*. These relationships were not widespread, were often within what would now be considered a single ethnic group, and were generally characterized by mutual respect and strong affective ties. State expansion prior to colonialism saw the extension of *ubuhake* and *ubureetwa,* where cows (in the case of the former), and labor or beer (in the case of the latter), were exchanged for more general political favor. However, under colonial rule, the use of *ubuhake* increased substantially and became more rigidly defined as a relationship between an individual patron and a single client, removing the protection offered by kinship obligations and leading to increasingly exploitative practices.[30]

The court's simplified story of migration and social organization helped the Rwandan ruling class to secure access to labor and land that was threatened by the colonisers' use of forces and their extractive economic practices. Such an account simultaneously mapped onto the colonialists' pseudo-scientific Hamitic hypothesis in which all "civilized" traits found in Africa could be traced to the more "evolutionary progressive" peoples of Europe and the Middle East. Within this construct, the Tutsi were identified as the more civilized, industrious group with their leaner and taller builds, long noses, and lighter skin. Their history of migration from the north made them a naturally superior "race" and the correct local leaders of Ruanda-Urundi.[31] Current historians contest the

---

[28] Maquet 10–14. *Ubuhake* was a type of voluntary vassalage initially applied between cattle owners who tried to resist the depletion of their herds as the king made claim to some of their animals. Later it provided a way for an individual to seek protection from a more powerful patron, in some instances facilitating class advancement. However, under colonial rule this practice of clientelism became increasingly exploitative.

[29] Newbury 7.

[30] Ibid. 74–114.

[31] Charles Gabriel Seligman, *Races of Africa* (Thornton Butterworth 1930).

linear account of settlement and rule in Rwanda. There were kingdoms long before the Nyiginya clan's rule, and the rituals of these previous clans included both "Tutsi" and "Hutu" practices that remained incorporated in the court structures.[32] The colonialists used the story of settlement in Rwanda, told to them by the Nyiginya court, to reinforce their own ideas of indirect governance. Equally, the telling of this history secured the immediate interests of the court and enabled shifts in patron-client relations that led to greater access to taxes and labor, enriching court officials who collaborated with the colonizers.

What emerges from this historical account is a more socially contingent understanding of the labels "Hutu" and "Tutsi," which gradually took on ethnic meaning and were infused with greater rigidity and stratification in the colonial era. Although a Tutsi identity developed through the consolidation of the Nyiginya Kingdom and the initial colonial state, the ethnic term "Hutu" was not, at this stage, an easily identifiable grouping, and direct clan ties remained far stronger than any other group identities.[33] Yet, in a society increasingly stratified by colonial rule, in which the commercial interests of both the Europeans and Tutsi chiefs were served through clientship relations and labor control mechanisms, the state's exercise of power gave rise to a new type of legitimate authority—that of moral resistance.

Historically, the right to exercise power was established through birthright or spiritual claim, limited to the king and to certain mystics. This changed over time and there evolved new means of legitimating power. Alison Des Forges records that, following the arrival of colonial powers, there emerged legitimacy to exercise power through the moral force of resistance against the oppressor.[34] By 1933, the introduction of ethnic identity cards by the Belgium administrators, who had taken control of the territory from Germany following World War I, ensured the oppressor was defined as both the colonialist and the Tutsi.[35] The claim of moral resistance to this exercise of power would come to full fruition in the Hutu uprising of 1959, by which stage it was deeply wedded to ethnic identity. As the political value of resistance grew, Newbury argues that Hutu identity, articulated in this Hutu party politics of the 1950s, emerged as a cohesive response to the Tutsi chiefs' and colonial administrators' use and abuse of their growing power.[36]

[32] Fujii 58.

[33] Ibid. 105. Fujii notes clan identity in Rwanda remains strong with seventy-nine of her eighty respondents being able to identify with their clan.

[34] Alison Des Forges, "'The Drum Is Greater than the Shout': The 1912 Rebellion in Northern Rwanda" in Donald Crummey (ed), *Banditry, Rebellion and Social Protest in Africa* (James Currey 1986) 321.

[35] Eltringham 18–19.

[36] Newbury 209.

2.2 POLITICAL ETHNICITY

Having previously aided in securing minority power through Tutsi ethnic identity, by the late 1940s, the Belgium administrators were under pressure to move toward self-governance in their colonies. On July 14, 1952, they established elective advisory councils for the administrative positions in Ruanda-Urundi.[37] This initial opening of political space drew attention to the schisms in the country. Those loyal to the monarch, now clearly identified as Tutsi, began pushing for the end of colonial rule, while there emerged a counter-call from an increasingly organized Hutu group directed at ending Tutsi oppression. In 1957 this call would take the form of the Bahutu Manifesto, which framed the independence struggle in ethnic rather than colonial terms.

Two opposition political parties were established, driven by a small, mostly seminarian-trained group of Hutu elite. Grégoire Kayibanda founded the Mouvement Social Muhutu (MSM), and Joseph Gitera, the l'Association pour la Promotion Sociale de la Masse (APROSOMA). At this early stage of political contestation, there were already clear divisions between the more isolationist northern Hutu interests and those of the increasingly middle class southern Hutu. Nonetheless, Hutu remained a fluid rather than unified identity, with Gitera still appealing to all Rwandans to resist the rule of an elite rather than that of an ethnic group.[38] By 1959, the Hutu ethnic categorization was a clear political construct articulated in opposition to the powerful articulation of Tutsi identity.[39]

Following identifiably ethnic-based violence in November 1959 against both local Tutsi elites and general citizens identified as Tutsi, Kayibanda established the Parti du Mouvement de l'Emancipation des Bahutu (Parmehutu). This party went on to win the communal elections in June–July 1960 on a clear ethnic platform. The elections were marred by intimidation and violence on both sides of the ethnic divide, but the Belgians continued to support a quick transfer of power to the Hutu elite. In the "*coup* of Giterama" in January 1961, the Parmehutu leaders declared the end of monarchical rule and, in September of that same year, Kayibanda was officially elected as president and led Rwanda to independence on July 1, 1962.[40]

Throughout the first half of the twentieth century, the effectiveness of consolidating power along ethnic lines as a means of both securing and contesting access to land, labor, and capital became increasingly embedded in Rwanda's political and social structures. Insecurity and interethnic tensions escalated from 1961 as Tutsi, exiled from the country following the ethnic violence of the 1959 revolution, engaged in sporadic cross-border raids. Inside the country, the violent response to these raids was not directed at the rebel

---

[37] René Lemarchand, *Rwanda and Burundi* (Pall Mall Press 1970) 81.

[38] Newbury 191–193.

[39] Lemarchand 154.

[40] Ibid. 188–197.

inyenzi[41] but rather at the remaining Tutsi civilians. By 1963, it is estimated that 14,000 civilians had been murdered and many more had fled the country.[42] Violence was galvanized along ethnic lines and accepted as a tool of politics. Although in some areas local officials did take action against those accused of involvement in the pillage,[43] at a national level, Kayibanda's state failed to arrest or punish the perpetrators, providing, at the very least, de facto support for the violence.

Despite its statements and actions of ethnic solidarity, the Parmehutu party remained divided. There were clear intra-ethnic contestations as some individuals continued to retain greater affinity to family and clan than to their Hutu identity. In the face of little economic and social change after independence, these divides, particularly between northern and southern interests, came to a head. In 1973, Major General Juvénal Habyarimana, an ambitious and well-connected northerner, came to power through a *coup d'état*. In the buildup, opportunistic violence was again left unpunished and Habyarimana promised to re-establish order. Such order took the form of a single party state. At birth, all Rwandans were now a member of the newly formed Mouvement Révolutionnaire pour le Développement (MRND).[44]

Habyarimana retained focus on central authority and required all Rwandans to perform community service once a week through *umuganda*.[45] In addition, principally to resist challenges from southern and central Hutu organizations, but also to further legislate rigid ethnic categories, he introduced ethnic and regional quotas in schools, universities, and the civil service.[46] Consistent with Rwanda's historical trajectory, a small elite retained power in Rwanda, following both the initial Hutu revolution and later under Habyarimana. Ethnicity was one means of securing or contesting this power, and as Fujii writes, "(w)hen authorities promoted ethnic violence, their goal was to seize, gain, or consolidate power."[47]

This historical account shows an active process of state building in Rwanda from the end of the nineteenth and throughout the twentieth century. This process concentrated political power within a small ruling class, but there remained regional and local resistance to this central power. Ethnicity was consistently used by Rwandan leaders as a means of securing or violently contesting state power, and was increasingly written into Rwandan law. The result was that citizens learned to identify themselves

---

[41] This term literally means "cockroaches" and was initially used in a non-pejorative way, possibly taken by the rebels themselves to denote their strength, determination, and indestructibility.

[42] Lemarchand 225.

[43] Fujii 95.

[44] Des Forges, *Leave None to Tell the Story: Genocide in Rwanda* 41.

[45] A state-implemented and mandatory community service program that requires one person from every household to participate in public works projects on a weekly basis. *Umuganda* continues once a month in Rwanda today.

[46] Des Forges, *Leave None to Tell the Story: Genocide in Rwanda* 41–43.

[47] Fujii 74.

by their ethnicity in interactions with the state.[48] However, at the local level, ethnicity remained "contextually configured"[49] and based on insiders' knowledge about how to tell the difference between the ethnic groups.[50] On occasion, it remained possible for individuals to move between ethnic categories and certainly to strategically use ethnic identity "in everyday, social settings as well as in interactions with the state."[51] This account of the formation of the Rwandan state and the political use and abuse of ethnic identity highlights the dynamic relationship in Rwanda between centralized policy and individual action. It is on this historical stage that a civil war began in 1990, political power was once again consolidated along ethnic lines, and a genocide unfolded.

The historical account of the formation of the Rwandan state as laid out in this section has important implications for understanding how the 1994 genocide occurred and how the post-genocide state operates. The coding and analysis of the empirical data collection through the interviews with participants from the ICTR, national courts, and *gacaca* is informed by this account of ethnicity and power in Rwanda. In Rwanda today, power remains centrally organized and access to power is tightly controlled. For the national courts, this central organization of power means that a key question is how, if at all, are the national courts trying to establish their independence from a powerful executive, and what is the current role of ethnic identity? The social context raises similarly important questions for *gacaca* and the ICTR. How has the extension of the *gacaca* courts as a central state policy been adopted, co-opted, or resisted on the political periphery of the country? The formation of the Rwandan state shows how domestic political actors have aligned themselves with external powers, raising the question of how the ICTR, as an external response to the genocide, has been aligned with or strategically adopted by national political objectives.

3. The Rwandan Genocide

In the buildup to the genocide, there were historical continuities in the structure of the Rwandan state and the political role of ethnicity. The next section highlights the crucial contestation for power inside the ruling elite in Rwanda before the genocide. Ethnic bipolarity was used to try to secure unity within this group. As the central message of ethnic racism became increasingly clear, at the local level, there was use, abuse,

[48] Ibid. 109.

[49] Catherine Newbury and David Newbury, "A Catholic Mass in Kigali: Contested Views of the Genocide and Ethnicity in Rwanda" (1999) 33 Canadian Journal of African Studies 292, 294.

[50] Fujii 114.

[51] Ibid. Fujii notes that the family of one of her respondents strategically changed her ethnicity from Tutsi to Hutu following the 1959 revolution. However, these shifts in identity had to be locally accepted, and as a result were subject to personal ties in the immediate local community.

and resistance to the central state messages, which helps to explain variation in the violence across the country.

3.1 THE CIVIL WAR

From October 1, 1990, the Rwandan state, under the leadership of President Habyarimana, was at war with the Rwandan Patriotic Front (RPF), a rebel force made up predominantly of Tutsi refugees who had fled to Uganda following the ethnic violence of the late 1950s and early 1960s. There was continued but sporadic military combat between these two groups up to and following the signing of the Arusha Peace Accords in August 1993.[52] This war framed the genocide. It was driven by both political factors in Uganda and those inside Rwanda. Despite the role played by key Rwandan soldiers in bringing Ugandan president Yoweri Museveni to power in 1986, shifts in domestic politics in Uganda challenged Rwandan refugees' claims to both land and citizenship.

President Habyarimana oscillated between a flat denial of this refugee problem and a refusal to allow mass return. By the 1980s, the predominantly Tutsi diaspora that had fled to Uganda was "without a political home in postcolonial Africa."[53] The creation of the RPF, most probably in early 1988[54] was tied to the political position of these Rwandan refugees. The refugees' shrinking foothold in Uganda and their emotively powerful connection with Rwanda propelled the RPF military offensive.

Inside Rwanda, the government responded to the initial offensive by tightening "security." After gunfire in Kigali on October 5, 1991, Habyarimana claimed that the RPF and its "accomplices" had infiltrated the capital.[55] The state's response showed an immediate, deliberate, and continued conflation of civilian and combatant identities. There was a mass arrest of Tutsi civilians and general political opponents, identified as "accomplices" of the *inyenzi.* This conflation of ethnic and combat identities appears as a deliberate policy that would be followed throughout the war, allowing for "military" operations against civilian targets.

At this early stage in the borderlands of Gisenyi and Ruhengeri, areas vulnerable to RPF attack, ensuring local "security" similarly manifested in the direct targeting of Tutsi civilians. Ten days after the initial RPF attack, Tutsi civilians were massacred in Kibilira Commume in Gisenyi Prefecture. A second attack, claiming between three

---

[52] Bruce D Jones, *Peacemaking in Rwanda: The Dynamics of Failure* (Lynne Rienner 2001).

[53] Mamdani 157.

[54] Filip Reyntjens, *Rwanda: Trois jours qui ont fait basculer l'histoire* (Centre d'Etudes et de Documentation africaines 1995), quoted in Danielle de Lame, *A Hill among a Thousand: Transformations and Ruptures in Rural Rwanda* (Helen Arnold tr, University of Wisconsin Press 2005) 473.

[55] Des Forges, *Leave None to Tell the Story: Genocide in Rwanda* 49. Both Des Forges and Reyntjens claim that the government staged the attack to justify the crackdown on civilians and opposition, although Straus suggests that this interpretation remains contested.

hundred and a thousand lives, occurred in Ruhengeri Prefecture in January 1991. Again this violence followed an RPF insurgency into the area.

At the time, the government framed the violence in terms of spontaneous uprisings by Rwandan citizens against local Tutsi supporters of the RPF—an "understandable response"[56] to the insecurity of the war. In establishing a macro account of the genocide, articulated as the current historical consensus on the conflict, these attacks are identified as testing grounds for genocidal extermination—planned, well-organized, and instigated in Habyarimana strongholds where success could be assured.[57] What is clear is that local authorities and rural elites led the attacks.[58]

The exact pattern of violence varied from commune to commune.[59] In Gisenyi, there were sectors with little to no violence and control was maintained, either because local officials preached peace, or Tutsi resisted. In both prefectures, the killing ended after pressure was exerted from the Rwandan capital, through the arrival of the military in the area. But this response was not immediate, and those involved in the violence were not arrested, charged, or prosecuted.[60] Violence, perpetrated in response to the stated insecurity, was solidified along ethnic lines, underpinned by local power dynamics, and, at the very least, implicitly condoned by the state.

The violence showed both a deliberate conflation of Tutsi civilians and RPF combatants and opportunistic behavior from local authorities and rural elites to gain power during a period of instability. Power was being violently contested. The tension, anxiety, and fear created by this contestation continued through the entire period of the genocide. Insecurity was heightened by the simultaneous introduction of multiparty politics and the "democratic" fight for control of the state.

3.2 POWER BECOMES CONTESTABLE

On June 10, 1991, parliament passed a new constitution establishing the right to form political parties.[61] In a country in which power was historically held in the hands of a few, there was an immediate and fervent emergence of political opposition. The pressure for this reform came from both donor countries and emerging interests inside Rwanda, highlighting underlying tensions in the country's social ties.

---

[56] Prunier 139 and 143.

[57] Des Forges, *Leave None to Tell the Story: Genocide in Rwanda* 87.

[58] Straus 192–193.

[59] Up until 2002, the state administrative structure in Rwanda was made up of four organizational tiers, namely prefectures, communes, sectors and *cellules*. A prefecture corresponded to a province, which was made up of several communes that in turn were comprised of several sectors containing several *cellules*. A *cellule* broadly corresponded to a neighbourhood in an urban setting.

[60] Ibid.

[61] Prunier 126.

Rwanda's rapid economic growth from 1975 to 1980 was heavily dependent on direct donor aid. This dependence was secured following the economic downturn of the 1980s in which the world price of coffee tumbled, government revenue declined, and unemployment rose. With the end of communist rule in Eastern Europe in the early 1990s, the increasingly vital Western aid packages came with democratic strings firmly attached.[62] Danielle de Lame argues that under Habyarimana's rule, the internal aid distribution had often been based on local affinities and was used to secure distorted patterns of power.[63] This same aid was now directly tied to opening such power relations to immediate challenge, deepening already present fissures in the local and national political arena.

At the national level, the major challenge to Habyarimana's party came in the form of the Mouvement Démocratique Républicain (MDR), whose political heartland lay in the central province of Gitarama. This was the former constituency of Kayibanda, and the MDR accessed a similar support base to Parmehutu. The historical intra-Hutu regional rivalry between the north and south was immediately apparent, despite the MDR framing its manifesto as an inclusive Rwandan response to the elite power of Habyarimana's inner circle, an approach more reminiscent of Gitera's position in 1959 than Kayibanda's political stance. In addition to the MDR, other opposition parties began to form along regional and socioeconomic lines. These included the Parti Social Démocrate (PSD), a center-left party based in the southern prefecture of Butare, and the Parti Libéral (PL), a center-right, urban-based party that attracted many businesspeople, including several prominent Tutsi.

With a newly emerging free press, the parties began voicing their criticism of the regime, directly challenging Habyarimana's and the MRND's ability to lead the country.[64] This occurred at a shaky political moment with doubts being expressed about Habyarimana's leadership inside the MRND and across the Rwandan hills.[65] As "the father of the nation"[66] tried to both stall and control the democratizing process, the political elite became increasingly focused on securing their existing privilege.

At the local level, multiparty activity significantly disrupted the political arena and, three years before the genocide began, set the stage for the competition of power among local elites.[67] Aggressive inter-party contestation, which through *kubohoza*[68] took the form of direct violence and intimidation, meant that genocide was but a short step from

---

62 Fujii 47.

63 de Lame 475.

64 Fujii 48.

65 de Lame 476.

66 James K Gasana, "La Guerre, la paix et al Démocratie au Rwanda" in André Guichaoua (ed), *Les Crises Politiques* (Karthala 1994) in de Lame 483.

67 Straus 123.

68 In Kinyarwanda the word means "to free or liberate." It referred to the practice of forced recruitment into political parties. Des Forges, *Leave None to Tell the Story: Genocide in Rwanda* 54–57.

the "mundane routinized violence that had already taken over everyday life."[69] The use of this violence to secure the influence of local elites is key to understanding the eventual spread of genocide throughout the Rwandan countryside.

The tension created by the civil war and multiparty politics continued to strain social ties and manifested in outbreaks of violence. In March 1992, another massacre of civilians was initiated by local elites supported from the center, this time in the Bugesera region of Kigali-Rural. In this instance, there was an explicit use of political party affiliation to foster the violence along with fear of the RPF and the conflation of Tutsi civilians and RPF combatants.[70]

Straus argues that this violence and the earlier massacres in Gisenyi and Ruhengeri were consistent with the historical patterns of ethnic violence perpetrated in Rwanda from 1957. They occurred in an environment of impending regime change, high tensions, and armed attack, or the threat of imminent armed attack. As with the violence in 1957–1962, 1962–1964, and the purges of 1973, at the local level, imminent shifts in power created a "period of political uncertainty, jostling for power, and divisions within the ruling elite."[71] In this context of uncertainly and insecurity, violence was used as a means to contest and assert power. "Ethnic" unity was key in such contestation.

3.3 CONSOLIDATING POWER: "UNITY" ALONG ETHNIC LINES

As the dynamics of war and multiparty contestation started to play out, ethnicity once again emerged as a means to paper over social inequities and mask political divides. This was consistent with the Rwandan state's historical development and political use of ethnic identities. Political elites invested in institutions they could control, including youth militia[72] and loyal military units. In a fragile political environment, arms flowed into Rwanda for "civil defense" and the hardliners in the political elite pursued extreme tactics through assassination plans and virulent propaganda.[73] The aim was to secure their increasingly fragile hold on power through Hutu unity.

Public speeches, radio programs, newspaper articles, and vulgar political cartoons showed the RPF, and intentionally by extension all Tutsi, as a foreign race bent on retaking the country by force. As with the early emergence of ethnic identity in the twentieth century, a clear articulation of this Tutsi identity also solidified a Hutu one. Hutu ethic

---

[69] Michele Wagner, "All the Bourgmestre's Men: Making Sense of Genocide in Rwanda" (45) 1 Africa Today 25, 34.

[70] Straus 193–194.

[71] Ibid. 195.

[72] Although there were a number of armed youth wings of the major political parties, including the *impuzamugambi* formed by the Coalition pour la Defence de la République (CDR), as the genocide unfolded they were increasingly referred to by the name of MRND's youth wing: the *interahamwe*.

[73] Straus 44.

"unity" was framed as a response to the insecurity of both the civil war and multiparty politics. It provided a point of commonality between the MRND and the MDR, and advocated such solidarity as a powerful and acceptable response to the civil war.

The hardliners' articulation of "Tutsi" collapsed civilians and combatants into a collective ethnic categorization.[74] In doing so, it provided the required link between national political events and local action. When roadblocks were finally set up and the genocide started, "killing Tutsi was inseparable from the language of war. Killing Tutsi, in fact, was equated with fighting the enemy."[75] Although the radio and print propaganda may not, on its own, have incited participation in the killings, it was crucial in collapsing the categories of combatant and noncombatant. This opened the way for the murder of women and children. In the extremist press, innocent civilians were deliberately and continually framed as supporters of the RPF, or soon to be front-line combatants who wanted to reinstate monarchical and exploitative rule. Presenting the conflict in strictly ethnic terms and drawing on clear ethnic stereotypes created the script from which the violence of the genocide was then enacted.[76]

On February 8, 1993, the RPF violated a ceasefire, attacking the government's northern front in the region of Byumba. The rebel group's relentless pressure gave uncomfortable credence to extremist messages that they were not out to share power, but to seize it by force.[77] The radical formation of the Coalition pour la Defence de la République (CDR), a Hutu political party with an overtly racist agenda, further perpetuated divisive politics. At the same time, Habyarimana appeared to try to keep open a more moderate political path. Following major protests, led by the MDR in Gitarama, spreading to Butare, and finally, Kigali, political opposition pressured Habyarimana to enter into an agreement with the MDR and ultimately to start peace talks with the RPF.[78]

On August 4, 1993, under intense international and regional pressure, Habyarimana signed a peace agreement, and the Arusha Accords ended the three-and-a-half-year civil war. The Accords laid the foundation for a power-sharing agreement and an interim government, but underlying tensions were not resolved. The RPF refused to include the CDR in the interim government, branding it the extremist wing of the MRND government. This secured the RPF's interests around the negotiating table, giving them the balance of power in the proposed transitional government. At the same time, inside Rwanda, hardliners continued to arm and prepare for a "war" directed not only at the RPF, but at all people identified as Tutsi.

By this stage inside Rwanda, ethnic polarization was an everyday reality. On October 21, 1993, Tutsi army officers in Burundi assassinated their country's first democratically

[74] Ibid. 162.

[75] Ibid. 151.

[76] Fujii 121.

[77] Ibid. 52.

[78] Prunier 145–150.

elected Hutu president. The force of this event reverberated across the political spectrum, increasing fears of Tutsi supremacy among Hutus in Rwanda. At the national level there was now a clear split in all of the major opposition parties along moderate and extremist Hutu Power lines, with the latter understood to be those who supported an overtly ethnic agenda and the former as those who did not.[79] Moderates and hardliners fought over the seats assigned to their party in the Arusha Accords, which delayed installation of the transitional government by several months.

At this early stage, the newly established United Nations Assistance Mission in Rwanda (UNAMIR), led by General Roméo Dallaire, deployed to monitor the implementation of the Accords, was already threatening withdrawal.[80] Fear and insecurity as a result of the civil war and multiparty politics created a volatile environment in which power was deliberately consolidated along ethnic lines. The assassination of President Habyarimana provided the final destabilizing event from which the genocide would emanate.

3.4 THE ASSASSINATION OF PRESIDENT HABYARIMANA

On the evening of April 6, 1994, President Habyarimana's plane was shot down. He and his entourage, along with the new Burundian president, Cyprien Ntaryamira, were returning from a meeting in Dar es Salaam. The plane was coming into land in Kigali airport when unknown assailants fired two missiles from a nearby hill. The plane crashed, killing everyone on board. This assassination ruptured Rwanda's strained political relations and elicited clear and immediate responses from the elites vying for power inside the country and from the RPF.

On the RPF side, fighting broke out immediately in the northern provinces of Ruhengeri, Byumba, and the eastern regions of Gabiro.[81] The RPF stationed in the parliament building, awaiting installation in the transitional government, took a defensive position. The country was at war. Within the Rwandan political and military structures, Colonel Théoneste Bagasora took decisive steps to establish control. On the night of April 6, 1994, he called and chaired a meeting of the top military officers at the army headquarters in Camp Kigali, arguing that the military should take immediate and effective charge of the state. He refused to recognize the authority of Prime Minister Agathe Uwilingiyimana, a moderate Hutu, over the Rwandan armed forces, and Colonel Marcel Gatsinzi was appointed as the interim chief of staff of the army.[82] Moderates

---

[79] Eltringham 76–78.

[80] Roméo Dallaire, *Shake Hands with the Devil: The Failure of Humanity in Rwanda* (Carroll & Graf 2005) 141–142, 155–157, 163–164.

[81] Ibid. 269.

[82] *Prosecutor v Théoneste Bagasora, Gratien Kabiligi, Aloys Ntabakuze and Anatole Nsengiyumva* (Judgment) ICTR-98-41-T, T Ch 1 (18 December 2008) para. 659.

inside the military, however, successfully argued for the retention of a civilian government. In direct resistance to this decision, early on the morning of April 7th, the prime minister's residence in Kiyovu was attacked in "an organized military operation."[83] The prime minister went into hiding but was found later that day, sexually assaulted, and killed.[84]

That same morning, the Presidential Guard and Para Commando Battalion, acting under the authority of Bagasora, killed four of the leading moderate politicians in the PSD, PL, and MDR parties.[85] Simultaneously, the Belgian and Ghanaian peacekeepers responsible for the security of the prime minister were taken to Camp Kigali where they were attacked by a crowd of Rwandan soldiers. During the attack, the peacekeepers were explicitly blamed for the death of Habyarimana. The violence was principally directed at the Belgian soldiers, all of whom were killed. The death of these peacekeepers prompted the withdrawal of that contingent from UNAMIR on April 18 to 19.[86] Two days later, the UN Security Council, concerned about the safety of its remaining personnel, passed a resolution reducing the number of UNAMIR troops from approximately 2,000 to 270.[87] Already without a mandate to use direct force, UNAMIR was left completely incapable of effectively responding to the rapidly escalating violence.

The space for moderate politics had been entirely closed down. This was achieved through the consolidation of power along ethnic lines, virulent propaganda, and the hardliners' immediate establishment of control over the armed forces following Habyarimana's assassination. The international actors inside the country and those involved in the initial peace agreement failed to protect Rwandans supporting a moderate political position in the buildup to, and following, the assassination of the president.

In addition to the power vacuum, to which the RPF and the hardliners responded, the death of Habyarimana reverberated through the political and social structures of Rwanda with huge symbolic weight. Historically, the king in Rwanda personified the country itself.[88] Drawing on Lemarchand's idea of "presidential *mwami*-ship"[89] under the Second Republic, Habyarimana as the chief of state did in fact personify power. He took on the *mwami's* authority, and was not challenged by the separate powers of the other branches of government.[90] Within this construct, an attack on the president was an attack on the nation. The two were inseparable. This played out in the actions of the government soldiers, as seen at Camp Kigali, and as the horror unfolded in the actions

---

83 Ibid. para. 720.

84 Ibid. para. 704–705.

85 Ibid. para. 751.

86 Ibid. para. 786–795.

87 UNSC Res 912 (21 April 1994) UN Doc S/RES/912.

88 Danielle de Lame, "Mighty Secrets, Public Commensality, and the Crisis of Transparency: Rwanda through the Looking Glass" (2004) 38 Canadian Journal of African Studies 287.

89 Lemarchand 269–273.

90 de Lame, *A Hill among a Thousand: Transformations and Ruptures in Rural Rwanda* 487

of the large number of Rwandans who ultimately participated in the killing. Given this symbolic weight, the death of the president became a rallying cry for the extremist media, most notably Radio-Télévision Libre des Mille Collines (RTLM).

Directly following the plane crash, "political order had been ruptured"[91] and power was contestable. This contest occurred at both a national and local level and was initially an *intra*-Hutu struggle for dominance and authority in a period of acute crisis. The Hutus promoting violence won.[92] The violence gained momentum and "once men started killing they themselves became increasingly violent and demanded conformity from their peers."[93] Although the propaganda was key in terms of collapsing the categories of combatant and non-combatant, it was military involvement, face-to-face mobilization, and the use of family, friendship, and group ties that initiated the actual violence. The violence was brutal and intimate. Once an individual was identified as a Tutsi that person was hunted down and killed. For months, militia armed with machetes, spears, and clubs routinely attacked churches, town halls, hills, and other areas of possible refuge. Fugitives were pursued relentlessly. For those few who did survive, the trauma of those hundred days of genocide remains deeply embedded.[94]

The account of the Rwandan genocide and civil war provided in this chapter is consistent with the initial discussion of the role of ethnicity and the construction of the Rwandan state. The conflict in Rwanda involved a deep and violent contestation for power among elites, in which those aligned with a violent and racist agenda won. The state pursued a violent agenda, and at the local level, Hutu civilians aligned and realigned themselves with different power groupings to pursue personal and group interests. At both the national and local levels, tensions manifested in intra- and interthnic relations with increasing social pressure to conform to violent racist behavior. The result was one of the great human horrors and tragedies of our time, leaving close to a million people dead.

The extreme violence of genocide and the civil war has irrevocably shaped Rwandan society. The conflict and killings have deepened ethnic divisions, distrust, and fear. As discussed in the next section, the immediate post-genocide transition has been highly uncertain. As a military force, the initial focus of the RPF was ensuring the territorial integrity of Rwanda. However, as a political force it was necessary for the RPF to form a new government with other existing parties, while not compromising political control. Much of the current scholarship on Rwanda emphasizes the increasing authoritarian tendencies of the RPF, particularly under the leadership of the incumbent president Paul Kagame. Yet, it is important that such a diagnosis does not obscure the historical

---

[91] Straus 88.

[92] Ibid. 89.

[93] Ibid.

[94] Jean Hatzfeld, *Into the Quick of Life: The Survivors Speak* (Gerry Feehily tr, Serpent's Tail 2005) and Jean Hatzfeld, *The Strategy of Antelopes: Rwanda after the Genocide* (Serpent's Tail 2009).

interactions between the exercise of power at the center and the social periphery. In the post-genocide state, it is clear that criminal law has been a crucial plank in the RPF's centralist governance. However, in the Rwandan social context, it is important to highlight the dynamic interactions among the international, national, and local use of criminal law. As will be seen in the discussion of the work of the ICTR, the national courts, and *gacaca* courts in Chapters 3, 4, and 5, judicial actors have influenced the orientation of the courts. Discussing the national courts, *gacaca,* and the ICTR exclusively in terms of the political decision-making of the RPF obscures a discussion of what the international, national, and localized courts have actually been orientated toward and why.

4. The Role of Law following the Genocide

From the start of the genocide in April 1994, the RPF had advanced steadily south down the eastern side of the country and then swept west. In most areas the arrival of the rebel troops prevented further execution of Tutsi civilians and quelled the violence.[95] The civil war strategy of the rebel troops was toward a military victory, not to the optimal rescuing of civilian lives, and Tutsi continued to be slaughtered in areas not yet under RPF control.[96]

When, on July 17, 1994, the RPF eventually gained effective control of Rwanda, the possibility of exacting immediate revenge was high. Churches, public meeting halls, and private homes filled with corpses confronted the advancing soldiers. There were serious allegations of reprisal killings of Hutu civilians[97] and a large number of civilians were killed in areas of direct combat between the government and RPF forces. The genocide had occurred in a climate of revenge and the gratuitous killing by some of the most violent militia had been "justified" by claims of avenging Habyarimana's death and defending the country.[98] In this environment, the retreating ex-Rwandan army fueled the fears and rumors of brutal RPF vengeance, and such fears resonated with an already terrified population. By July 1994, with the support of the French *Opération Turquoise*, over 2 million Hutu civilians had fled to refugee camps in eastern Zaire, Tanzania, and Burundi. This mass exodus comprised predominantly Hutu civilians, but also included the full retreating army and militia who had participated in the hundred-day massacre.[99]

---

95 Des Forges, *Leave None to Tell the Story: Genocide in Rwanda* 692.

96 Ibid. 698.

97 Ibid. 726–731. Des Forges suggests that the most comprehensive report of RPF atrocities was compiled by Robert Gersony for the United Nations High Commission for Refugees (UNHCR) and, quoting this report, that in the months directly following the genocide thousands of civilians were killed per month.

98 Straus 141.

99 Gérard Prunier, "Opération Turquoise: A Humanitarian Escape from a Political Dead End" in H. Adelman and A. Suhrke (eds), *The Path of a Genocide: The Rwanda Crisis from Uganda to Zaire* (Transaction Publishers 1999).

The reaction of the newly constituted Rwandan government was shaped by both the perceived and real security threat posed by this refugee population. These actions initially led to the request by the Rwandan government to establish the ICTR, coupled with the broad arrest of lower-level genocide suspects, and later, the prosecution of these accused. At its most violent, the RPF's response to the fear of further invasion culminated in Rwanda's involvement in the first Congolese war that brought Laurent Desiré Kabila to power in May 1996, and the second Congolese war in 1998 and 1999.[100] As Phil Clark notes, "Rwanda's ongoing involvement in conflict in the Democratic Republic of Congo (DRC) underlines the extent to which, sixteen years after the genocide, it is still a heavily militarised state."[101] However, if in July 1994, the RPF soldiers had exacted widespread revenge inside the country, it would have made Rwanda ungovernable. Rather than revenge, "justice" was adopted as the mantra of the new dispensation, leading to the wide-scale arrest of suspected *génocidaires* and the establishment of the ICTR, the Special Chamber of the Rwandan Supreme Court, and finally, the *gacaca* courts.

The establishment and structure of these concurrent post-genocide courts, although often examined in isolation, have in fact influenced one another, further supporting the need for an integrated analysis of their practice. The ICTR was the first of the three courts to be established. On September 28, 1994, in a letter to the President of the United Nations Security Council (UNSC), the Permanent Representative of Rwanda to the UN identified an international criminal tribunal as one means to respond to the security concern raised by the remaining ex-government fighters and *génocidaires* on the borders of the Rwandan territory.[102]

However, on November 8, 1994, when the UNSC finally adopted Resolution 955 establishing the ICTR, it was with one dissenting vote: that of Rwanda. In her account of the reasons for the breakdown in the negotiations between the Rwandan state and the UNSC, Madeline H. Morris focuses on three central concerns. The first was that the Tribunal was to have jurisdiction only from January 1, 1994 through December 31, 1994, while Rwanda felt it should extend to 1990 to include crimes committed by the previous regime during the civil war period. This was viewed by the new Rwandan government as key to proving the planning and preparation of the genocide. Second, the number of judicial personnel designated to staff the Tribunal was seen by the Rwandan government

---

100 United Nations Office of the High Commission for Human Rights, "Report of the Mapping Exercise Documenting the Most Serious Human Rights and International Humanitarian Law Committed within the Territory of the Democratic Republic of the Congo between March 1993 and June 2003" (Report) (August 2010). This report provides evidence to suggest that the most fervent reprisal killings of Hutu civilians occurred in the Democratic Republic of Congo following July 1994 and were perpetrated by the newly constituted Rwandan Defence Force (RDF).

101 Phil Clark, *The Gacaca Courts, Post-Genocide Justice and Reconciliation in Rwanda: Justice without Lawyers* (Cambridge University Press 2010) 25.

102 Letter from the Permanent Representative of Rwanda Addressed to the President of the Security Council (Sept. 28, 1994), UN Doc. S/1994/1115.

as insufficient to deal with the number of suspects, whose arrest had been key to securing control of the country. Finally, the Tribunal was to prohibit the use of capital punishment, which was still in force in Rwanda at the time.[103]

The first two criticisms of the ICTR can certainly be viewed as legitimate, and it was in response to these concerns that the Rwandan legislature passed the 1996 Organic Law, establishing a Special Chamber of the Supreme Court to try acts sanctioned under that Rwandan Penal Code that constituted genocide and crimes against humanity, with a temporal jurisdiction from October 1990 until December 1994. When the Special Chamber began its operations, it was severely understaffed and faced with the overwhelming task of trying over 100,000 suspects. Partly as a result of these two enormous challenges, the initial trial proceedings were severely criticized. The criticisms focused on three principal issues: judicial personnel, particularly the limited number of defense counsel;[104] Rwanda's continued use of capital punishment;[105] and the restricted appeal procedure.[106]

Despite the continued international criticisms of Rwanda's domestic trials, on April 24, 1998, twenty-two people convicted of genocide before the national courts were executed in five different locations in Rwanda. This occurred five months before the ICTR handed down its first conviction of genocide and crimes against humanity, sentencing Jean-Paul Akayesu to life imprisonment.[107] The Rwandan executions would be the only death sentences for the offense of genocide carried out in the country. Two weeks later, amid international outrage, then-president Pasteur Bizimungu opened discussions on alternative justice mechanisms. These talks ultimately led to the establishment of the new *gacaca* courts.[108]

The timing of these events is notable: just as the establishment of the domestic courts was in part a reaction to the criticisms that the Rwandan government raised against the ICTR, so *gacaca* was in part a response to the international criticisms and domestic challenges raised against the national courts' prosecutions. The different criminal justice processes in Rwanda have influenced one another at the time of their establishment and, as discussed in detail in the next four chapters, in their practice.

The concurrent establishment of the ICTR, the national courts, and *gacaca* shows that criminal law and the pursuit of trials for serious human rights violations have been

---

103 Madeline H. Morris, 'The Trials of Concurrent Jurisdiction: The Case of Rwanda' (1996) 7 Duke Journal of Comparative and International Law 349, 353–357.

104 Mark Drumbl, "Rule of Law amid Lawlessness: Counselling the Accused in Rwanda's Domestic Genocide Trials" (1998) 29 Columbia Human Rights Law Review 545, 550.

105 Navanethem Pillay, "The Rwanda Tribunal and Its Relationship to National Trials in Rwanda" (1998) 13 American University International Law Review, 1477.

106 International Crisis Group, "Five Years after the Genocide in Rwanda: Justice in Question" (Report) (April 7, 1999), 15.

107 *Prosecutor v Jean-Paul Akayesu*, (Judgment and Sentence) ICTR-96-4-T, T Ch 1 (2 September 1998 and 2 October 1998).

108 Clark 61–62.

an important part of the Rwandan government's exercise of post-genocide authority. On first analysis, this response appears to support a legalist perspective on transitional justice, in line with the trend toward individual criminal accountability. Yet, in Rwanda, law was not only used as a means of quelling immediate calls for revenge through retributive justice. In addition to criminal trials, law has played a broader role in structuring the Rwandan state. There have been extensive constitutional changes, coupled with broad judicial reforms.[109] In addition, law has been explicitly adopted as the means through which the government has chosen to approach ethnicity. In 2004, any public reference to ethnic identity was banned by presidential degree, in what Lemarchand has described as a bid to "legislate ethnic identity out of existence"[110]

Lemarchand criticizes this use of law, proposing that its application has enforced a memory of the genocide in which all Tutsi were victims and all Hutu perpetrators. In refusing to acknowledge the specific identity of the victims, Lemarchand suggests that such identity is assumed to be Tutsi, effectively establishing the collective guilt of all Hutu and running counter to any ideas of individual criminal accountability or RPF culpability in the crimes of the civil war. In addition, this move has complex historical resonance as a similar proposal for the legal removal of ethnic identification was rejected in 1959 on the basis that doing so would have rendered invisible the specific exploitation of the rural Hutu peasantry and undermined the development of Hutu political consciousness.[111] While both Lee Ann Fujii and Helen Hintjens agree that the legacy of genocide has exacerbated ethnic divisions[112] and even created ethnic hatred,[113] Hintjens is supportive of the legal removal of explicit reference to ethnicity, suggesting that it has "allowed other, more complex, perspectives on political identity to emerge."[114]

The broad resort to law following the Rwandan genocide is clear and could be coherently read in line with the early transitional justice literature in which law is deployed to facilitate a move to democracy. However, Lars Waldorf contests the value of a democratizing perspective on this use of law, arguing that Rwanda "does not fit the teleological transitional justice paradigm, in which a successor regime is presumed to be democratising."[115] For Waldorf, it is Rwanda's increasingly authoritarian politics that has set the parameters for accountability and reconciliation. From this

---

109 Rwanda's new constitution entered into force in May 2003 and, as discussed in Chapter 3, stimulated further legislative reform. Constitution of the Republic of Rwanda, Law No. Special of 2/05/2003.

110 René Lemarchand, "The Politics of Memory in Post-Genocide Rwanda" in Phil Clark and Zachary D. Kaufman (eds), *After Genocide: Transitional Justice, Post-Conflict Reconstruction and Reconciliation in Rwanda and Beyond* (Hurst 2008) 66.

111 Newbury 193.

112 Helen Hintjens, "Reconstructing Political Identities in Rwanda" in Phil Clark and Zachary D. Kaufman (eds), *After Genocide: Transitional Justice, Post-Conflict Reconstruction and Reconciliation in Rwanda and Beyond* (Hurst 2008) 94.

113 Fujii 183.

114 Hintjens 97.

115 Lars Waldorf, "Mass Justice for Mass Atrocity: Rethinking Local Justice as Transitional Justice" (2006) 79 Temple Law Review 88, 11.

position, since 1994 there has been escalating oppression in Rwanda, heightened at the moments when power has been contestable.[116] This has been most clearly seen in the lead-up to the first post-genocide elections in 2003. There were restrictions on civil society, allegations of the "disappearances" of political dissidents, the arrest[117] or exile[118] of prominent government critics, and the banning of three opposition parties, including the MDR.[119] Seven years later, at the next presidential elections, the Rwandan government responded in a similar fashion. Just before the 2010 polls, two senior RPF political and military leaders went into exile and were heavily critical of Kagame's leadership,[120] followed by a similar clamping down on the press and the refusal to register two of the opposition political parties.[121]

In their recent scholarship on Rwanda, Straus and Waldorf point to a number of reasons that they see the regime as having chosen this increasingly oppressive path. They draw attention to the RPF's military background and ideology, its uncontested control of the country following the genocide, its effective use of international support, the county's history of powerful state-centered social control, and the narrowing support-base of the party.[122] Filip Reyntjens argues that most important among these considerations is the position that "the RPF would simply lose power if it accepted a competitive political system."[123]

---

116 Ibid. 3.

117 The most prominent of these arrests was that of the first post-genocide Rwandan president Pasteur Bizimungu, who resigned from office in 2000, was arrested in 2001 while attempting to create a new political party, and imprisoned until he received a presidential pardon in 2007.

118 Included among those in exile was Bosco Rutagengwa, a genocide survivor and founder of the survivors' group *Ibuka* (the Kinyarwanda word for "remember").

119 Waldorf 3 and Filip Reyntjens, "Rwanda, Ten Years On: From Genocide to Dictatorship" (2004) 103 African Affairs 177, 182.

120 General Kayumba Nyamwasa, former army chief of staff, and Colonel Patrick Karegeya, former director of Rwanda's external security services, both went into exile. In January 2011, along with Theogene Rudasingwa, Kagame's former chief of staff and ambassador to the United States, and Gerald Gahima, former Prosecutor General, Nyamwasa and Karegeya were tried and convicted in absentia by the Rwandan military courts on allegations of forming a terrorist group, threatening state security, undermining public order, promoting ethnic divisions, and insulting the president. On December 31, 2013, Karegeya was murdered in an alleged political assassination in a hotel room in Johannesburg, South Africa. At the time of this writing police investigations into his death are ongoing.

S. Kinzer, "Kagame's Authoritarian Turns Risk Rwanda's Future" *Guardian* (London January 27, 2011) http://www.guardian.co.uk/commentisfree/cifamerica/2011/jan/27/rwanda-freedom-of-speech accessed January 28, 2011.

121 X. Rice, "Rwanda Election Set to Return Kagame to President" *The Guardian* (London August 9, 2010) http://www.guardian.co.uk/world/2010/aug/09/rwanda-election-kagame-president accessed February 14, 2011.

122 Scott Straus and Lars Waldorf, "Introduction: Seeing Like a Post-Conflict State" in Scott Straus and Lars Waldorf (eds), *Remaking Rwanda: State Building and Human Rights after Mass Violence* (University of Wisconsin Press 2011).

123 Filip Reyntjens, "Constructing the Truth, Dealing with Dissent, Domesticating the World: Governance in Post-Genocide Rwanda" (2011) 110 African Affairs 1, 33.

Reyntjens is by far the most definite in his position on the current dictatorial nature of the Rwandan state, arguing that "the regime seeks full control over people and space."[124] Rather than an incremental shift since 1994 toward the restriction of freedoms, Reyntjens argues that from as early as May 1995, the enactment of the new "Fundamental Law" signaled the RPF's clear intention to establish military control.[125] In Reyntjens's view this law was "a piece of subtle and smart constitutional engineering that allowed concealment of the monolithic nature of the exercise of power."[126] He suggests that the 2003 constitution proceeded from the same logic, with the Senate and the Consultative Forum for Political Organisation (CFPO), both of which were dominated by the RPF, officially empowered to "discipline" political parties.

Clark argues that it is both incorrect and misleading to examine the RPF as a monolithic entity.[127] He proposes that serious political dissent occurs inside the party structures and can be seen in the sometimes-conflicting positions of different government departments. For Clark this is principally seen in the debates over the formation and implementation of the *gacaca* process in Rwanda. There was serious contestation and disagreement over the structure and implementation of *gacaca*. Some members of the government, including Kagame, viewed the localized courts as insufficiently retributive. As discussed in Chapter 4, political compromises were made in the buildup to and during *gacaca's* establishment. In addition, the structure of *gacaca* has transferred a significant amount of power to the local level, and Clark argues that the requirement of public dialogue in the hearings appears to run counter to the RPF's attempts to quash dissent.[128]

From an interpretive perspective, to use as a starting point the view that the Rwandan state is authoritarian flattens the contours of how the concurrent transitional justice processes have worked and interacted. At the same time, however, the political history and current social context of Rwanda remains central to the analysis here. Understanding the formation of the Rwandan state is key to analyzing the work of the post-genocide courts. It highlights the strategic but constrained engagement between state officials and external players and draws attention to the exercise of centralized power while acknowledging the differences between central administrative accounts of state policies and local experiences. As a result, an empirical examination of the understandings of all three of

---

124 Ibid. 2.

125 Promulgated on May 26, 1995, the Fundamental Law entered into force retroactively on July 17, 1994, the day the RPF officially declared victory. Along with the Protocol of Agreement from November 24, 1994, this law had supremacy over the Arusha Accords drawn up as part of the initial civil war Peace Agreement and the 1991 Constitution. Filip Reyntjens, "Constitution-Making in Situations of Extreme Crisis: The Case of Rwanda and Burundi" (1996) 40 Journal of African Law 234.

126 Reyntjens, "Constructing the Truth, Dealing with Dissent, Domesticating the World: Governance in Post-Genocide Rwanda," 16.

127 Phil Clark, "Book Review: International Justice in Rwanda and the Balkans: Virtual Trials and the Struggle for State Cooperation" (2008) 22 Ethics and International Affairs 433.

128 Clark, *The Gacaca Courts, Post-Genocide Justice and Reconciliation in Rwanda: Justice without Lawyers* 23.

the transitional justice processes in Rwanda helps to illuminate how the post-genocide courts have attempted to legitimize their authority. Such an enquiry highlights where the courts' power has been eroded and how the legitimacy of all three of the courts could have been strengthened.

5. Conclusion

The Rwandan social context, described in this chapter, informs how the actions of the ICTR, the national courts, and *gacaca* have been interpreted. The next four chapters take seriously the points of agreement and dissent within Rwanda's post-conflict courts. Chapters 2, 3, and 4 outline how the processes of the courts have been understood inside their implementing institutions. What becomes clear is that the ICTR, the national courts, and *gacaca* have pursued increasingly divergent objectives, and this has affected the work of the courts and their ability to complement one another. Chapter 5 then explains why this divergence has occurred and its implications for the ability of concurrent international, national, and localized criminal courts to provide a legitimate and just response to the crimes of the civil war and the genocide in Rwanda.

In each chapter, the social context of Rwanda remains salient. In relation to the ICTR, as discussed above, international criminal law provided a response to real postwar security concerns. Inside Rwanda, as with previous responses to foreign involvement, the court has been subject to strategic co-option by the Rwandan state. At the national level, the strategic use of the ICTR is buttressed by an increased scepticism toward international intervention following the failure of the UN to protect Rwanda civilians during the genocide. It is within this social context that, as a legal institution, the ICTR has endeavored to insulate itself from complicated domestic politics and, as discussed in detail in Chapter 2, purposely oriented itself toward an international legal audience.

Similarly, when examining the national courts and *gacaca*, it is necessary to remain conscious of what Rwanda is transitioning from and to. This chapter has drawn attention to how the country's political power has historically been held in the hands of a few elites, and current analyses suggest that this remains the case. However, as argued above, the current "legal, political and military landscape"[129] of post-genocide Rwanda requires an analysis of the use of law that does not assume that the state is homogenous or that the executive exclusively determines how state policies are implemented. In examining the actions of the national courts in the Rwandan social context, Chapter 3 acknowledges the role that these courts have played in aiding the security agenda of the Rwandan government and their use and resistance to international law. Nonetheless, the chapter takes seriously the means through which the courts have endeavored to establish their independence.

---

129 Ibid. 25.

Similarly at the local level, current scholarship on the Rwandan genocide rightly emphasizes the importance of the processes through which central state policies of ethnicity and violence were locally implemented. The establishment of the Rwandan state and the causes and processes of the genocide are not perfectly explained through a discussion of the central power of the state. In Chapter 4, Rwanda's historical background of central control and local action helps to explain the regional variation in the interpretations of the work of the localized *gacaca* courts. What emerges is that the central government's interpretation of what *gacaca* courts have achieved differs from the more localized understanding held by the *gacaca* judges.

Finally, this chapter's account of the Rwandan social context draws attention to how ethnic identity emerged and has been used as a means of contesting centralized power. The extreme violence of the genocide, expressed in stark ethnic terms, has deepened divisions within communities. Given this post-genocide social reality, Chapter 5 examines how the concurrent work of the ICTR, the national courts, and *gacaca* has been understood to respond to the crimes committed during the conflict. In examining the interpretations of the courts' work offered by general participants, it is important to remain mindful that Rwandan citizens have complex political identities. Historically, citizens have exercised their capacity to strategically align themselves with state policies and to conform to social norms but, similarly, there have been consistent moments of resistance to the exercise of power from the center, leading to notable local variance in the strength and impact of the Rwandan state. This continues today and informs the understandings of transitional justice in Rwanda.

2 Inside the United Nations International Criminal Tribunal for Rwanda

1. Introduction

The judge strode across the runway toward the UN-branded light aircraft. I followed, eager to continue our discussion. As we boarded the plane he turned to me:

> You must remember that the Tribunal is not just about Rwanda—it is about the world. It was set up by the United Nations to apologize because they had not acted when Dallaire had called them to act.[1]

I had spent the two months before this brief exchange in Rwanda, grappling with how the ICTR was being understood in light of the concurrent operation of national criminal prosecutions and the *gacaca* courts. My realization, as we fell into silence, ascended and started our journey back to Arusha, Tanzania, was that in a comparative discussion of post-genocide justice in Rwanda, it was useful to evaluate how those at the Tribunal understood their own work.

[1] Informal Discussion with a Trial Chamber Judge (Participant 25), Chambers, UN ICTR (Kigali, Rwanda, September 8, 2008) notes on file with author.

Clifford Geertz suggests that through culture, an action is ascribed meaning.[2] This chapter addresses the question: How have the ICTR judges and lawyers understood the Tribunal's actions, and what does this indicate about the legal culture of international criminal law and its operation in post-genocide Rwanda? Answering this question places the judges and lawyers at the center of the analysis. The legal culture of the ICTR comprises the collection of concepts, practical experience and professional intuitions that give meaning to the actions of the judges and lawyers.[3] The concepts used by the judicial actors to describe what the courts are trying to achieve both reflect and constitute the culture of the international institution[4] and help to explain the court's interaction with Rwanda's domestic systems of post-genocide criminal justice.

In written law, the ICTR, the national courts, and *gacaca* are meant to be complementary, with each court seeking to establish accountability for the crimes committed during the Rwandan genocide. This chapter examines the concurrent work of the courts, in practice. The chapter argues that how the work of the ICTR has been understood, inside the institution, has impacted upon the international court's formal and informal interactions with the concurrent domestic courts. For the ICTR, the compatibility of the three courts depends on the domestic courts' supporting the international proceedings.

Although there is extensive scholarship on post-genocide justice in Rwanda, few studies have explored the implications of the concurrent operation of an international, national, and localized set of transitional mechanisms. Madeleine H. Morris, writing in 1996 on the disputes over the distribution of suspects between the ICTR and the Rwandan national courts, argues that there is a need to clarify the specific purpose of each jurisdiction if there is to be effective prosecution of genocide at both the national and international level.[5] Alexander Betts, in 2005 after the extension of domestic post-genocide justice to include the *gacaca* courts, proposes that political tensions and elite interests in all three tiers of justice have created contradictions that undermine judicial credibility and compatibility between the courts.[6] However, an evaluation of the Tribunal as entirely determined by elite political interests, as Betts suggests, fails to take account of any normative objectives that may have driven the work of the courts or how this work has been received, reproduced, or disrupted by the interpretations and actions of everyday Rwandans.[7]

---

[2] Clifford Geertz, "Thick Description: Toward an Interpretive Theory of Culture" in Clifford Geertz (ed), *The Interpretation of Cultures: Selected Essays* (Fontana Press 1993) 6.

[3] This interpretive cultural account draws strongly on David Garland's notion of the constituent elements of penal culture. David Garland, *Punishment and Modern Society: A Study in Social Theory* (Oxford University Press 1990) 210.

[4] David Nelken, "Using the Concept of Legal Culture" (2004) 29 Australian Journal of Legal Philosophy 1, 10.

[5] Morris, 350.

[6] Alexander Betts, "Should Approaches to Post-conflict Justice and Reconciliation Be Determined Globally, Nationally or Locally?" (2005) 17 The European Journal of Development Research 735.

[7] These local interpretations of the work of the ICTR and the other post-genocide courts are discussed in greater detail in Chapter 5.

This chapter responds to Morris's call for greater clarity, while taking seriously the broad set of potential objectives of the ICTR, outlined in the general literature on transitional justice and international criminal law, discussed in the Introduction. An empirical evaluation of the ICTR's objectives, as understood inside the institution, highlights the court's focus on the development of international criminal case law. This is the dominant understanding of the ICTR's work, and it has shaped its formal interaction with Rwanda's concurrent national and local transitional justice processes. Inside the Tribunal, the actions of the Rwandan national courts and *gacaca* are explained in a way that is consistent with the ICTR's focus on building an international legal regime. The work of the Rwandan domestic courts is interpreted within the ICTR's cultural context, better explaining the Tribunal's decisions on the transfer of its remaining cases to Rwanda, and its scepticism toward the evidentiary value of the *gacaca* proceedings.

The chapter is structured around three sections. The first reviews the current literature on the ICTR, showing how it has centered on the court's ability to fulfil its legal mandate, articulated in Security Council Resolution 955. When examined together, these writings highlight the international orientation of the Tribunal; yet, they fail to take account of the agency of the judicial actors inside that institution. Responding to this failure, the interpretive approach pursued in this chapter establishes the specific relevance of detailed empirical work inside the ICTR.

The second section outlines the findings of the empirical research conducted in 2008, 2010, and 2012, with a selection of judges, prosecutors, defense counsel, and registry staff working at the Tribunal. The ICTR's contribution to a substantive body of international case law emerges as the judges' and lawyers' dominant interpretations of the court's actions alongside its contribution to removing key political players and, to a much lesser extent, its contribution to a historical account of the genocide and to reconciliation in Rwanda. These understandings of the practice of the ICTR are significantly narrower than those envisioned at the outset of the process, or within the established literature on transitional justice and international criminal law. In part, this narrowing is explained by several practical constraints on the process, as the ICTR has attempted to insulate itself from the complicated social and political context of post-genocide Rwanda.

Stepping inside the ICTR allows the researcher to take the Tribunal on its personnel's own terms. The final section analyzes the implications of how the work of the ICTR has been "produced, perceived and interpreted"[8] for the concurrent practice of local, national, and international transitional justice. For a group of genocide suspects who have testified before the ICTR and have been prosecuted by the national courts or *gacaca*, the post-genocide courts have interacted through their own personal experiences. At these points of informal contract, the ICTR's institutional focus on international case law emerged as one of the criticisms raised against the work of the Tribunal. However, at points of formal interaction, such as when the ICTR has reviewed the

[8] Geertz 7.

practice of the Rwandan national courts or has made use of the *gacaca* records in its judgments, the ICTR's actions are consistent with the court's internal understandings of Rwandan domestic processes.

The legal culture of the ICTR is illuminated by the ways in which the judges and lawyers have understood the Tribunal's practice. In this cultural context, the work of the national courts and *gacaca* are examined in a similar manner to how the international judges and lawyers have interpreted their own work. The words used by the ICTR participants are key to understanding the social institutions and the cultural formations that surround the actions of the post-genocide criminal courts.[9] For the judges and lawyers at the ICTR, the compatibility of an international, national, and localized system of criminal justice rests on the assumption that the work of the Rwandan national courts and *gacaca* should support the international court's activities. As the domestic institutions are not perceived to do this sufficiently, the ICTR's personnel raise strong criticisms against the domestic courts, and the ICTR is intentionally distanced from, and resistant to, the development of domestic judicial institutions.

The purpose of this chapter's analysis of international criminal law is to make observations "offered in the spirit of improving a relatively new discipline,"[10] taking the lead from scholarship pursued by Darryl Robinson. Robinson suggests that we need to reflect on *how we think* about international criminal law, because it affects not only the way we implement the law but also how the law is practiced. Due to the international humanitarian law principles within international criminal law, "prosecution and conviction are often conceptualized as the fulfilment of the victims' human right to a remedy."[11] Robinson argues that this sits in tension with the fundamental principles of liberal criminal law where "liberal sensitivities focus on constraining the use of the state's coercive power against individuals."[12] In practice the focus on the duty to prosecute plays out in the "sweeping modes of liability, expanding definitions of crimes, and reticence towards defences in international criminal law."[13]

As Robinson suggests, the comfortable liberal discourse on international criminal law often obscures the need to critically interrogate how it is being practiced. This applies not only to the case law, with its expanding net of culpability as discussed by Robinson, but also to its interactions with domestic criminal justice systems. Rather than remaining settled in its moral basis and buttressed by its dedication to procedural fairness, this chapter critically examines how the ICTR has interacted with domestic criminal practice and alternative accountability mechanisms in Rwanda.

---

[9] Sally Engle Merry, "Legal Pluralism" (1988) 22 Law & Social Review 869, 886.

[10] Darryl Robinson, "The Identity Crisis of International Criminal Law" (2008) 21 Leiden Journal of International Law 925, 931.

[11] Ibid. 930.

[12] Ibid.

[13] Ibid. 927.

2. The Mandate of the ICTR

On November 8, 1994, the ICTR was established by the UNSC through Resolution 955. The Tribunal was mandated to:

- respond to a threat to international peace and security by putting an end to the crimes and taking effective measures to bring to justice the persons who are responsible for them.
- contribute to the process of national reconciliation and to the restoration and maintenance of peace.
- stress the need for international cooperation to strengthen the Courts and Judicial System of Rwanda, having regard in particular to the necessity for those Courts to deal with large numbers of suspects.

In the literature on the ICTR, its work is predominantly assessed against this original mandate. Peter Uvin and Charles Mironko concur with the judge with whom I flew to Arusha, and argue that the establishment of the ICTR was underpinned by the international community's desire to reaffirm its own morality in light of its failure to respond to the genocide.[14] This guilt is often identified as a central driving factor behind the court.[15]

William Schabas and Zachary D. Kaufman, in separate but complementary pieces, provide further insight into the political considerations underpinning the Tribunal's establishment. Kaufman postulates that it was the United States' prior support for the ICTY that drove support for a similar vision of justice for Rwanda.[16] In a discussion of the statements of UN representatives, religious leaders, and diplomats at the time, Schabas suggests that there is evidence that an international tribunal was contemplated from the earliest days of the genocide[17] and there was certainly a growing perception that an international response was required.

Common across these commentators' analyses is the internationalized nature of the processes establishing the ICTR. Victor Peskin proposes that another initial indication

---

14 Peter Uvin and Charles Mironko, "Western and Local Approaches to Justice in Rwanda" (2003) Global Governance 219.

15 Virginia Morris and Michael P Scharf, *The International Criminal Tribunal for Rwanda*, vol 1 (Transnational Publishers 1998). A similar argument has recently been raised by Thierry Cruvellier, *Court of Remorse: Inside the International Criminal Tribunal for Rwanda* (Chari Voss tr, The University of Wisconsin Press 2010).

16 Zachary D Kaufman, "The United States Role in the Establishment of the United Nations International Criminal Tribunal for Rwanda" in Phil Clark and Zachary D. Kaufman (eds), *After Genocide: Transitional Justice, Post-conflict Reconstruction and Reconciliation in Rwanda and Beyond* (Hurst and Company 2008).

17 William Schabas, "Post-Genocide Justice in Rwanda: A Spectrum of Opinions" in Phil Clark and Zachary D. Kaufman (eds), *After Genocide: Transitional Justice, Post-conflict Reconstruction and Reconciliation in Rwanda and Beyond* (Hurst and Company 2008).

of the intended audience of the court was the decision to locate it in Arusha, Tanzania, rather than in Rwanda. He argues that this was done "in a large part, to insulate the court from political forces that could harm the integrity of this experiment in international law."[18] The location of the ICTR in Tanzania was an intentional decision to distance the court from the compromised post-genocide social context. Crucially, in both the ICTY and ICTR, the international basis of the courts meant that the decision of whether and how to prosecute human rights abuses was taken out of the hands of domestic state structures and placed within the discretionary power of a Prosecutor appointed by the Security Council.[19]

Under Security Council Resolution 955, the Office of the Prosecutor (OTP) is charged with the duty to effectively prosecute persons alleged to have committed war crimes, crimes against humanity, or genocide in the territory of Rwanda in 1994. In the exercise of their discretion, the Prosecutors of the ICTR have focused on those deemed most responsible for the genocide. The literature supporting the work of the ICTR focuses on the court's mandate to contribute to justice and security. Rwandan commentators writing from outside of the country identify the Tribunal's ability to arrest and incapacitate senior public figures whose continued involvement in the political arena could have resulted in the "political and military destabilization of the peace in Rwanda."[20]

Further supportive commentators, such as Schabas, have determined that the Tribunal has effectively pursued the mandate to take "measures to bring to justice the persons who are responsible for the crimes."[21] He writes, "the ICTR has managed to try and convict many of the most prominent and important participants in the 1994 genocide"[22] while avoiding the criticism of "being unrepresentative and, therefore, biased against the majority Hutus."[23] However, the Tribunal's pursuit of accountability has also been seriously challenged.

As with its achievements, the criticisms leveled against the ICTR focus on the court's original mandate and reflect its international orientation. Indicative of an increasingly held position, Luc Reydams argues that the ICTR's failure to initiate proceedings against RPF officials suspected of violating international humanitarian law in 1994 compromises the achievement of the court's mandated objectives of justice, reconciliation,

---

18 Victor Peskin, "Courting Rwanda: The Promises and Pitfalls of the ICTR Outreach Programme" (2005) 3 Journal of International Criminal Justice 950, 950.

19 Helena Cobban, "The Legacies of Collective Violence: The Rwandan Genocide and the Limits of Law" (2002) 27 Boston Review http://new.bostonreview.net/BR27.2/cobban.html accessed November 26, 2014.

20 Jean Marie Kamatali, "The Challenge of Linking International Criminal Justice and National Reconciliation: The Case of the ICTR" (2003) 16 Leiden Journal of International Law 115, 127. This argument is also made in Francois-Xavier Nsanzuwera, "The ICTR's Contribution to National Reconciliation" (2005) 3 Journal of International Criminal Justice 944, 948.

21 Schabas 211.

22 Ibid.

23 Ibid. 212.

and maintenance of peace in the Great Lakes region.[24] This position holds that prosecuting only one side of the civil war risks compromising "the very idea of international criminal justice."[25] This is a challenge to the Tribunal by the international community, its main constituency, and so it manages this criticism very carefully and with great effort. In 2009, a group of NGOs and academics working on Rwanda signed a petition directed to the ICTR, calling for the indictment of RPF suspects.[26] In response, the current Prosecutor, Hassan Jallow, argued that there is currently insufficient evidence to issue indictments against members of the RPF, while defending the OTP's efforts to investigate the allegations.[27]

The achievements and current critiques of the ICTR highlight the court's international positioning, epitomized in the discussions of the court's location, its ability to apprehend and remove key political players, and its capacity to justly determine the guilt or innocence of these senior accused. The importance of this international audience is similarly seen in the Tribunal's careful management of the criticism that it has failed to account for RPF crimes. However, these appraisals of the ICTR are static. They center on the original mandate of the Tribunal and fail to acknowledge that the emphasis of this mandate may have shifted over time due to the agency of the judicial actors within that institution. There is a need to examine the practice of the Tribunal from the perspective of those who argue the law, make the legal decisions, and implement the judgments.

The Tribunal has operated as a functional legal institution for twenty years. The lawyers and judges working inside the institution have made crucial decisions about the purpose and direction of the ICTR. Their understanding speaks to both the purpose of the trials and the compatibility of the ICTR's legal practice with the concurrent domestic transitional justice processes.

---

[24] Luc Reydams, "The ICTR Ten Years On: Back to the Nuremberg Paradigm?" (2005) 3 Journal of International Criminal Justice 977.

[25] Ibid.

[26] Kenneth Roth, "Letter to the Prosecutor of the International Criminal Tribunal for Rwanda Regarding the Prosecution of RPF Crimes" (May 26, 2009) http://www.hrw.org/node/83536 accessed August 31, 2009.

[27] Hassan Jallow, "Letter in Response to Kenneth Roth, Executive Director of Human Rights Watch" (June 22, 2009 OTP/2009/P/084') http://www.hrw.org/sites/default/files/related_material/2009_06_Rwanda_Jallow_Response.pdf accessed August 31, 2009.

In 2008, following joint investigations by the Rwandan Public Prosecutor and the ICTR's OTP, four RPF soldiers were arrested and tried for the murder of fifteen clergymen in Kabgayi, Mihanga District, in central Rwanda in June 1994. Two of the officers, Captain John Butera and Captain (Rtd) Dieudonné Rukeba, pleaded guilty and were sentenced to eight years in prison. This sentence was later reduced to five years on appeal. The other two more senior accused were acquitted, as the Military Court held that the Prosecutor had failed to establish command responsibility. Following these domestic proceedings, the call for an internationalized response continued.

"Rwandan Military Court Acquits Two Officers and Sentences Two Others" *Hirondelle* (Arusha October 24, 2008) http://www.hirondellenews.com/content/view/11594/291/ accessed March 7, 2011.

3. Inside the Institution

As discussed in the Introduction, the empirical research underpinning this study was conducted in four phases: first, through eighteen months of participant observations at the Tribunal; second, a two-month period of intensive data collection through semi-structured interviews, participant observations, informal discussions, and the analysis of grey material and case law in June and July 2008; third, through the presentation of the research findings to the ICTR staff in April 2010 for feedback and refinement; and, finally, through a follow-up set of semi-structured interviews and informal discussions in March 2012.

Forty interviews were held with personnel across Prosecution, Defence, Chambers, and the Registry. In these interviews, the Tribunal was credited with making four contributions through its practice: the creation of a body of international criminal case law, the removal of key political players who were primarily responsible for the genocide, the construction of a historical record of the genocide, and the reconciliation in Rwanda. As will be discussed, these contributions were not uniformly endorsed, and must be assessed in light of the constraints on the practice of international criminal justice. It is through an analysis of these perceptions of the court's work that this research is able to take a first step in providing a "thick description" of the legal culture within the ICTR, enabling an examination of the implications of the court's culture for the effective practice of concurrent local, national, and international criminal justice.

3.1 A CONTRIBUTION TO INTERNATIONAL CASE LAW

As Prosecutor Jallow succinctly stated in 2008, "The first [contribution the Tribunal has made] is the jurisprudence. This has been tremendous, particularly in relation to the substantive law. It has fleshed out the elements of the crimes, defining the contours of the law."[28] In a similar vein in 2012, Judge President Joensen remarked,

> The major general contribution is that the international community has set up a system that challenges impunity for leaders here, and elsewhere. It has laid the groundwork for the ICC. With respect of more concrete results, it has developed the jurisprudence, it was the first court to apply the Genocide Convention and the first to try a head of state.[29]

---

[28] Interview with Prosecutor Hassan Jallow, OTP, UN ICTR (Arusha, Tanzania, December 1, 2008) notes on file with author.

[29] Interview with Judge President Vagn Joensen, Chambers, UN ICTR (Arusha, Tanzania, March 27, 2012) notes on file with author.

These words encapsulate the sentiment expressed by the majority of the participants across the Prosecution, Chambers, and Defence of the ICTR.[30] These judges and lawyers identified the development of international jurisprudence as the primary contribution of the Tribunal. The common emphasis on the ICTR's case law was particularly striking, given the initial methodological assumption that Prosecution, Defence, and Chambers would hold quite different positions on the work of the court.

As Joensen's and Jallow's statements suggest, respondents tended to identify two key components to this understanding of the court's work: first, the contribution of the Tribunal in defining the elements of the crimes within the Statute, particularly with regard to the crime of genocide; and, second, the creation of a body of case law that has provided the building blocks for the ICC. The court's work was described by one respondent as creating a "global movement"[31] and another as "an international model of justice."[32]

The ICTR's clear focus on developing international case law illustrates a narrow understanding of the legalist justification for transitional judicial processes. From a legalist position, case law is seen as the basis for the pursuit of criminal trials, not the end point of the process. The development of a body of case law supports courts in establishing criminal liability and punishment for particular violations of international law, the deterrence of future violations, or the public denunciation of such conduct as unacceptable.[33] Equally, from a democratizing perspective, it is through the body of case law and the establishment of judicial institutions that the consistent and equal application of the law assists in the movement toward a liberal democratic state. The role of law is to transform the prevailing meaning of legality in the transitional moment.[34] An interpretive examination of how the ICTR's judges and lawyers make sense of their own actions shows that the Tribunal's contribution is now significantly distanced from the transitional moment in Rwanda. It is directed toward the transition to an international criminal regime.

---

[30] Ten to fourteen participants from each section of the Tribunal were selected on the basis of their involvement in the recent Rule 11 *bis* transfer decisions or their participation in the *Karemera* case. Two participants were interviewed in the Registry.

[31] Interview with Trial Attorney (Participant 14), OTP, UN ICTR (Arusha, Tanzania, July 17, 2008) notes on file with author.

[32] Interview with Associate Legal Officer (Participant 19), Chambers, UN ICTR (Arusha, Tanzania, July 17, 2008) notes on file with author.

[33] As discussed in the Introduction, this position was broadly raised in José Zalaquett, "Confronting Human Rights Violations Committed by Former Governments: Principles Applicable and Political Constraints" in Neil J. Kritz (ed), *Transitional Justice: How Emerging Democracies Reckon with Former Regimes* vol 1 (United States Institute of Peace 1995) and more forcefully advocated by Diane Orentlicher in her debate with Carlos Nino in 1991. Retributive, deterrent, and expressivist justifications for the pursuit of criminal trials during transitions continue to underpin a large amount of transitional justice scholarship. For a summary of this literature, see chapter 1 of Tricia D Olsen, Leigh A. Payne, and Andrew G. Reiter, *Transitional Justice in Balance: Comparing Processes, Weighing Efficiency* (U.S. Institute of Peace Press 2010).

[34] Ruti G. Teitel, *Transitional Justice* (Oxford University Press 2000) 19.

One of the reasons for this narrowing is self-evident: while the objectives of peace, security, and reconciliation are difficult to quantify, the case law provides something definite in its neatly printed words. As one judge, who has dedicated a significant part of her career to international criminal law, articulated in relation to the ICTR and ICTY cases, "something concrete has been done."[35] Although the ICTR's actions are shaped by its original mandate, its practice has also actively molded its participants' understandings of these objectives. As a senior prosecutor articulated, "international criminal justice has been perceived as the cure-all and it isn't, but we have learnt from experience."[36] What emerges from the dialectic between the ICTR's original mandate and its practice is an increasing focus on building an international legal order, rather than a focus on the ICTR's contribution to justice, peace, or reconciliation inside Rwanda.

Just as Anderson argued that newspapers and novels provided the images and symbols of the imagined community of a nation, so the case law of the ICTR provides solidity to the illusive notion of the "international community," reinforcing this community's ability to respond to the Rwandan genocide.[37] In doing so, the case law contributes to the broader project of building an international consciousness.[38] However, as illustrated below, this orientation has also shaped the Tribunal's ability to make sense of the practice of the national and localized post-genocide courts.

The Tribunal's increasingly clear focus on its contribution to international criminal case law, rather than the broader objectives articulated in its initial mandate, shows the dynamic nature of transitional justice. The practice of the court and the challenges it has faced have shaped what the institution is understood to have achieved. A similarly dynamic ascription of meaning is seen in the other emergent objectives of the court.

3.2 REMOVAL OF KEY POLITICAL PLAYERS

The second central understanding of the actions of the ICTR, in this instance held most strongly among participants in the OTP and Chambers, was the perception that the Tribunal has contributed to peace and security through the removal of key figures from the Rwandan political arena. Respondents most often placed this contribution second to, but in close conjunction with, the Tribunal's development of international case law. The ICTR judges and lawyers argued that the international character of the Tribunal allowed it to exercise effective jurisdiction over fugitives whom the Rwandan state would not

[35] Interview with Trial Chamber Judge (Participant 4), Chambers, UN ICTR (Arusha, Tanzania, July 9, 2008) notes on file with author.

[36] Interview with Senior Trial Attorney (Participant 10), OTP, UN ICTR (Arusha, Tanzania, July 15, 2008) notes and recording on file with author.

[37] Benedict Anderson, *Imagined Communities: Reflections on the Origins and Spread of Nationalism* (Verso 1983) 25.

[38] Ibid. 44.

have been able to extradite. From this perspective, international criminal justice is one of a plethora of tools to remove certain influential individuals from the political stage. As a participant in Chambers articulated,

> The first contribution of the Tribunal is a factual one. The Tribunal has apprehended over sixty people who otherwise would not have been brought to justice. The Rwandan government would not have negotiated the extraditions to the country.[39]

Understandably, this view was closely linked with the Tribunal's achievement in terms of accountability, again attributed in part to the international character of the institution. As one participant in OTP concisely stated,

> I think that its major contribution has been holding persons accountable. It has shifted the focus from state responsibility to the recognition that individuals committed these crimes. In punishing and seeking to punish, it will be a deterrent too, as potential human rights violators will recognise that this is an international process.[40]

This participant's interpretation sits comfortably with a number of external commentators' appraisals of the work of the Tribunal. Payam Akhavan, a strong proponent of international criminal justice and its deterrent potential, argues that the incapacitation of the Hutu extremist political and military leadership is the primary contribution of the Tribunal.[41]

However, from as early as 1996, Morris contested the argument that the international criminal tribunal should try the leaders simply because it could gain custody of them. The claim rests on the assumption that countries would not extradite suspects to Rwanda, an assumption that was initially challenged by the extradition of Ferdinand Karamera from Ethiopia to Rwanda.[42] However, this position was recently reasserted with the refusal of extradition of Rwandan genocide suspects in Finland,[43] France,[44]

---

[39] Interview with Trial Chamber Judge (Participant 28), Chambers, UN ICTR (Arusha, Tanzania, September 12, 2008) notes on file with author.

[40] Interview with Trial Attorney (Participant 23), OTP, UN ICTR (Arusha, Tanzania, July 25, 2008) notes on file with author.

[41] Payam Akhavan, "Beyond Impunity: Can International Criminal Justice Prevent Future Atrocities?" (2001) 95 The American Journal of International Law 7, 23–24.

[42] Morris 363.

[43] Redress, "Report on Universal Jurisdictional Developments" (January 2006—May 2009) http://www.redress.org accessed October 1, 2009.

[44] Ibid.

Germany,[45] and the United Kingdom.[46] These decisions were heavily influenced by the ICTR's own refusal to transfer cases to the Rwandan national courts. However, as discussed in detail in the final section of this chapter, the ICTR has now transferred the cases of Jean Uwinkindi and Bernard Munyagishari to Rwanda, and Canada and Norway have extradited Léon Mugesera and Charles Bandora respectively, increasing the likelihood of further extraditions.[47]

The removal of key players from the political arena is a more modest contribution than that of establishing peace and security in current-day Rwanda. None of the respondents made the claim that removing these individuals had secured peace in the Great Lakes region. Repeatedly since the 1994 genocide, eastern DRC has experienced insecurity and violence, in part due to ongoing military mobilization around the ethnic divisions that drove the genocide.[48] As seen in the predominant focus on developing international criminal case law, inside the Tribunal, the court's actions are understood to be more specific and narrower than the initially envisaged mandate. In addition to being the most routinely cited justifications, all participants who mentioned the development of case law and the trial of certain key politicians framed these contributions positively, and there was consensus regarding their value. It is notable that these elements are understood as the main justifications for the process. The other two emergent justifications, namely the creation of a historical record and reconciliation, were contested across participants. The criticisms of these understood contributions support the emerging position that the Tribunal's central endeavor has been to contribute to the establishment of an international legal order.

3.3 CREATION OF A HISTORICAL RECORD

In his recent appraisal of the ICTR, Schabas credits it with clarifying the historical truth of the genocide and, in doing so, putting this account beyond the reach of deniers and negators.[49] However, inside the institution there was strong contestation over the perspective that international criminal law is justified through its contribution to the

---

45 Ibid.

46 Brown, Munyaneza, Nteziryayo, and Ugirashebuja v The Government of Rwanda and the Secretary of State for the Home Department, [2009] EWHC 770 (Admin).

47 *Prosecutor v. Jean Uwinkindi* (Decision on the Prosecutor's Request for Referral to the Republic of Rwanda) ICTR-2001-75-R11bis, T Ch (28 June 2011) [hereinafter *Uwinkindi* Rule 11 *bis* Trial judgment]; *Prosecutor v. Bernard Munyagishari* ICTR-05-89-R11bis, T Ch (6 June 2012) [hereinafter *Munyagishari* Rule 11 *bis* Trial judgment] and the Cour Superiéure, Canada, Province de Québec, District de Montréal, No 500-17-069828-120 (23 January 2012).

48 The most recent cases of such violence have centered on the actions of two rebel groups, the *Forces démocratiques de libération du Rwanda* (FDLR) and a newer formation known as M23. These groups claim to represent the interest of Hutu and Tutsi civilians, respectively. For a discussion of the actions of M23 and allegations of the Rwandan government's support of this rebel group, see "Interim Report of the Group of Experts on the DRC Submitted in Accordance with Paragraph 4 of Security Council Resolution 2021 (2011)" http://www.un.org/sc/committees/1533/egroup.shtml accessed November 21, 2012.

49 Schabas 221.

creation of a historical record. The distinct positions emerged from the interview material. The first perspective fervently opposed such an understanding. As a senior member of Chambers articulated,

> Creating an historical record was certainly one of the initial rationales for setting up the Tribunal. This is problematic as the ICTR is staffed by legal experts, not historians. In the cases there can be an over-abundance of historical material and allowing this excessive detail on contested histories can undermine the fairness of the trial and is contrary to any efforts to streamline the process. Worse than this, there is a danger of bad history; they can get it wrong. This objective needs to be seriously re-evaluated. A criminal trial is not an instrument of history. I think to use it as such can be futile and dangerous.[50]

The second perspective was to support the idea that the Tribunal had contributed to the creation of a historical record with the caveat that this record was restricted to the activities of the selected individuals who have been indicted. Respondents emphasized the use of the criminal justice processes as a means of establishing certain historical facts, but noted that it provided only a part of the picture.[51]

The third position was in ardent support of a historical justification for the Tribunal's activities. As a judge in Chambers highlighted,

> We are contributing to an historical record, particularly at the ICTR. At the end of the day, we are trying the same case again and again. The events occurred over a very small area, in a very brief space of time and they are the same witnesses, testifying to the same events.[52]

Similarly, other participants argued that, through its judgments, the ICTR has contributed to the prevention of genocide revisionism or denial. In this reading, the court provided a mechanism, outside of the Rwandan state, that acknowledged that the genocide occurred.[53]

---

[50] Interview with Senior Legal Officer (Participant 2), Chambers, UN ICTR (Arusha, Tanzania, July 4, 2008) notes on file with author.

[51] Interview with Legal Officer (Participant 7), Chamber, UN ICTR (Arusha, Tanzania, July 15, 2008) notes on file with author; interview with Senior Defence Council (Participant 9), Defence, UN ICTR (Arusha, Tanzania, July 15, 2008) notes and recording on file with author; interview with Trial Attorney (Participant 14), OTP, UN ICTR (Arusha, Tanzania, July 17, 2008) notes on file with author; and interview with Senior Trial Attorney (Participant 34) OTP, UN ICTR (Arusha, Tanzania, December 1, 2008) notes on file with author.

[52] Interview with Trial Chamber Judge (Participant 4), Chambers, UN ICTR (Arusha, Tanzania, July 9, 2008) notes on file with author.

[53] Interview with ICTR Personnel (Participant 1), OTP, UN ICTR (Arusha, Tanzania, July 3, 2008) notes on file with author.

The creation of a historical record was not explicitly included in the Tribunal's mandate in 1994. In line with the perspectives articulated by some of the ICTR judges and lawyers, Zackin challenges the role that the Tribunal should play in fulfilling broader transitional objectives, stating that "criminal courts exist for the purpose of establishing individual accountability—not to uncover the fates and locate the remains of loved ones. Nor is it their purpose to provide an official history."[54] From a democratizing perspective, if a criminal trial is to contribute to "historical justice,"[55] the recorded history must connect with the affected population and stimulate democratic deliberation.[56] In some of the early writing justifying the pursuit of criminal trials during transitions, Mark Osiel argued that clarifying historical events bolsters the didactic function of trials and aids in restoring solidarity among social antagonists.[57] More recently in response to this position, Mark Drumbl has questioned the success of international criminal trials in performing this instructive role, suggesting that, when responding to mass atrocity, other accountability processes may be more effective at communicating social mores.[58]

In a recent detailed empirical examination of the role of history in international criminal trials, R.A. Wilson argues that it is necessary to take account of the legal rationale for introducing historical evidence and the legal actors' motivations for using history in their arguments.[59] He suggests that legal actors have strategically used history to pursue particular legal objectives, and these strategies have changed over the course of the courts' operations. He argues that some of these endeavors have been crucial to establishing legal categories such as genocide, which emphasize the collective nature of international crimes,[60] while others run the risk of entrenching polarized narratives of the conflict.[61]

In line with Wilson's analysis, the discussions within the ICTR centered on the role of history as it impacts, or is contained within, the trial process. Among the judges and

[54] Ralph Zacklin, "The Failings of Ad Hoc International Tribunals" (2004) 2 Journal of International Criminal Justice 541, 544.

[55] Teitel 72–75.

[56] Priscilla B. Hayner, *Unspeakable Truths: Facing the Challenge of Truth Commissions* (Routledge 2002) 208.

[57] Mark Osiel, *Mass Atrocity, Collective Memory and the Law* (1997) 36–56.

[58] Mark Drumbl, *Atrocity, Punishment and International Law and Policy* (Cambridge University Press 2007). Drumbl's argument has led some current international criminal law scholars to focus on international courts' contribution to case law as its central justification. For example, see Kevin Jon Heller, *The Nuremberg Military Tribunals and the Origins of International Criminal Law* (Oxford University Press 2011). For a favorable review of the overall contribution of this publication that nonetheless questions whether this should be accepted as the central justification for the legal practice of international criminal law, see Nicola Palmer, "Book Reviews: The Nuremberg Military Tribunals and the Origins of International Criminal Law" [2012] European Human Rights Law Review 246.

[59] Richard A. Wilson, *Writing History in International Criminal Trials* (Cambridge University Press 2011) 70.

[60] Richard A. Wilson, "Judging History: The Historical Record of the International Criminal Tribunal for the Former Yugoslavia" (2005) 27 Human Rights Quarterly 908.

[61] Wilson 168.

lawyers interviewed in this study, none of the respondents discussed the Tribunal's contribution to the creation of a historical record in terms of its impact on the Rwandan population. It is clear that where, if at all, the creation of a historical record was seen as a contribution of the Tribunal, it was in a far narrower way to what is envisaged in the literature regarding the role that law can play in providing historical justice and facilitating a transition to democracy.[62] The ICTR's practice has shaped the understandings of its purpose. Inside the institution, the court's contribution is narrower than what is attributed to international criminal justice in the dominant legalist and democratization writings.

3.4 RECONCILIATION

As an emergent theme, the ICTR judges and lawyers seldom invoked reconciliation as a justification for international criminal justice. Many respondents, across Defence, Prosecution, and Chambers, offered scathing critiques of the Tribunal's capacity to contribute to reconciling Rwandans. As one OTP participant said in 2008, "If reconciliation is a criterion by which to measure the work of the Tribunal, is has failed dismally."[63] Meanwhile in 2012, a Senior Defence Council said,

> The contribution [of the ICTR] has been mixed . . . I do not believe that these trials have had an impact on reconciliation in Rwanda. If they wanted to contribute to this, there needed to also be trials for RPF crimes.[64]

Similarly in Chambers one respondent stated, "If it is truth or reconciliation that is being sought, then Rwandans may be generally disappointed."[65]

If at all, reconciliation was introduced as an adjunct to other objectives. For example, one judge suggested that the creation of a historical record would lead to reconciliation:

> There is a body of thought that the underlying factors that assist in reconciliation include recording the facts, the establishment of a reliable historical record. This has seemed to many people as an important way of assisting reconciliation in Rwanda. And so you find that as you read the decisions, there is a lot of information that is unnecessary to prove the specific elements of the crimes with which

---

62 Teitel 69–117.

63 Interview with Senior Trial Attorney (Participant 22), OTP, UN ICTR (Arusha, Tanzania, September 9, 2008) notes on file with author.

64 Interview with Senior Defence Counsel (Participant 40), Defence, UN ICTR (Arusha, Tanzania, March 27, 2012) notes on file with author.

65 Interview with Legal Officer (Participant 3), Chambers, UN ICTR (Arusha, Tanzania, July 7, 2008) notes on file with author.

> they are charged. And I think that the reason for this has to do with an attempt to satisfy the reconciliation objectives that the Security Council laid out in the establishment of the Tribunal.[66]

This statement illustrates how Security Council Resolution 955 continues to shape what the ICTR is understood to have achieved but that these achievements are much more modestly phrased after years of legal practice.

Reconciliation was also invoked in connection with the removal of key figures: "I think it is important to reconciliation that the leaders are tried and I don't think that Rwanda would have been able to do it."[67] Similarly, regarding the act of confession, one OTP participant stated, "This is what leads to reconciliation, when someone says I was wrong, I did this, I apologise."[68] However, none of the respondents strongly supported the Tribunal's direct contribution to reconciliation. One senior participant in Chambers expressed it as a possible future aspiration: "There have been some negative and some positive aspects to it all, but I believe that we will contribute to reconciliation, at least in the long term."[69]

The need for this broad understanding of the Tribunal's contribution to reconciliation was honestly acknowledged by this same participant in his discussion of the challenges of the process:

> There was an issue of addressing new and complex issues. There is an underlying problem in interpreting the Security Council Resolutions that set up the Tribunal in which it described an objective of reconciliation.[70]

This response similarly indicates the importance of framing documents such as the Security Council Resolutions in shaping people's expectations of what transitional justice institutions can and should achieve. In the literature on the ICTR, Resolution 955 provides the point of departure, and the court's work is assessed against its original mandate. Despite explicit mention of reconciliation in the founding document, in the empirical work of this study, reconciliation did not consistently or broadly emerge as a contribution of the Tribunal's work. In contrast, the creation of international case law, a far more definite and concrete product of the ICTR's work, was identified as the

---

66 Interview with Trial Chamber Judge (Participant 21), Chambers, UN ICTR (Arusha, Tanzania, July 25, 2008) notes and recording on file with author.

67 Interview with Appeals Counsel (Participant 12), OTP, UN ICTR (Arusha, Tanzania, July 17, 2008) notes on file with author.

68 Interview with Senior Trial Attorney (Participant 20), OTP, UN ICTR (Arusha, Tanzania, July 24, 2008) notes on file with author.

69 Interview with Trial Chamber Judge (Participant 28), Chambers, UN ICTR (Arusha, Tanzania, September 12, 2008) notes on file with author.

70 Ibid.

dominant contribution, which allowed the ICTR lawyers and judges to actively imagine themselves as contributory members of an "international community."

The practice of the ICTR, in which reconciliation has been difficult to see and case law far more easily quantifiable, has affected the Tribunal personnel's understandings of what they are working toward and why they are doing this work. The mandate of the Tribunal shapes and is shaped by its practice. As will be discussed in the subsequent chapters on the national courts and *gacaca*, malleable understandings of criminal justice are not restricted to the international court. The shifts in what the courts have been understood to achieve has led to an increasing divergence in the objectives of the concurrent Rwandan criminal justice processes.

The narrowing of the ICTR's objectives can partly be explained by the impact of a number of practical constraints on the operation of the court, identified by the ICTR personnel and discussed in the next section. While a more modest appraisal of what international criminal justice can achieve is perhaps expected, and even admirable, the ICTR's specific institutional appraisal of its own work has serious implications for the concurrent operation of the Rwandan national courts and *gacaca*. How the judges and lawyers interpret the ICTR's actions starts to build a detailed description of its legal culture, illuminating some of the ideas, reasoning, practical experience, and institutional wisdom that allow the judges and lawyers to infuse the court's social actions with meaning. As argued in the final section of this chapter, the work of the other concurrent post-genocide justice processes are understood in a way that is consistent with this description. The ICTR's achievements underpin its formal interactions with *gacaca* and the national courts. For the ICTR, the result is that, despite being complementary in law, in practice, the compatibility of the three courts depends on the domestic courts' supporting the international proceedings.

4. Practical Constraints

There is little doubt that at the start of its operation, the ICTR functioned in a remarkably challenging environment. Established only a few months after the genocide, in a politically fraught context, there were considerable constraints on its operation. Judge Erik Møse, in his appraisal of the main achievements of the ICTR, describes the first four years of operation of the court as "a difficult beginning,"[71] citing the logistical and location-related challenges the court faced.

In 2008, bolstered by fourteen years of institutional experience, the challenges identified by the ICTR staff help to explain why the articulated achievements of the ICTR have narrowed. For the international judges and lawyers at the ICTR, the practical constraints on investigations and the need for state cooperation highlight the difficulties of

[71] Erik Møse, "Main Achievements of the ICTR" (2005) 3 Journal of International Criminal Justice 920, 921.

working in post-genocide Rwanda. Consistent with the understandings of these constraints, the ICTR's focus on the development of international criminal case law helps to insulate the institution from Rwanda's complicated domestic context.

4.1 INVESTIGATION

The challenges and shortcomings of the investigations conducted during the early stages of the Tribunal's work were the most consistently identified constraint on the effective practice of the court. The factors recognized as undermining effective investigation included the choice of personnel, the reality of working in post-genocide Rwanda, and the challenges of relying on detainee testimony.

Coming from two very different angles, but identifying a similar problem, a Senior Defence Counsel challenged the initial investigations, criticizing the ways in which witnesses were identified and the investigators' reliance on translation from Kinyarwanda to English or French from a translator supplied by the Rwandan government. He concluded, "There is no record at any stage of what they [the witnesses] actually said. There is no record of this whatsoever. This investigation process is eminently corruptible and completely un-robust."[72] Echoing this view, but from the other side of the courtroom, a Trial Attorney in OTP succinctly articulated, "The initial stages of investigation were problematic and then the system was built upon these initial processes."[73]

Sets of investigators unfamiliar with the Rwandan context and heavily dependent on translation were operating in the harrowing reality of post-genocide Rwanda. As another Trial Attorney reflected,

> In 1999, four human rights workers were killed during an infiltration from the DRC and as a result, ICTR personnel were not allowed to leave Kigali without a Rwandan military convoy. This posed a huge logistical challenge to doing basic investigation.[74]

Another OTP participant further highlighted initial challenges on the ground: "What we had were returnees who wanted to get on with their lives in the aftermath of a war that they hadn't participated in, didn't know who the victims were, or if they knew the victims, didn't know who the perpetrators were. So it was really hard."[75]

---

72 Interview with Senior Defence Counsel (Participant 9), Defence, UN ICTR (Arusha, Tanzania, July 15, 2008) notes and recording on file with author.

73 Interview with Trial Attorney (Participant 23), OTP, UN ICTR (Arusha, Tanzania, July 25, 2008) notes on file with author.

74 Ibid.

75 Interview with Senior Trial Attorney (Participant 10), OTP, UN ICTR (Arusha, Tanzania, July 15, 2008) notes and recording on file with author.

In the interviews it was suggested to the participants that some of the challenges associated with investigations could have been alleviated if the Tribunal had been located in Rwanda. However, as a number of the ICTR participants were quick to remark, attempts to do so in other contexts such as Sierre Leone, Iraq, and Cambodia have raised their own set of problems. As one prosecutor noted, "Sometimes the local can be problematic."[76] Acknowledging the practical constraints on ICTR investigations helps to explain the court's limiting of its understood objectives. A focus on the court's contribution to international criminal case law provides the judges and lawyers with a means of traversing the "problematic" reality of the local environment. In concentrating on the development of the legal rules, the ICTR is protected from a difficult social context, which was understood to have hampered the initial gathering of evidence.

Similarly, the ICTR's orientation toward the development of international criminal law helps the judges and lawyers to clearly identify what the ICTR has been able to achieve, despite the other major practical constraint of gaining state cooperation. Effective investigation and the need for state cooperation are closely interlinked. As one judge noted,

> [The first challenge was] the collection of evidence in the very beginning. The Tribunal is not a state and the investigators do not have police powers, so the conduct of the enquiries was vastly different to that of a domestic context where they are supported by police power legislation. Then you had a situation where a lot of people we wanted to interview were scattered over the world for different reasons. The logistical problems in the conduct of investigations were enormous.[77]

State cooperation from both Rwanda and other third-party states was identified as the second major practical constraint on the work of the ICTR.

4.2 STATE COOPERATION

State cooperation has been a long-standing challenge facing international criminal justice. Without a standing police force, cooperation from individual nation-states is required at every stage of an international criminal court's proceedings, from investigations to arrests to the provision of witnesses during trials. Peskin examines the ICTY's and ICTR's approach to state cooperation. He argues that international shaming of states at points of noncooperation has been key to the Tribunals' ability to balance conciliatory and confrontational approaches toward obtaining cooperation.

---

[76] Interview with Senior Trial Attorney (Participant 34), OTP, UN ICTR (Arusha, Tanzania, December 1, 2008) notes on file with author.

[77] Interview with Trial Chamber Judge (Participant 21), Chambers, UN ICTR (Arusha, Tanzania, July 25, 2008) notes on file with author.

However, for Peskin, in the case of the ICTR, the Rwandan government has been able to gain a "monopoly on the mobilisation of shame,"[78] successfully focusing international attention on the ICTR's shortcomings rather than on the government's own noncooperation with the Tribunal. In building this argument, Peskin examines, among other examples, the Rwandan government's refusal to allow sixteen ICTR witnesses to leave Rwanda following the Tribunal's 1999 decision to release Jean-Bosco Barayagwiza on procedural grounds. Peskin also notes the Rwandan government's effective resistance to the international prosecution of RPF-related atrocities.

Inside the ICTR in 2008, participants were conscious of the political difficulties raised by the requirement of state cooperation. As one prosecutor noted,

> It would be wrong to say that politics has engulfed the entire Tribunal. It has a role to play. You have to get cooperation from the states. If you want this cooperation, you have to go to the politicians. But once the trials start, it doesn't play a role at all.

This was similarly articulated in Chambers: "In this particular instance, the issue of the political climate is an important element to our work. It is a factor that plays into this work."[79] In order to navigate what was understood as a complicated political relationship with the Rwandan state, inside the ICTR, state cooperation was discussed strictly in terms of what states could do for the Tribunal. As a senior trial attorney noted,

> Government's willingness to help us ranges from 10%–77% and they don't give us 100% cooperation and sometimes it is that last 23% that is really needed to secure prosecutions. Where a state has an interest in the case then cooperation is much more difficult.[80]

This same respondent went on to describe the impact of this constraint on the functioning of international criminal justice: "It is like a table with no legs that is meant to remain at the level of a table."[81]

As noted at the start of this chapter, an interpretive approach allows the researcher to take account of the agency of the judges and lawyers working at the Tribunal. A study inside the ICTR has shown that the achievements of the court have changed over time and have been shaped by both the court's initial mandate and its practice. Inside the ICTR, the development of international criminal case law is understood as the

---

[78] Victor Peskin, *International Justice in Rwanda and the Balkans: Virtual Trials and the Struggle for State Cooperation* (Cambridge University Press 2008) 152.

[79] Ibid.

[80] Interview with Senior Trial Attorney (Participant 20), OTP, UN ICTR (Arusha, Tanzania, July 24, 2008) notes on file with author.

[81] Ibid.

dominant contribution made by the court, given the practical challenges facing international criminal justice. However, the ICTR has not operated in isolation, and the meanings ascribed to its actions reflect broader aspects of the court's legal culture. The next section will examine the impact of the internal appraisal of the ICTR's work at points of interaction with domestic post-genocide justice. In doing so, the chapter examines the compatibility of the ICTR with its domestic counterparts, from the vantage point of the judges and lawyers within the international court.

5. Concurrent Transitional Justice

The ICTR, the Rwandan national courts, and *gacaca* do not challenge each other jurisdictionally; nonetheless, the three courts have intersected in crucial practical ways. This section examines the points of formal and informal contact among them, illustrating the impact of the ICTR's understanding of its own activities on its engagement with the concurrent domestic post-genocide trials.

As established in the previous section, the Tribunal's work has been principally understood to contribute to the creation of an international legal order. At a point of transition in Rwanda, where the domestic legal landscape has been shifting substantially, the focus of the ICTR has been on a shifting international—rather than domestic—legal order. Although seen as its major strength by many inside the institution, the focus on the international contribution of the ICTR poses one of the biggest challenges to its effective operation in a concurrent system.

How the ICTR participants ascribe meaning to the actions of the court illuminates the institution's legal culture. Inside the ICTR, the work of the national courts and *gacaca* are understood within the international court's cultural context. Rwanda's domestic transitional justice processes are viewed and understood in a manner that is consistent with how the ICTR judges and lawyers have described their own work. The implications of the ICTR's consistent interpretations of its own work and that of the domestic courts come to the fore at points of intersection among the three courts.

The first point of intersection among the ICTR, the national courts, and *gacaca* is informal. It occurs through a common group of participants who have appeared before two or more of the post-genocide courts. Due to the importance of accomplice evidence and the need to establish, or contest, chains of command, a large number of the ICTR witnesses have also faced trial in Rwanda, either before the national or the *gacaca* courts. For these individuals, the three courts have intersected through their personal experiences. As discussed below, among some of these witnesses who were interviewed, the ICTR's institutional focus on case law was directly challenged. The internationalized legal rules of the Tribunal were described as foreign and inappropriate. More commonly, the procedural and sentencing disparities among the three courts were used to challenge both the international and the domestic justice processes.

Examining these interpretations of the ICTR's practice extends the study beyond the judges and lawyers to include not only how social meanings of criminal justice are produced, but also how they shift when interpreted within Rwanda. This aspect of interpretive research, as Rod Rhodes and Mark Bevir suggests, is in line with bottom-up approaches in the social sciences.[82] It provides an account of the justice processes "from below," examining the interpretations provided by the prisoners and witnesses who are subject to the authority of the courts. Insights into these informal interactions among the courts create the foundation for a discussion, in Chapter 5, on how interpretations of post-genocide justice are "reproduced, or disrupted, by—the everyday consciousness and conversations"[83] of the Rwandans who interact with the courts, in different ways, in their everyday lives. What emerges from this initial analysis of these informal interactions is that there are clear differences in the interpretations of the international court's actions, highlighting tensions among the concurrent courts.

The second point of intersection among the concurrent courts is formal. It occurs when there is the potential for the transfer of cases from one court to another, or when one court has made official use of the other court's evidence or legal findings. At these points of formal interaction, the ICTR's legal culture has impacted the three courts' ability to complement one another. There have been misunderstandings between the ICTR and the national courts, and the ICTR has failed to fully engage with the *gacaca* proceedings. An analysis of how the ICTR lawyers have made use of the evidence brought before the *gacaca* courts, and how the international judges have received this evidence, highlights the practical limitations imposed by the ICTR's international orientation.

5.1 INFORMAL INTERACTIONS: A COMMON GROUP OF PARTICIPANTS

While the importance of developing international criminal case law is very clearly articulated inside the ICTR, it is much less clear "from below." Seventeen prisoners were interviewed in three jails corresponding to the research sites in the Northern Province, the Western Province, and Kigali. The prisoners had overlapping experiences of the ICTR, the national courts, and *gacaca*. Seven of the participants had been tried by the national courts and were appealing their cases through *gacaca,* and ten of the prisoners had been tried and sentenced by *gacaca*. Out of this mixed experience of domestic prosecution, ten of the participants had appeared as witnesses before the ICTR.

Among the participants who had given evidence before the ICTR, the external nature of the laws was one of the points of criticism of the international court. In the words of Marie, a female detainee, who had testified before the ICTR and had been

---

[82] Rod Rhodes and Mark Bevir, "Defending Interpretation" (2006) 5 European Political Science 69.

[83] Ian Loader and Aogán Mulcahy, *Policing and the Condition of England: Memory, Politics and Culture* (Oxford University Press 2003) 50.

sentenced to twenty-eight years by a *gacaca* court, "[The ICTR] follows on the UN laws . . . the international community is getting the criminals tried outside and that leads to less punishment."[84] The notion of the "outside" was regularly iterated. "The rules are from people from the outside," said Ascel, another ICTR witness jailed in Rwanda for fourteen years at the time of the interview,

> It is not the same as people going from the inside. The people accused in Arusha ought to be brought here because to have them all the way over there, and the foreigners making up the rules, I do not think that this is a good idea.[85]

In evaluating the "outside" rules, the Rwandan prisoners, who had testified before the ICTR, expressed two clear distinctions between the work of Rwanda's domestic courts and that of the international court: the sentencing disparities between the courts, and the differing length of the legal proceedings.

In the words of Athanase, a middle-aged man facing a life sentence handed down by the national courts, "The ones at the top are not being punished the same, it is not equal justice."[86] André, whose life sentence was later reduced to twenty-four years on appeal before *gacaca*, was similarly critical: "Arusha is about people living in good conditions. We are serving their interests. We are here because of them and they are getting light sentences and we are being heavily condemned."[87]

Prosper, who was tried by the national courts in 1994, was more supportive of the international court: "Although it does not judge many cases, the ICTR does a good job. It has a balance, it has to listen to prosecution and defence. I have gone there often and seen it . . . but you have to say in ten words at the ICTR what you can say in one."[88] The procedural and sentencing distinctions between the ICTR and the national courts were apparent to the participants, and the practice of one court was often used as the basis to criticize the other concurrent processes.

For Alphonse, a former local leader who was arrested in 1996 and sentenced by *gacaca* in 2007, the length of proceedings before the ICTR was seen as a strength:

> Arusha is a good answer to the problems with *gacaca*. In *gacaca* you are not free. I was tried for three hours and in Arusha I would have been tried for ten years![89]

---

[84] Interview with Marie (Participant 6), (Kigali, Rwanda, April 16, 2009) notes on file with author.

[85] Interview with Ascel (Participant 2), (Rural District, Northern Province Rwanda, September 5, 2009) notes on file with author.

[86] Interview with Athanase (Participant 16), (Western Province, Rwanda, April 21, 2009) notes on file with author.

[87] Interview with André (Participant 8), (Kigali, Rwanda, April 20, 2009) notes on file with author.

[88] Interview with Prosper (Participant 17), (Western Province, Rwanda, April 21, 2009) notes on file with author.

[89] Interview with Alphonse (Participant 9), (Kigali, Rwanda, April 20, 2009) notes on file with author.

For Leopold, who was approached to be an ICTR witness after he named a number of senior accused in his initial guilty plea, the time taken on the proceeding was a point of criticism: "Over there things never end, they just keep going and going. At least here you feel like sometimes you are getting somewhere. There they just go on and on . . ."[90]

As seen in Leopold's response, the notion of the prisoner's experience of post-genocide criminal trials "here" and the idea that the trials before ICTR occur over "there" was a common and consistent articulation. The ICTR was not identified as a means of leading the way for domestic prosecutions through building robust procedural and substantive precedent. Rather, the externalized nature of the processes was criticized by those subject to the courts' authority. The different orientations of the courts led to critical comparisons among all three of their practices, of which the wider implications for the legitimacy of the courts' work are discussed more fully in Chapter 5. However, in addition to these critiques "from below," as will be outlined in the next section, inside the ICTR the external orientation of the Tribunal's work has impacted the international court's formal interactions with the Rwandan national courts and the localized *gacaca* proceedings.

5.2 UNDERSTANDINGS OF THE NATIONAL COURTS

Inside the ICTR, the national courts were evaluated in ways consistent with how the personnel inside the Tribunal interpreted their own work. The appraisals of the domestic justice processes were shaped by the cultural context of the international institution. A number of ICTR participants were explicit that the achievements of the ICTR provided the basis against which the national courts were measured. As one OTP participant stated,

> We have also undertaken substantial capacity-building in Rwanda, trying to improve the entire judicial sector to be compliant with the international standards, standards that I think the ICTR has established.[91]

These international standards of criminal justice have been set through the case law of the ICTR. As one judge stated, "The standard has already been fixed, there is a lot of jurisprudence on this issue."[92] Robinson argues that the focus of the ICTR's legal standards has been on the realization of procedural rights.[93] Inside the ICTR, the work

[90] Interview with Leopold (Participant 1), (Rural District, Northern Province Rwanda, September 5, 2009) notes on file with author.

[91] Interview with Trial Attorney (Participant 23), OTP, UN ICTR (Arusha, Tanzania, July 25, 2008) notes on file with author.

[92] Interview with Trial Chamber Judge (Participant 21), Chambers, UN ICTR (Arusha, Tanzania, July 25, 2008) notes and recording on file with author.

[93] Robinson 927.

of the national courts was evaluated consistently with the Tribunal's own focus on the development of international case law and the court's application of procedural rights.

The judges and lawyers who were interviewed held two broad positions on the national courts. The first was a strident view that the Rwandan national courts had failed to meet the ICTR's legal standards. As one judge stated in relation to the initial need for an international response, "The Rwandan judiciary did not in any way stand up to the standards of international justice."[94] Similarly, as an OTP investigator, who was working on the transfer of ICTR indictees to Rwanda in 2008 said, "The UN offers a better standard than any national tribunal."[95]

However, the more common position was to adopt a paternalistic appraisal of the work of the national courts. Participants generally felt that, if given the right guidance, the Rwandan national courts could achieve the same objectives as the ICTR. As one senior prosecutor stated in relation to the possibility of transferring cases to Rwanda, "Sending these cases to Rwanda and holding them to specific standards, may teach them something that they can be proud of."[96] Similarly a prosecutor in Appeals, commenting on the initial decisions by the ICTR Trial Chambers not to transfer four of its remaining cases to Rwanda, stated, "Rwanda has come a long way and most of the transfer decisions do acknowledge this, but they say more needs to be done."[97] However, there was deep contestation as to whether the ICTR should have played a direct role in the Rwandan national courts' domestic judicial development.

Consistent with the emphasis on the creation of international case law, participants principally saw the activities of the Tribunal as a means of establishing an international system of criminal justice for violations of humanitarian law. Although some participants expressed a normative preference for domestic prosecution, they argued that in the case of Rwanda, international intervention was a necessity. Among the ICTR judges and lawyers there was contestation over whether, in addition to this international process, intervention should also take the form of domestic judicial development. Some ICTR practitioners argued that, in theory, interventions should develop the justice system in the post-conflict country. Others strongly opposed the demand for domestic judicial development, placing exclusive emphasis on the international contribution. "This is not just for Rwanda," one participant in Chambers articulated,

> . . . nor is it our way to fix the Rwandan judiciary. The ICTR does not exist to please the Rwandan community. If the issue had been about strengthening the

---

[94] Interview with Trial Chamber Judge (Participant 28), Chambers, UN ICTR (Arusha, Tanzania, September 12, 2008) notes on file with author.

[95] Interview with Investigator (Participant 5), OTP, UN ICTR (Arusha, Tanzania, July 10, 2008) notes on file with author.

[96] Interview with Senior Trial Attorney (Participant 20), OTP, UN ICTR (Arusha, Tanzania, July 24, 2008) notes on file with author.

[97] Interview with Appeals Counsel (Participant 12), OTP, UN ICTR (Arusha, Tanzania, July 17, 2008) notes on file with author.

> Rwandan judiciary then the trials should have happened in Rwanda, there could have been assistance through foreign staff and training and there would have been an application of Rwandan law. In this instance there was a need for an international response.[98]

From this perspective, international criminal justice is not about instilling the rule of law in a domestic context but rather instilling the rule of law globally. This was coupled with a strongly articulated position that the money used in the establishment and running of the Tribunal should not have gone to Rwanda. In the words of one judge,

> The [Rwandan] Minister of Justice should be ashamed. The reason that the ICTR has taken so long and cost so much is because he could not create a sufficient judicial system. The idea that the money should have gone to the Rwandan judiciary from the international community, to do what they should have done themselves, is just wrong.[99]

When acknowledged, the contribution to the domestic legal system was distanced. "The ICTR has hopefully had a positive impact on the Rwandan judicial system," said another senior member of Chambers. "It has spearheaded the fight against impunity."[100] There was a widely held perspective that the ICTR offered a better standard of justice to that offered in Rwanda, and in upholding this standard, it provided the impetus for the domestic realization of the standard within the East African and Great Lakes region as a whole. This sits at odds with the opinions expressed by the ICTR witnesses who are imprisoned in Rwanda. In the three courts' informal interactions inside the Rwandan prisons, the differences between the domestic and international proceedings provided the basis for criticizing *both* the international court and the domestic trials. Yet, in formal interactions with the Rwandan national courts, the ICTR's appraisal of the domestic courts has informed the Tribunal's decisions on the transfer of its remaining cases to the Rwandan national courts.

5.2.1 Interpreting the Rule 11 *bis* Decisions

In October 2008, the ICTR Appeals Chamber upheld the decision not to transfer the case of Yussuf Munyakazi from the jurisdiction of the Tribunal to the Rwandan

[98] Interview with Legal Officer (Participant 3), Chambers, UN ICTR (Arusha, Tanzania, July 7, 2008) notes on file with author.

[99] Interview with Trial Chamber Judge (Participant 4), Chambers, UN ICTR (Arusha, Tanzania, July 9, 2008) notes on file with author. This position is in line with that taken by the Bureau of the Assembly of State Parties (ASP) to the Rome Statute. Following the review conference in Kampala, Uganda, in 2010, the States Parties articulated a strong stance that positive complementarity should be conducted "without involving the Court in capacity building, financial support and technical assistance"; see Kevin Jon Heller, "A Sentenced-Based Theory of Complementarity" (2012) 53 Harvard International Law Journal 202, 222.

[100] Interview with Senior Legal Officer (Participant 2), Chambers, UN ICTR (Arusha, Tanzania, July 4, 2008) notes on file with author.

national courts. This was followed by two consistent appeals decisions relating to Gaspard Kanyarukiga and Ildephonse Hategekimana, with the Prosecutor electing not to appeal the fourth case of Jean-Baptiste Gatete. On June 28, 2011, following changes to Rwandan legislation, a newly constituted referral bench ruled in favor of transferring the case of Jean Uwinkindi to Rwanda.[101] This decision was upheld on appeal and laid the foundation for the transfer of Bernard Munyagishari along with the cases against six fugitives, who have been indicted by the ICTR but remain at large, including that of Fulgence Kayishema, which had initially been refused.[102] These differing decisions highlight the impact of the ICTR's legal culture on its formal interactions with domestic accountability processes. The Trial Chambers' reasoning is consistent with the Tribunal's international orientation and its focus on developing international criminal case law. However, the decisions assume that the Rwandan national courts should have been oriented in a similar direction.[103]

The transfer decisions were made according to Rule 11 *bis* of the Rules of Evidence and Procedure of the ICTR, which governs the transfer, to competent national jurisdictions, of individuals indicted but not yet tried by the ICTR. The rule was intended to create a bridge between the Tribunal's practice and Rwanda's domestic criminal justice processes, by ensuring that domestic courts had an adequate legal framework to try international crimes and provide suitable fair trial guarantees.

Although there are a series of differences in the initial four Trial Chamber decisions that refused transfer to Rwanda, all three Appeal decisions were upheld on two grounds common to all cases:

(1) that there existed a legal ambiguity in Rwandan law that meant that the Rwandan courts may be empowered to hand down a sentence of "life imprisonment with special provisions," which could constitute prolonged incarceration in isolation, with insufficient legal safeguards to ensure that such incarceration did not amount to torture; and

---

[101] *Uwinkindi* Rule 11 *bis* Trial judgment.

[102] *Prosecutor v Fulgence Kayishema*, (Decision on the Prosecutor's Request for Referral to the Republic of Rwanda) ICTR-01-67-R11bis, RT Ch (22 February 2012); *Prosecutor v Aloys Ndimbati*, (Decision on the Prosecutor's Request for Referral of the Case of Aloys Ndimbati to the Republic of Rwanda) ICTR-95-1F-R11bis, RT Ch (25 June 2012); *Prosecutor v Phénéas Munyarugarama*, (Decision on the Prosecutor's Request for Referral of the Case to the Republic of Rwanda) ICTR-02-79-R11bis, RT Ch (28 June 2012). *Prosecutor v Ladislas Ntaganza*, (Decision on the Prosecutor's Request for Referral of the Case to the Republic of Rwanda) ICTR-96-9-R11bis, RT Ch (8 May 2012); *Prosecutor v Charles Sikubwabo*, (Decision on the Prosecutor's Request for Referral of the Case to the Republic of Rwanda) ICTR-95-1D-R11bis, RT Ch (26 March 2012).

[103] This argument was initially developed and published in Nicola Palmer, "Transfer or Transformation?: A Review of the Rule 11 *bis* Decisions of the International Criminal Tribunal for Rwanda" (2012) 20 The African Journal of International and Comparative Law 1.

(2) that it would be impossible to raise an effective defense in Rwanda due to the subjective fear of witnesses, both inside and outside of the country, of testifying for the accused, thus undermining the possibility of a fair trial.

The first ground for refusal fits with the legislative requirements of Rule 11 *bis* and relates to the broad wording adopted in the 2007 law abolishing the death penalty in Rwanda.[104] Following the Appeals Chamber decisions, and in consultation with international lawyers in OTP, the legal ambiguity has been addressed through an amendment to the law governing the transfer of suspects from the ICTR.[105] Life imprisonment is now the maximum sentence in respect of transferred cases.[106] The ICTR's second grounds for refusal to transfer, that of the fear of witnesses to testify in defense, appeared far more intractable. The Trial Chambers' evidentiary basis through which they determined the subjective fear experienced by defense witnesses illustrates the impact of the ICTR's international orientation on its Rule 11 *bis* decisions and, as discussed below, has had unexpected reverberations in the domestic arena.

The ICTR made the unequivocal decision, in all four Trial Chamber decisions, to go beyond the written legislation relating to transfer. This is a shift away from the jurisprudence of the ICTY. The Appeals Chamber held that when determining whether an accused would receive a fair trial in that state, the court was not required to look further than the state's relevant legislation.[107] The *Hategikimana* decision makes explicit what the Trial Chambers undertook in both the *Kanyarukiga* and *Munyakazi* decisions, namely, "The Chamber considers that it may and should look beyond the relevant legislation to examples of the practices of Rwandan courts."[108] What underscores this decision is, as

[104] Organic Law No. 31/2007 of 25 July 2007 Relating to the Abolition of the Death Penalty. (Official Gazette of the Republic of Rwanda. Year 46, no. special, 25 July 2007).

[105] Rwanda's Organic Law No. 66/2008 of 21 November 2008 modifying and complementing Organic Law No. 31/2007 of 25 July 2007 relating to the Abolition of the Death Penalty. This law had been passed before Hategekimana's appeal hearing; however, it was not yet in force. The Appeals Chamber held that "should this new law enter into force in its current form, the ambiguity as to the applicable punishment for transfer cases ... would be resolved." *Hategekimana* Rule 11 *bis* Appeal judgement at para. 38.

[106] Organic Law No. 11/2007 of 16 March 2007 Concerning the Transfer of Cases to the Republic of Rwanda from the International Criminal Tribunal for Rwanda and from Other States. (Official Gazette of the Republic of Rwanda. Year 46, no. special, 19 March 2007).

[107] For example see *Prosecutor v. Zeljko Mejakic, Momcilo Gruban, Dusan Fustar, Dusko Knezevi* (Decision on Joint Defence Appeal against Referral Decision under Rule 11 bis) IT-02-65-AR11bis.1, App Ch (7 April 2006) para. 69 in which the Appeal Chamber ruled that the Referral Bench did not err by focusing on the legal framework in BiH.

[108] *Prosecutor v Ildephonse Hategekimana* (Decision on the Prosecutor's Request for Referral to the Republic of Rwanda) ICTR-00-55B-R*11*bis-T, T Ch 1 (19 June 2008) para. 35.

one senior ICTR judge articulated in an interview, the fear that "there have only been cosmetic changes, but much comes from practice."[109]

In determining the legislative framework in Rwanda, the Rule 11 *bis* decisions examined some of the case law of the national courts, as recorded by Avocats Sans Frontières (ASF).[110] However, in determining the practice of genocide prosecution, and in reaching the decisions that the four accused would not be able to raise an effective defense inside Rwanda, the Trial and Appeals Chamber decisions drew exclusively on non-Rwandan sources. The decisions rely on the experience of ICTR Defence counsel and witnesses and two amicus curiae briefs submitted by Human Rights Watch (HRW) and the International Criminal Defence Attorneys Association (ICDAA). In doing so, the decisions failed to take careful account of how and under what circumstances defense evidence has been provided before the *gacaca* courts or the Rwandan national courts.

The evidentiary bases of the Rule 11 *bis* decisions are consistent with the ICTR's interpretation of its own work and reflect the international orientation of the court. While the national courts and *gacaca* proceedings are not immediately intelligible to the international judges and lawyers, HRW and ICDAA are both advocacy groups that communicate specifically to an international legal audience on fair trial rights. The position of these groups is consistent with the ICTR's own focus on developing the fair procedural application of international criminal law and leading domestic judicial development by example. As a result, the court is more comfortable relying on this evidence. If evidence relating to the practice of the Rwandan national courts had been framed in terms of the "international best practice" in providing witness security, it may have been more immediately accessible to the ICTR judges. However, as discussed in the next chapter, this has not been the orientation of the domestic courts. The Rule 11 *bis* decisions illustrate the ICTR's assumption that the national courts should have focused on the domestic application of international criminal law.

In the more recent transfer decision relating to Jean Uwinkindi, the Trial Chamber returned its focus to Rwanda's legislative framework. The court ruled in favor of transfer and held that the recently included "immunities and protections provided to the witnesses under the [Rwandan] Transfer Law are adequate to ensure a fair trial of the Accused before the High Court of Rwanda."[111] The court found that "the relevant Rwandan laws must be given a chance to operate before being held to be defective."[112] As noted, the decision was upheld on appeal, and paved the way for further transfers from the ICTR and extraditions from third states.

---

109 Interview with Trial Chamber Judge (Participant 4), Chambers, UN ICTR (Arusha, Tanzania, July 9, 2008) notes on file with author.

110 Avocats Sans Frontières, Vade-Mecum: Le Crime de Genocide et les Crimes Contre L'Humanite devant les Juridictions Ordinaires du Rwanda [The Crime of Genocide and Crimes against Humanity in Rwanda's Courts] (2004) available at http://www.asf.be/fr/publication accessed January 13, 2011.

111 *Uwinkindi* Rule 11 *bis* Trial judgment para. 90.

112 Ibid. para. 103.

In these decisions, the ICTR's return to the legislative framework remains consistent with the international court's notion of leading legal development through setting the example of what constitutes international standards. These more recent decisions, while upholding the transfer of suspects, still fail to provide a careful and detailed analysis of the practice of *gacaca* and the national courts, where the majority of defense witnesses have testified. The decisions do not show a change in the engagement between the ICTR and the concurrent domestic courts. but rather that, by refocusing attention on Rwanda's legislation, the court has aligned its position with that of the ICTY.

At the domestic level, the ICTR's focus on witness protection has led to an increasing use of anonymous testimony as the major form of protection offered before the national courts.[113] As Goran Sluiter, in his analysis of ICTR case law, argues, witness protection measures through the provision of pseudonyms, the use of in camera hearings, and the confidentiality of the identity of the witness vis-à-vis the public and the media are now "adopted as a matter of routine in practically every case"[114] before the Tribunal. This approach to witness protection has been exported to the practice of the national courts through the Rule 11 *bis* decisions.

In turn, such an approach to witness protection has given rise to unexpected legal arguments in the domestic arena that perhaps challenge the Chambers' initial reasoning. According to the most recent ICTR monitoring report on Uwinkindi's trial before the Rwandan High Court in Kigali, the accused's counsel has argued that prosecution witnesses should not automatically be able to testify under a pseudonym, stressing that "as a principle, all hearings should be public"[115] and that "because public hearings are the rule and protective measure the exception, the witnesses should be required to show why they fear testifying in public."[116] As will be discussed in Chapter 4, this is consistent with the emphasis on open testimony in *gacaca*, but is inconsistent with the argumentation in the Rule 11 *bis* decisions, which centered on ensuring that witnesses would be able to testify under pseudonyms, in line with ICTR practice.

The Rule 11 *bis* decisions are consistent with the ICTR's interpretations of its own work and that of the Rwandan national courts. However, as will be laid out in the next two chapters, the decisions sit less comfortably with the understood objectives of post-genocide justice inside Rwanda. Within the ICTR, a complementary system of national and international justice depends on the domestic courts' supporting the development and application of the international criminal case law. The ICTR's appraisal of the *gacaca* courts is similarly consistent with what the judges and lawyers at the

---

[113] Redress, "Testifying to Genocide: Victim and Witness Protection in Rwanda" Redress (October 2012) with P. Clark and N. Palmer http://www.redress.org/africa/rwanda accessed August 28, 2014.

[114] Göran Sluiter, "The ICTR and the Protection of Witnesses" (2005) 3 Journal of International Criminal Justice 962, 976.

[115] *Prosecutor v. Jean Uwinkindi* (Monitoring Report June 2014) MICT-12-25, (16 July 2014) para. 11.

[116] Ibid. para. 20.

international court saw themselves as having achieved, impacting the Tribunal's formal use of *gacaca* records in its own judgments.

5.3 UNDERSTANDINGS OF THE *GACACA* COURTS

During the course of the ICTR's operation, the court has had increasing and extensive formal interactions with the *gacaca* courts. Out of the seventy-four cases tried by the ICTR, fifty-two have referred to the *gacaca* courts. More strikingly, since the nationwide implementation of *gacaca* in 2005, forty-seven out of forty-nine ICTR cases have discussed evidence gathered by the *gacaca* courts.[117]

On the surface, this degree of interaction is unsurprising. As noted in the Introduction, the ICTR and *gacaca* deal with the same conflict and, in many cases, with the same crimes. The jurisdictional distinction of the courts is based on the seniority of the accused and their alleged level of responsibility in the orchestration of the genocide. However, despite a clear and unavoidable overlap, the empirical research undertaken in this book shows that, inside the Tribunal, participants stressed the distance between the two processes, and this has impacted the use of *gacaca* evidence in the ICTR cases.

Inside the ICTR, the international judges and lawyers emphasized the distinct nature of *gacaca*, suggesting that the Tribunal and *gacaca* have operated very separately. One Rwandan ICTR employee described the two courts as "two worlds working very separately."[118] Another Rwandan lawyer working in defense described them as two "completely different systems."[119] The majority of non-Rwandan ICTR participants claimed that they did not know very much about the *gacaca* process. As one senior prosecutor said, "I have to be honest, I know very little about the process,"[120] while a senior defense counsel stated, "I have never been near a *gacaca* court."[121]

In addition, there was a careful and consistent distancing of the ICTR's work from that of *gacaca* in order not to be too critical. As a senior participant in Chambers stated, "The ICTR has adopted a hands-off approach to *gacaca*. It is not our job to

---

[117] I reviewed all of the Trial Chamber judgments handed down by the ICTR and drew up a table of every reference to *gacaca*. I then analyzed how the legal parties made use of *gacaca* evidence and the assessment of this evidence and legal argument as reflected in the reasoning of the Trial Chambers in their judgments. The judgments were downloaded from the official website of the International Criminal Tribunal for Rwanda, http://www.unicrt.org accessed January 1, 2014.

[118] Interview with Registry Officer (Participant 1), Registry, UN ICTR (Arusha, Tanzania, July 3, 2008) notes on file with author.

[119] Interview with Defence Investigator (Participant 17), Defence, UN ICTR (Arusha, Tanzania, September 12, 2008) notes on file with author.

[120] Interview with Senior Trial Attorney (Participant 20), OTP, UN ICTR (Arusha, Tanzania, July 24, 2008) notes on file with author.

[121] Interview with Senior Defence Counsel (Participant 9), Defence, UN ICTR (Arusha, Tanzania, July 15, 2008) notes on file with author.

criticise it."[122] Among the lawyers and judges who did engage on this issue, there were a number of scathing critiques. As one Trial Attorney stated, "The problem with *gacaca* is that it is based on rumour and erroneous testimony. People are hauled in front of *gacaca* and there is room for manipulation of the process."[123]

Some participants felt that *gacaca* did provide information to the Tribunal, particularly in respect of the credibility of the witnesses, who had also appeared before *gacaca*. As noted above, the number of witnesses who have testified before both the ICTR and *gacaca* is significant, given the number of detainees who have testified at the Tribunal. The most generous of these participants in Chambers made the following diagnosis:

> *Gacaca* has had a tremendous impact. It has created a paper trail that allows for a direct challenge of the credibility of the witnesses. It has provided a good source of information to the Tribunal and provides a nice lens through which to understand what has happened. It has shown that you can have open proceedings.[124]

The focus by this participant is very clearly on the use of *gacaca* to support what the international court seeks to achieve. Like the national courts, the actions of *gacaca* are explained in terms of what the ICTR itself is understood to have contributed.

When criticisms were raised against *gacaca,* they similarly related to the localized courts' impact on the ICTR's work. As one Senior Trial Attorney stated,

> It is a failed process . . . *Gacaca* has undermined the integrity of international justice. The attempt to further domestic criminal justice has undermined international justice. How was the evidence assessed? It is not clearly documented. In fact I feel that it undermines the system of accountability.[125]

Both of these participants explained the work of *gacaca* in terms of the ICTR's own perceived purpose, namely that of creating an international legal order for the trial of international crimes. There is a consistent interpretation of the international and localized courts' actions. Generally the ICTR participants tried to distance their work from the *gacaca* courts. and there was an assumption that when there was interaction, *gacaca* processes should support the ICTR's objective. However, this was not underpinned by a deep understanding of how the domestic courts had worked, which in turn has influenced the interpretation of *gacaca* evidence in the ICTR's judgments.

---

122 Interview with Senior Legal Officer (Participant 2), Chambers, UN ICTR (Arusha, Tanzania, July 4, 2008) notes on file with author.

123 Interview with Trial Attorney (Participant 14), OTP, UN ICTR (Arusha, Tanzania, July 17, 2008) notes on file with author.

124 Interview with Legal Officer (Participant 3), Chambers, UN ICTR (Arusha, Tanzania, July 7, 2008) notes on file with author.

125 Interview with Senior Trial Attorney (Participant 22), OTP, UN ICTR (Arusha, Tanzania, September 9, 2008) notes on file with author.

5.3.1 Interpreting Evidence from *Gacaca*

As with the national courts, the ICTR's appraisal of its own work has shaped its formal interaction with *gacaca*. During the course of the ICTR's operation, there has been increasing and extensive formal interaction between the two courts. An analysis of the Trial Chamber judgments shows five distinct uses of the *gacaca* records in the fifty-two ICTR trial judgments in which the local courts are mentioned. The ICTR refers to *gacaca* in relation to the introduction of potentially exculpatory evidence from *gacaca* proceedings, the use of *gacaca* documents and previous trial records to challenge witness credibility, the introduction of general hearsay evidence from *gacaca* proceedings, and the court's reference to *gacaca's* sentencing practice; on one occasion, the ICTR makes use of *gacaca* documents to determine the details of a specific murder.

By and large, the use of *gacaca* proceedings to assess credibility, admit general hearsay evidence, and establish the sentencing practice in Rwanda is uncontested and generally accepted by the ICTR Trial Chambers. However, *gacaca* judgments, guilty pleas, and witness statements are most regularly used to provide potentially exculpatory evidence, in an effort to establish that the particular accused was not mentioned in the *gacaca* proceeding relating to the same set of crimes. The Trial Chambers have been highly sceptical of this, the first and dominant, use of the localized courts' evidence. Meanwhile, it is the final reference to *gacaca*—using the local courts' records to determine the deaths of specific individuals—that is the most rare, and arguably the most useful. As a result these two references to the *gacaca* records, the most common, on the one hand, and arguably the most useful, on the other, best illustrate how the ICTR's understandings of *gacaca* have impacted the Tribunal's own legal work.

Since 2004, ICTR defense counsel have used oral and written evidence from *gacaca* proceedings to argue that their clients have not been mentioned in Rwandan domestic proceedings relating to the same crimes as those charged in the ICTR indictments. In the *Muhimana* case in 2005, the Chamber was clear that it "did not consider the evidence that the accused was not mentioned in *gacaca* persuasive."[126] However, the next reference to *gacaca* in September 2006 was in the acquittal decision of André Rwamakumba, where this evidence was read more favorably. The Chamber, in finding that there was reasonable doubt that the accused was involved in the distribution of weapons, noted that the accused was not mentioned in the *gacaca* hearings in relation to this charge.[127] This inconsistency is, in part, due to the Trial Chamber's incomplete knowledge of how *gacaca* has operated, consistent with the ICTR's intentional distancing from the local courts.

By 2010, in the *Muvunyi* decision, the Trial Chamber took a clear position on the naming of the accused in a guilty plea provided to *gacaca*, rejecting this evidence and

---

[126] *Prosecutor v Mikaeli Muhimana* (*Judgment*) ICTR-95-1B-T, T Ch (28 April 2005) para. 254 and 342.

[127] *Prosecutor v André Rwamakuba* (*Judgment*) ICTR-98-44C-T, T Ch III (20 September 2006) para. 101–103.

holding that "authority figures are not typically included in *gacaca* guilty pleas since they do not fall under *gacaca* jurisdiction."[128] The Chamber takes this position from an explanation of the *gacaca* proceedings provided by a single witness. The judgment provides no further details to demonstrate an understanding of how *gacaca* has worked. In practice, the guilty pleas before *gacaca* have varied substantially. Some guilty pleas, such as that provided by Leopold, one of the participants in this study, did include senior accused.[129]

To correctly determine whether an accused was mentioned at a specific *gacaca* case would have required a very thorough review, not only of the guilty pleas but also of the *gacaca* judgments on the particular crime. This documentary evidence would have best been supported by the testimony of one or more of the *gacaca* judges presiding over the hearing, due to the more discursive nature and structure of the *gacaca* proceedings. A fuller understanding of the *gacaca* proceedings would have enabled the ICTR to more effectively assess the evidence before it. It would also have enabled the court to make a more constructive use of *gacaca* evidence, as seen in a decision handed down just two weeks after the *Muvunyi* judgment.

The *Setako* judgment shows the most interesting and engaged understanding of the *gacaca* proceedings. Despite extensive reference to *gacaca* since 2004, the case of Ephrem Setako is the first before the ICTR in which an expert on *gacaca* provided evidence before the international court. Bert Ingeleare prepared a report and provided oral testimony on the function of *gacaca*, particularly on the possibility of a senior accused being mentioned in the local court hearings. As will be discussed in the next chapter, Ingeleare is generally quite critical of the role of *gacaca* in Rwanda; nonetheless the impact of a better informed Chamber is evident throughout the judgment.

The reasoning of the Trial Chamber in the *Setako* judgment is generally consistent with previous uses of *gacaca* records. The Chamber dismissed the exculpatory evidence provided by a series of defense witnesses that the accused had not been mentioned at the *gacaca* hearings, while accepting the use of *gacaca* records to challenge the credibility of both prosecution and defense witnesses and the admission of general hearsay evidence.[130] However, the Chamber's determination of how one of Setako's alleged victims died shows a more interesting and informed use of the *gacaca* records.

As will be discussed in detail in Chapter 4, the determination of individual deaths, the naming of the victims, and the location of their bodies have been the principal concerns of the *gacaca* courts. In the *Setako* decision, in finding that the prosecution had not established beyond a reasonable doubt that Rachel Mukarutamu was killed by Setako on April 8, 1994, at his home in Nkuli commune, the Chamber referred to a number of

---

[128] *Prosecutor v Tharcisse Muvunyi (Judgment)* ICTR-00-55A-T, T Ch III (11 February 2010) para. 85.

[129] Interview with Leopold (Participant 1), (Rural District, Northern Province Rwanda, September 5, 2009) notes on file with author.

[130] *Prosecutor v Ephrem Setako (Judgment)* ICTR-04-81-T, T Ch I (25 February 2010) para. 137.

gacaca documents relating to the victim's death in which it had been recorded that the victim was killed in a different commune in the prefecture of Gisenyi.[131] Although, in this case, the Chamber once again did not request the full set of *gacaca* documents relating to her death, this reasoning does show the potential for the detailed use of the *gacaca* documents when examining the death of specific individuals.

Despite this more appropriate use of *gacaca* evidence, the failure of the ICTR prosecution and defense to use this evidence subsequent to the *Setako* judgment shows the continued reluctance of the international court to fully engage with the *gacaca* proceedings. The ICTR's use of *gacaca* records illustrates the impact of the court's more general appraisal of the local community courts. A more detailed understanding of how *gacaca* works and its central objectives could have aided the ICTR in its work. However, the ICTR's internal focus on contributing to the development of an international legal order meant that the ICTR personnel distanced their work from that of the *gacaca* courts.

6. Conclusion

This chapter opened with the proposition that in a comparative discussion of post-genocide justice in Rwanda, it was useful to evaluate how those at the Tribunal understood their own work. The current literature on the ICTR has not taken full account of the agency of the judicial actors inside the institution when examining the objectives of the international court and its interactions with the domestic post-genocide justice processes. The resultant empirical research challenges how we think about international criminal law. Embedded in its local context, the judicial actors at the ICTR identified the creation of international criminal case law as their central contribution, a far narrower vision than that of accountability, peace, reconciliation, and domestic judicial development articulated at the start of the court's mandate. Drawing on the explanations provided during the ICTR interviews, this narrowing was in part due to the practical constraints on the practice of international criminal justice.

The impact of the ICTR's consistent focus on international criminal case law comes to the fore at points of interaction between the ICTR and the Rwandan domestic courts. Inside the ICTR, the effective concurrent work of local, national, and international transitional justice processes has been predicated on the assumption that the domestic courts are, or at least should be, pursuing objectives that support the establishment of an international legal order. This chapter has taken the ICTR on its own terms. The next two chapters examine the national courts and *gacaca* in the same manner, exploring how actors inside these domestic transitional justice processes have understood their own work. Such a comparative institutional analysis allows for an examination of the congruence of the objectives and practices of the post-genocide courts.

---

[131] Ibid. para. 256.

3 Inside the Rwandan National Courts

1. Introduction

The Rwandan Prosecutor General, Martin Ngoga, leaned forward to emphasize his point, "Justice in this country has been contextual. What they call double standards is justice in a contextual environment."[1] He was responding to the ICTR Trial Chamber decisions not to transfer Yussuf Munyakazi's case to the Rwandan domestic courts. Despite Rwanda's prosecution of international crimes, through both the national and the *gacaca* courts, the Rwandan legislature enacted a new law, *lexis specialis,* to govern the trial of any accused transferred from the ICTR.[2] Rwanda's approach to receiving cases from the ICTR relied on the continued use of a three-tiered justice system that has applied different procedures at the international, national, and local levels.

The initial decision by the ICTR judges not to transfer cases to the national courts suggests that, from the Tribunal's perspective, Rwanda's domestic rule of law was not secured by the promulgation of the specific Transfer Law nor any previous domestic genocide trials, and required further legislative amendments. As argued in Chapter 2, these Rule 11 *bis* decisions are consistent with the ICTR's own understanding of the

[1] Interview with Martin Ngoga (Participant 9) Prosecutor General for Rwanda, Parquet Général (Kigali, Rwanda, September 5, 2008) notes on file with author.

[2] Organic Law No. 11/2007 of 16 March 2007 concerning the Transfer of Cases to the Republic of Rwanda from the International Criminal Tribunal for Rwanda and from Other States. (Official Gazette of the Republic of Rwanda. Year 46, no. special, 19 March 2007).

role of international criminal justice. However, the decisions assume that the national courts have held a complementary position toward the ICTR. The Rule 11 *bis* decisions are underpinned by the assumption that the ICTR leads by example, and that the national courts, like the ICTR, are aimed at developing the application of international criminal law.

While consistent with the ICTR's approach to post-genocide justice, inside Rwanda, the Rule 11 *bis* decisions raise the important question of what the work of the national courts has been understood to achieve. An empirical analysis of the objectives of the national courts shows a clear focus on improving legal educational standards. The national courts' personnel have expected the concurrent justice processes of the ICTR and *gacaca* to support their internal objective of the domestic development of the judiciary and the broader legal fraternity. However, as the previous chapter outlined, the staff at the ICTR are quite explicit that they have not focused on the direct development of Rwanda's domestic courts. This chapter argues that the divergence between the understood objectives of the ICTR and the national courts has led to an increasingly competitive system of international and national criminal justice.

Consistent with an interpretive approach to transitional justice, the chapter examines the objectives and practice of the Rwandan courts, as understood inside the institution, and experienced by a group of prisoners subject to the courts' authority. The argument is structured around three sections. In the opening section, grounded empirical research is used to examine how a selection of Rwandan judges and lawyers have interpreted the work of the national courts. In 2008 and 2009, these legal practitioners argued that the national courts had principally contributed to the transitional period through improved legal education standards, drawing specific attention to substantial domestic legal reforms in 2004. However, this interpretation of the courts' work must be examined in the context of the use of law in post-genocide Rwanda. A focus on the legal reforms in 2004 differentiates the current practice of the national courts from both the pre-genocide period and the immediate post-genocide criminal trials.

The second section argues that the national courts' current focus on legal education allows the judges and lawyers a means of navigating the initial international criticisms raised against their practice. Since 1994, there has been a tension in the use of international law in Rwanda. International criminal law was drawn on to justify the arrest of thousands of genocide suspects, while international human rights law has formed the basis for the criticism of the resultant incarcerations and trials. The national courts' narrower focus on legal reform in the post-2004 period responds to the tensions raised by the practical and political constraints on the courts' work, while asserting the judges' and lawyers' current legal capacity.

The third section then lays out the Rwandan judges' and lawyers' interpretations of the national courts' work and its impact on the courts' engagement with the ICTR and *gacaca*. For a group of witnesses who have been tried by the national courts, the competition between the concurrent courts is an everyday reality, with one process routinely being used as the basis for criticizing the other concurrent courts. However, inside the national courts, there is still an assumption of complementarity. The actions of the ICTR and *gacaca* are understood in a way that is consistent with the national courts' articulated efforts of trying to improve legal education, and through this to reinforce their independence from a historically and currently strong executive. The result is that the Rule 11 *bis* decisions show the national courts' assumption that the ICTR will support domestic capacity building, while the transfer of cases to *gacaca* increased pressure on the local *gacaca* judges to move toward formal procedures in their work.

When read alongside Chapter 2, which highlighted the ICTR's focus of building an international legal order, this chapter demonstrates that the concurrent post-genocide courts have conceived of themselves as pursuing very different objectives. In addition, these objectives are at variance with both the collective and individual objectives generally ascribed to transitional justice processes in the established literature. These different institutional understandings of transitional justice have impacted the courts' interactions with one another and have led to points of friction among the ICTR, the national courts, and *gacaca*.

2. Inside the Institution

As discussed in the Introduction, the nature of a transitional period means that the social structures being studied are undergoing substantial transformation. An interpretive perspective draws attention to the movement associated with transition, detailing how the processes of the national courts have operated during a period of substantial change. Equivalent to the approach taken inside the ICTR, twenty-four current Rwandan judges and lawyers were interviewed in the national courts. In addition, interviews were conducted with High Court and District Tribunal judges, along with prosecutors and criminal lawyers in the two districts outside of the capital Kigali, in the Northern Province, and in the Western Province.[3] These judges and lawyers drew attention to the capacity of the law to drive change in a transitional society.

Inside the national courts, legal reform was central to the courts' current work. The participants described how reforms in 2004 that required higher educational standards for admission into the judiciary and the national prosecuting authorities better enabled the Rwandan domestic courts to drive change during the transitional period. When

[3] As discussed in the Introduction, all interviews were conducted with the express consent of the participants, following either a verbal or written explanation of the aims and structure of the research as approved by the University of Oxford's ethics committee. The interviews were semi-structured, and all began with the general question: "What do you see as the central contribution of this court?" Quotes included in this chapter are not attributed to individuals, although not all respondents requested anonymity. In each instance, they are always representative of a broader category of how participants ascribed meaning to the courts' work.

examined "in-context," these interpretations of the national courts' actions have helped the judges and lawyers to separate their current work from both the pre-genocide period and the immediate post-genocide criminal trials, while challenging the court's interaction with the ICTR and *gacaca*.

2.1 LEGAL TRAINING

As noted in Chapter 1, law has been central to the Rwandan government's policies during the transitional period. The judges interviewed within the domestic courts explicitly identified the transformative role that law has played in Rwanda since the 1994 genocide. As one judge noted, "Like everywhere else, here in Rwanda, social development is moved through laws."[4] Another judge more stridently articulated, "This judiciary brought the country out of the doldrums. Our new laws have changed the country."[5] When examining which laws were understood to have had the greatest influence, the majority of Rwandan judges, prosecutors, and private lawyers focused on the 2004 judicial reforms. As one judge succinctly noted,

> There has been a large amount of positive evolution in judicial capacity and this needs to be recognised. 2004 was a turning point: a whole lot of new judges were employed and they had received better training.[6]

As the above quotation suggests, the judges and lawyers primarily saw the national courts as having contributed to the Rwanda transition through overall improvements to the professional capacity of the Rwandan legal fraternity. "We wanted to bring into the Rwandan judiciary competent and skilled personnel," said one prosecutor, "because for so many years from the 1960s, 70s, 80s the Rwandan judiciary was manned by poorly educated magistrates. Some of them had other qualifications but very few of them were lawyers."[7]

In 2004, separate but complementary legislation determined the educational requirements of Rwandan judicial[8] and prosecutorial staff.[9] This was followed in 2013 by

[4] Interview with National Court Judge (Participant 3) Supreme Court (Kigali, Rwanda, August 7, 2008) conducted in conjunction with P. Clark, notes and recording on file with author.

[5] P. Clark, Interview with National Court Judge (Participant 20) High Court (Kigali, Rwanda, April 14, 2010) notes on file with author.

[6] Interview with National Court Judge (Participant 12) High Court (Regional, Rwanda, August 27, 2008) conducted in conjunction with P. Clark, notes on file with author.

[7] Interview with National Prosecutor (Participant 4), Parquet Général (Kigali, Rwanda, August 13, 2008) notes and recording on file with author.

[8] Organic Law No. 6 bis/2004 of April 14, 2004 on the Statutes for Judges and Other Judicial Personnel, art. 8.

[9] Organic Law No. 22/2004 of August 13, 2004 on the Statute of Public Prosecutors and Personnel of the Public Prosecutions, art. 8.

similar requirements set out for admission to the Rwandan Bar Association.[10] There was a notable focus by the Rwandan judges and lawyers on the use of this legal regulation to improve judicial capacity. Such regulation was routinely cited in response to the open-ended question, equivalent to that asked inside the ICTR, "What would you see as the major contribution of the national courts to the Rwandan transition?" In the words of another judge,

> The most important aspect of judicial reform has been hiring competent judges because, before 1994, and actually, before the reforms, the majority of judges were not qualified in law. I don't know what criterion was used to hire them, but it wasn't a law degree. From 2004, to become a judge you must have a law degree. All except the lowest magistrates now have law degrees, so that at least the people who are dealing with cases know the law and apply it.[11]

Ruti Teitel argues that during transitions, changes in a country's law are used as a means to differentiate between the current and previous regimes. What is particularly striking about this judge's statement is that he differentiates the courts' current work, not only from the pre-1994 period, but also from the ten years immediately following the genocide, during which time the RPF was already in power.

Inside the national courts, the clear focus on judicial capacity building after 2004 has allowed the current judges and lawyers a means of delineating their work from both the pre-genocide regime and the initial post-1994 arrests and trials. The national court participants were explicit about the challenges faced in the earlier trials. In the words of one senior prosecutor,

> The 1990s were a crisis in the justice sector. There was much effort, but limited outcomes due to limited personnel, legal information, logistical ability and infrastructure. We were also dealing with prison congestion and needed to work on an appropriate legal framework.[12]

A senior member of the Rwandan Bar Association was particularly critical of the level of legal expertise during the initial post-genocide prosecutions: "The first genocide judges weren't qualified, but today all of them are qualified. They're the intellectuals who work according to their consciences."[13] These statements highlight the focus on education

[10] Organic Law No. 83/2013 of September 11, 2013 on Establishing the Bar Association in Rwanda and Determining Its Organization and Functioning, art, 6. This legislation replaced the earlier Organic Law No. 03/1997 of March 19, 1997.

[11] Interview with National Court Judge (Participant 3) Supreme Court (Kigali, Rwanda, August 7, 2008) conducted in conjunction with P. Clark, notes and recording on file with author.

[12] Interview with National Prosecutor (Participant 9) Parquet Général (Kigali, Rwanda, April 12, 2010) conducted in conjunction with by P. Clark, notes on file with author.

[13] P. Clark, Interview with Private Lawyer (Participant 17) Rwandan Bar Association (Kigali, Rwanda, April 15, 2010) notes on file with author.

levels, not only as a means of differentiating between the previous and current regimes, but also as a means of asserting the current capacity of the Rwandan judges to conduct fair trials. Gerald Gahima, who served as Deputy Minister of Justice from 1996 to 1999, and the Prosecutor General from 1999 to 2003, in acknowledging the constraints on the initial genocide trials similarly focuses on the issues of legal training: "In retrospect, it is evident that the training that was provided to recruits to the various justice sector institutions may not have been adequate,"[14] but nonetheless "offered the only prospect of commencing genocide trials with a minimum delay."[15]

As with the ICTR's increasing focus on international criminal case law, so the national courts have focused on increasing judicial capacity. The ICTR and the national courts were both initially mandated to bring to justice the persons responsible for crimes committed during the 1994 genocide and civil war, ensuring both security and peace.[16] In practice, both jurisdictions have been understood to make a far more limited contribution than was envisaged at their outset, or within transitional justice literature more generally. As a consequence, the objectives of the ICTR and the national courts have narrowed and diverged.

2.2 REFORM IN PRETRIAL DETENTION

The other area of legal reform that was specifically referred to in the national courts was the improvements in pretrial detention. When articulating this contribution, participants similarly acknowledged the weaknesses in the early genocide trials. As discussed in the next section, one of the major human rights critiques raised against the Rwanda government throughout the 1990s was that its extended pretrial detention processes violated human rights, and at the extreme, amounted to cruel, inhuman, and degrading treatment. The focus on improved pretrial detention was identified by close to half of the participants and is shown in the wording of a district court judge:

> There have been important reforms in pre-trial detention, which is only permitted in exceptional circumstances. There is an emphasis on awarding bail and a suspect is only retained in custody for long periods under exceptional circumstances. You can be detained for 72 hours before being charged and you have to be brought before a judge within 24 days.[17]

---

14 Gahima 136.

15 Ibid.

16 The details of the mandate and empowerment of the national courts to try international crimes is discussed in detail in Section 3.1 of this chapter.

17 Interview with National Court Judge (Participant 12) High Court (Regional, Rwanda, August 28, 2008) notes on file with author.

A private lawyer coupled this acknowledgment of reforms in pretrial detention with improvements in the overall processing time of cases: "Before, cases would have taken three years; now the emphasis is on completion in six months, although this time limit is not ascribed for more serious cases."[18] As with the focus on improved judicial training, this identification of judicial reform similarly differentiates between the practice of the national courts in the 1990s and their current operation. The earlier efforts to regularize the law on pretrial detention in 1996, 1999, and 2001 were met with serious criticisms by international NGOs for the failure to adhere to the requirements laid out in the International Covenant on Civil and Political Rights (ICCPR).[19]

While the participants drew particular attention to an area of law criticized for failing to meet international legal standards, there was a focus on the courts' current capacity to respond to these criticisms. One judge highlighted that the drafting of the laws in 2004 took account of international legal bodies, with specific reference to the ICTR:

> Since 2004 we have had reform of our civil and criminal procedure and our laws of evidence. We drafted these laws looking at associates, including international organisations, and so they bear a strong resemblance to the laws of the ICTR.[20]

These dominant interpretations of the national courts' work must be examined in the social and political context of post-genocide Rwanda. In the immediate aftermath of the genocide, international law provided both the justification for action and the basis for critique, and the national courts operated in a transitional period, characterized by continued insecurity and mass arrests, carried out by domestic law enforcement agencies.

The next section argues that the national courts' focus on judicial expertise has been shaped by tensions in Rwanda's earlier use of international law. These tensions are identified in the existing literature on the courts and are supported by the Rwandan judges' and lawyers' own discussions of the practical constraints on their work. In 2008, the national court personnel's focus on judicial capacity affirms the courts' ability to receive cases from the ICTR and distances the national courts from the initial post-genocide trials, while endeavoring to reinforce their independence from other branches of government.

---

18 Interview with Private Lawyer (Participant 13) Rwandan Bar (Regional, Rwanda, August 28, 2008) notes on file with author.

19 International Covenant on Civil and Political Rights (adopted December 16, 1966, entered into force March 23, 1976) 999 UNTS 171 (ICCPR).

20 Interview with National Court Judge (Participant 3) Supreme Court (Kigali, Rwanda, August 7, 2008) conducted in conjunction with P. Clark, notes and recording on file with author.

3. The Constraints on the National Courts in Post-Genocide Rwanda

The prosecution of international crimes in the Rwandan transition takes us into the heart of post-genocide politics. From July 1994 until 1999, the work of the national courts was heavily shaped by the Rwandan government's prioritization of ongoing security concerns and the consolidation of political power. This resulted in wide-scale arrests, allegations of "disappearances," and extensive detention without charge. In line with the general legalist arguments for the use of trials in transitional periods, arrests were justified by the international legal requirement to prosecute the crime of genocide, an objective lauded and encouraged outside the country.[21] However, the resultant trials were criticized for their failure to adhere to international due process standards and the inadequacy of available defense.[22]

Although limited, the existing scholarship on the national courts highlights a tension between the use of international law both as the grounds for action and a basis of critique. This tension goes part of the way to explaining the Rwandan judges' and lawyers' interpretation of the courts' practice in the post-2004 period and is similarly supported by the practical constraints explicitly acknowledged inside the national courts.

3.1 INTERNATIONAL CRIMINAL LAW AND THE SECURITY OF THE RWANDAN STATE

It was clear from July 1994 that the Rwandan government intended to pursue the broad prosecution of all individuals suspected of involvement in the genocide. The proposal for a South African–style truth commission was repeatedly rejected on the basis that it would allow for a conditional amnesty, particularly for lower-level perpetrators.[23] The early appraisals of the decision to arrest and prosecute genocide suspects aligned with a growing argument in international law that, given the treaties ratified by Rwanda, there was a legal obligation to pursue prosecutions for serious human rights violations.

---

[21] International Crisis Group, "Five Years after the Genocide in Rwanda: Justice in Question" (Report) (7 April 1999) at 13; Amnesty International, "Rwanda—Unfair Trials: Justice Denied" (Report) (8 April 1997) AI-Index AFR 47/08/197,1 and Michael P. Scharf, "Responding to Rwanda: Accountability Mechanisms in the Aftermath of Genocide" (1999) 52 Journal of International Affairs 621.

[22] Ibid and Amnesty International, "Rwanda—The Troubled Course of Justice" (Report) (April 2000) AI-Index AFR 47/10/00.

[23] This occurred at a conference in Kigali in October/November 1995 and was reiterated following a Rwandan delegation's trip to South Africa in 1997. William Schabas, "Justice, Democracy, and Impunity in Post-Genocide Rwanda: Searching for Solutions to Impossible Problems" (1996) 7 Criminal Law Forum 523, 528; International Crisis Group, "Five Years after the Genocide in Rwanda: Justice in Question" (Report) (7 April 1999) 5 and Phil Clark, "Hybridity, Holism, and 'Traditional' Justice: The Case of the *Gacaca* Courts in Post-Genocide Rwanda" (2007) 39 The George Washington International Law Review 765, 781.

Articulating a position taken by many advocates of international criminal law, Michael P. Scharf argued that amnesty in Rwanda was not an option as it would have been a violation of the Genocide Convention, to which Rwanda was a party,[24] and "served as a virtual license to repeat the crimes."[25]

In line with the international support for prosecutions, the 1996 Organic Law established a Special Chamber of the Rwandan Supreme Court to try both genocide and crimes against humanity, with a temporal jurisdiction from October 1990 until December 1994. While the ICTR had been mandated to contribute to international peace and security and to establish national reconciliation, the mandate established under the national courts was more simply articulated: To organize criminal proceedings against those accused of acts sanctioned in the Penal Code that constituted genocide and crimes against humanity.[26] In 1998 Theogene Rudasingwa, then-Rwandan Ambassador to the United States, wrote, "This law simply proceeds from the premise that everyone who committed genocide would be made individually accountable for the crime that he or she committed."[27] International law and a legalist perspective on transitional justice were drawn on to justify the Rwandan government's "policy of maximal accountability"[28] in which all senior and lower level participants would be brought to trial.

International criminal law provided the basis for much of the action of the Rwandan criminal justice sector in the ten years following the genocide. Yet, just as international criminal law was being carefully incorporated into Rwandan law, international human rights law was being drawn on to criticize its implementation as the forced repatriation of the refugees began, the conditions of incarceration for those arrested rapidly deteriorated, and the justice system was put under increasing strain. Between June and July 1994, it was estimated that around 2 million Rwandans, predominantly of Hutu ethnicity,

---

[24] Rwanda had ratified the following treaties but had not specifically incorporated them into its penal code: Convention for the Prevention and Punishment of the Crime of Genocide (adopted December 9, 1948, entered into force 1 2 January 1951) 78 UNTS 277; Geneva Convention Relative to the Protection of Civilian Persons in Time of War (adopted 12 August, 1949, entered into force October 21, 1950) 75 UNTS 287 (Geneva Convention IV); Protocol Additional to the Geneva Conventions of 12 August 1949, and Relating to the Protection of Victims of International Armed Conflicts (adopted June 8, 1977, entered into force December 7, 1978) 1125 UNTS 3, and the Convention on the Non-applicability of Statutory Limitations to War Crimes and Crimes against Humanity (adopted November 26, 1968, entered into force November 11, 1970) 754 UNTS 73.

[25] Scharf 625.

[26] Organic Law No. 08/96 of August 30, 1996.

[27] Theogene Rudasingwa, "The Rwanda Tribunal and Its Relationship to National Trials in Rwanda" (1998) 13 American University International Law Review 1484, 1486. As noted in Chapter 1, in a deeply concerning turn of events on January 14, 2011, a Rwandan military court sentenced Theogene Rudasingwa to a prison term of twenty to twenty-four years. Rudasingwa is currently in exile in the United States. S. Kinzer, "Kagame's Authoritarian Turns Risk Rwanda's future" *Guardian* (London 27 January 2011) http://www.guardian.co.uk/commentisfree/cifamerica/2011/jan/27/rwanda-freedom-of-speech accessed January 28, 2011.

[28] Jones 80.

fled their homes in fear of reprisal killings from the advancing RPF forces. The majority of these displaced persons settled in a series of refugee camps in eastern Rwanda, the DRC, Burundi, and Tanzania. Although most of the refugees were civilians, they included the retreating armed forces and militia involved in the genocide and civil war. The camps posed a serious military threat to the newly established Rwandan government.

Closure of the refugee camps began on April 22, 1995, with the forced repatriation of over 150,000 internally displaced persons in Kibeho camp, the largest refugee camp on Rwandan soil, located in the southwest of the country. The United Nations' voluntary repatriation program had floundered amid rumors that inside Rwanda revenge killings and arbitrary arrests were taking place. In contrast, the newly constituted Rwandan Defence Forces (RDF) acted far more quickly and brutally, unwilling to accept the potential for the consolidation of fighting forces in the refugee camps. It was estimated that over four thousand people died during the closing of the Kibeho camp. The official figure, accepted by the then-precarious government of national unity, was 338 deaths, largely attributed to "criminal elements" operating in the camp.[29] This large-scale forced repatriation was coupled with the arrest of genocide suspects and a rapidly escalating prison population.

The literature on the national courts shows how the Rwandan government's decision to broadly prosecute the crimes perpetrated in the 1994 genocide was in line with global legal trends toward pursuing prosecutions for international crimes. However, authors have also noted that the arrest of suspected *génocidaires*, regardless of their level of responsibility, served a domestic political purpose as it helped to prevent any potential military resistance to RPF control.[30] Certainly many of the accused were worthy of arrest, and creating stability was rightly prioritized. However, the use of force when enacting the arrests, such as those in Kibeho, was excessive and often arbitrary.[31] Law was drawn on to secure the post-genocide political arrangement. As a result, although useful as a means to secure power after the genocide, the wide-scale arrests had very severe practical and legal implications.

Inside the Rwandan national courts in 2008 and 2009, some participants acknowledged the influence of executive power on the early operation of the courts. One private lawyer, who was broadly supportive of the improvements in the criminal justice system, stated that in evaluating the work of the national courts it was necessary to take into account that "there is official authority and influence over the whole justice system."[32] Similarly, another participant said, "There is the strong and invisible hand of the

---

[29] Prunier, *From Genocide to Continental War: The "Congolese" Conflict and the Crisis of Contemporary Africa* 41.

[30] Ibid.

[31] Linda Polman, *We Did Nothing: Why the Truth Doesn't Always Come Out When the UN Goes In* (Viking 2003).

[32] Interview with Private Lawyer (Participant 11) (Regional, Rwanda, August 27, 2008) notes on file with author.

executive that is guiding everything."[33] A current sitting judge argued forcefully that, if very senior accused had been brought before the national courts early on, "There would have been problems with government involvement with the cases."[34] However, another participant, who acknowledged some level of political involvement, was quick to point out that the incidence of such pressure had been reduced in recent practice:

> Before 2003, there was much more political involvement in judicial cases and we had to deal with these in the High Legal Council. There were significant differences after the Constitutional changes in 2003.[35]

The judges' and lawyers' focus on later judicial reforms differentiated between the earlier, more overt political use of law, and the current contributions of the Rwandan justice sector. There was explicit acknowledgment of the role of executive power, and more recent law reforms were drawn on as a means of arguing for the increased insulation of the courts from this centralized pressure. In addition to these political pressures, the pursuit of the initial wide-scale arrests of genocide suspects led to increasing tensions between Rwanda's use of international criminal law and international human rights law.

3.2 INTERNATIONAL HUMAN RIGHTS LAW IN RWANDA

The exact number of people incarcerated in Rwanda throughout the 1990s is difficult to verify. Quoting HRW, Gerard Prunier estimates that "from 1000 prisoners in August 1994, the numbers had risen to 6000 at the end of the year and kept growing exponentially to reach 23,000 by March 1995."[36] Later he suggests that the prison population was 9,000 in February 1995 and jumped to 44,000 by June 1995.[37] What is clear is that while some arrests were happening across the country, the closure of the camps such as Kibeho in April 1995, and those in the DRC in September 1996 and again in 1998, caused the numbers to spike dramatically.

As the numbers of genocide inmates grew, so the conditions of detention rapidly deteriorated. By 1998, there were officially two categories of civilian prisons in Rwanda: those under the authority of the Ministry of Justice, and those run by the Ministry of the Interior.[38] Conditions in the prisons, with an estimated capacity of only 15,000 inmates,

---

33 Interview with Private Lawyer (Participant 22) (Kigali, Rwanda, August 13, 2008) notes on file with author.

34 Interview with National Court Judge (Participant 12) (Regional, Rwanda, August 27, 2008) notes on file with author.

35 Interview with Private Lawyer (Participant 18) (Kigali, Rwanda, April 15, 2010) conducted by P. Clark, notes on file with author.

36 Prunier, *From Genocide to Continental War: The "Congolese" Conflict and the Crisis of Contemporary Africa* 9.

37 Ibid. 45.

38 Drumbl, "Rule of Law amid Lawlessness: Counselling the Accused in Rwanda's Domestic Genocide Trials" 572.

were "harsh and life-threatening,"[39] with minimal sanitation and overcrowding so pronounced that in some cases prisoners had to take turns to sit down. The "prisons" under the Ministry of the Interior—called *cachots communaux*—were at the extreme end of this spectrum. Organized at the local level, these holding areas were initially under the exclusive control of the local majors or *bourgmestres*[40] and took many forms, from warehouses and private homes to shipping containers and latrines.[41] Of the 183 places of detention listed by the International Committee of the Red Cross (ICRC) during this period, only 16 were actual prisons. International human rights law formed the basis for the argument by human rights NGOs that such conditions of incarceration constituted cruel, inhuman, and degrading treatment.[42]

As the Rwandan prisons and *cachots* filled, so the Constitution was amended[43] to allow for continued detention without charge as the burgeoning criminal justice system struggled to regularize prisoner arrest records. By May 1997, Amnesty International (AI) estimated that more than 100,000 people were held in prisons and detention centers across Rwanda, the majority charged with genocide. In an effort to respond to this unmanageable caseload, the 1996 legislation relied heavily on a plea-bargaining system that was intended to meet international procedural standards while processing the enormous number of cases.

The plea-bargaining system was based on categorizing the accused into four groups, according to the severity of their offense. Category 1 was reserved for people suspected of being in positions of responsibility and engaging in the organization of the genocide at the national, prefecture, sector, or *cellule* level.[44] Category 2 consisted of those accused of being perpetrators and accomplices of murder. Category 3 applied to persons accused of serious assaults against the person, and Category 4 related to those accused solely of committing property offenses.[45] This categorization formed the backbone of a confession and guilty plea procedure.

---

[39] U.S. Department of State. "Rwanda Country Report on Human Rights Practices for 1998" (Report) (February 26, 1999) 4.

[40] International Crisis Group, "Five Years after the Genocide in Rwanda: Justice in Question" (Report) (7 April 1999) 12.

[41] Drumbl, "Rule of Law amid Lawlessness: Counselling the Accused in Rwanda's Domestic Genocide Trials" 571–547.

[42] Amnesty International, "Rwanda—Unfair Trials: Justice Denied" (Report) (April 8, 1997) AI-Index AFR 47/08/197, 1.

[43] Article 6 of The Constitutional Amendment I, January 18, 1996, authorized derogation from Article 12(2) of the 1991 Constitution in cases of "exceptional danger threatening the existence of the nation." The then-Rwandan Constitutional Court initially held this legislation to be invalid; however, prisoners continued to be incarcerated for an indefinite period of time. The Rwandan parliament eventually pushed through a constitutional amendment to prevent any further challenges to legislative derogations of prisoners' rights.

[44] As noted in the previous chapter, a prefecture corresponds to a provincial structure and is made up of several communes, sectors and *cellules*.

[45] In 2004, Category 2 and 3 were amalgamated. However, by this stage the *gacaca* courts were in operation and had jurisdiction over Categories 2 and 3, leaving only Category 1 in the remit of the national courts.

Under Articles 15 and 16 of the 1996 Organic Law, in return for a full confession and apology, offenders in the second, third, and fourth categories could benefit from substantial reduction in penalties. This reduction was increased if perpetrators confessed before the start of prosecution proceedings against them.[46] Despite these efforts, in practice the domestic genocide trials, just like the initial arrests and conditions of incarceration, were heavily criticized by international and domestic human rights NGOs for failing to meet international procedural standards. The criticisms focused on three principal issues: the paucity of judicial personnel, particularly the limited number of defense counsel;[47] Rwanda's continued use of capital punishment;[48] and the restricted appeal procedure.[49] It was in the midst of these critiques of the national courts that twenty-two individuals who had been domestically tried were executed, four years after the start of the genocide. As discussed in Chapter 1, soon after this, in the wake of international outrage, *gacaca* was introduced as a possible response to the crisis in the criminal justice sector.

Plea-bargaining did not resolve the tension in Rwanda's use of international law, as the efforts to streamline the process failed to address the unmanageable caseload. By 1999 the national courts had heard only 1,274 cases, 1 percent of the total number of detainees then held in custody.[50] By early 2000, this number had nearly doubled, and some external commentators noted that the trials conformed with "international standards."[51] However, progress remained slow, and fewer than 20 percent of the accused had pleaded guilty. The caseload remained unmanageable and, as discussed in more detail in the next chapter, after 2004 it was the *gacaca* courts that ultimately provided a procedural solution to the desperately overcrowded prisons.

Inside the Rwandan court system in 2009, the caseload was identified as the clearest practical constraint on the national courts, readily discussed by all the participants in this study. Respondents repeatedly opened their interview with an acknowledgment of the challenge of pursuing broad and wide-ranging prosecutions. As a lawyer in the Ombudsman's Office said, "We had an overloaded system."[52] However, this was generally identified as an early constraint that has been mitigated since the advent of *gacaca*.

---

[46] Offenders in the first category could participate in the guilty plea procedure and benefit from the mitigated penalties, provided their names had not previously been published in the Official Gazette. Article 9 of Organic Law No. 08/96 of August 30, 1996.

[47] Drumbl, "Rule of Law amid Lawlessness: Counselling the Accused in Rwanda's Domestic Genocide Trials" 550.

[48] Pillay 1477.

[49] International Crisis Group, "Five Years after the Genocide in Rwanda: Justice in Question" (Report) (7 April 1999) 15.

[50] Drumbl, "Rule of Law amid Lawlessness: Counselling the Accused in Rwanda's Domestic Genocide Trials" 291.

[51] M. Moussalli, "Report on the Situation of Human Rights in Rwanda" (Report) (25 February 2000) Economic and Social Council E/CN.4/2000/41, 27.

[52] P. Clark, Interview with Private Lawyer (Participant 18), Office of the Ombudsman (Kigali, Rwanda, April 15, 2010) notes on file with author.

As one senior judge observed, by 1998, the national courts were "going to collapse,"[53] and it was this practical reality that drove the search for alternative forms of accountability. A regional judge noted that the initial genocide trials took up the majority of his courts' resources, and *gacaca* had now made these resources available for the trials of common crimes.[54] The transfer of the majority of the genocide cases to the *gacaca* jurisdictions allowed for the 2004 judicial reforms, and the Rwandan judges' and lawyers' current focus on this post-2004 period distinguishes the courts' current practice from the initial genocide trials.

Inside the ICTR, a focus on international criminal law provided the legal practitioners with a means of distancing their work from what was perceived as a difficult and constrained domestic context. Similarly, the Rwandan judges' and lawyers' focus on legal expertise allowed them to traverse the initial tensions in the use of international law and the practical constraints that arose from the Rwandan government's decision to pursue wide-scale genocide prosecutions. However, a narrower focus within the national courts on the post-2004 period has impacted the Rwandan judges' and lawyers' engagement with both the ICTR and *gacaca*.

4. Concurrent Transitional Justice

This chapter opened with a description of how participants inside the national courts have understood the work of these courts since the 1994 genocide. A hermeneutical approach to cultural analysis examines the meanings that render intelligible the practice of law in Rwanda's transition. The Rwandan judges and lawyers identified the 2004 judicial reforms as the crucial legal change during the transitional period, focusing on the improved legal education standards in Rwanda and the reforms to pretrial detention. As discussed above, this interpretation has been shaped by the earlier tensions in Rwanda's use of international law, the pressures of a strong executive, and the practical constraints identified within the national courts. A focus on the improved legal education of the judges and lawyers asserts the Rwandan national courts' current judicial capacity, but it is a transitional objective that is distinct from the emergent objectives of the ICTR.

Although both the ICTR and the national courts were mandated to bring to justice those accused of genocide crimes, fifteen years later, the concurrent courts were understood to have pursued and contributed very different outcomes. The national courts focused on domestic legal education standards, while the ICTR has been concerned

[53] Interview with former National Court Judge (Participant 7), Ministry of Justice (Kigali, Rwanda, September 3, 2008); interview conducted in conjunction with P. Clark, notes on file with author.

[54] Interview with National Court Judge (Participant 12) High Court (Regional, Rwanda, August 27, 2008) notes on file with author.

with developing the legal definitions and procedural standards for trying the international crimes of genocide, war crimes, and crimes against humanity. In both instances, the interpretations of the courts' actions provide a response to the criticisms of the courts and the practical challenges that have constrained their practice. However, as discussed below, the divergent objectives of the national and international courts have led to a mismatch of expectations, crucially affecting how the courts have practically engaged with one another formally and informally.

4.1 INFORMAL INTERACTIONS: A COMMON GROUP OF PARTICIPANTS

This section argues that, for a group of prisoners who were convicted by the Rwandan national courts, the ICTR, the national courts, and *gacaca* are understood to be in competition with one another. The distinct objectives of the ICTR and the national courts, while clearly articulated inside the institutions, were not articulated "from below." During the interviews inside the Rwandan prisons, participants generally focused on one aspect of their trial process and then evaluated all three of the courts against this ideal. Routinely, the work of one court was used as the basis to critique the others. For these prisoners, the courts competed with one another to provide what the prisoners perceived as a more just trial.

Seven of the participants in the Rwandan prisons had been tried by the national courts and were appealing their cases through *gacaca*. Three of these prisoners had also testified before the ICTR. All of the participants were critical of the early national court cases. This opinion is consistent with the current Rwandan national judges' and lawyers' own acknowledgment of the early challenges facing the genocide trials, as discussed above. However, the inmates' views on the national courts' current capacity and the trials before *gacaca,* and the ICTR differed substantially. Participants often made unprompted comparisons between the different courts, as the work of one court provided a means of critiquing the others.

Michel, previously a guard in Virunga National Park, was most concerned with the capacity of the courts to gather reliable evidence. When interviewed in 2008, he had been imprisoned in Ruhengeri Central Prison for fourteen years. He was tried by the national courts and had testified before *gacaca* and the ICTR. In July 1994, "after the RPF took hold of the country"[55] he had fled across the Rwandan border into the DRC. On return to Rwanda he was arrested and charged with the murder of sixteen people. Michel claimed that he was told by "the higher authorities"[56] that the people were RPF infiltrators, so he shot them. In his own words, "Of course I admitted my guilt. I told the truth so that God could forgive me, to make it easier on everyone, instead of trying to

[55] Interview with Michel (Participant 4), (Rural District, Northern Province Rwanda, September 5, 2008) notes on file with author.

[56] Ibid.

fight . . . I confessed because the government said I would receive forgiveness but I feel that I was deceived."[57]

In 1997, his case was heard before the national courts, and he was sentenced to life imprisonment. "I asked for defence counsel but I never received one . . . In 1997 I feel that those courts were not seeking for the truth, they were seeking for conviction at the time . . ."[58] For Michel, *gacaca* offered an opportunity to better obtain this "truth":

> *Gacaca* is good because you go to where the people who know you, and know what happened and they can speak the truth, for or against you. In the classical courts I have been accused of killing a lady who is still alive. When I gave testimony at *gacaca* they cleared me of this charge.

For Michel, the weakness of the national court's investigation was interpreted as the central strength of the *gacaca* process. One court's practice provided the basis for the critique of the other concurrent courts.

Like Michel, Jean-Baptiste was also critical of his initial trial before the national courts. He was tried alongside four co-accused; three of them were acquitted, although, in his words, "The case was the same against all of us."[59] In Jean-Baptiste's account, he was in Rwanda for only two weeks of the genocide, after which he fled to Burundi because he feared for his life. He returned to Rwanda in July 1994 to restart his transport business, and flew to Europe that same year, although he was later arrested on his return to Rwanda. He did not confess and was tried by the national courts in 1999, sentenced to death in 2002, and appealed in that same year. Like Michel, Jean-Baptiste's case was recently transferred to the *gacaca* courts for review. However, unlike Michel who was supportive of *gacaca,* Jean-Baptiste remained sceptical, despite the possibility of *gacaca* providing an opportunity for further review:

> I would rather go before the ordinary courts because under the ordinary courts you get factual evidence. *Gacaca* is just about emotional feelings . . . There is also hatred because of the conflict, many people can falsely charge you and this is from the side of both Hutu and Tutsi. In *gacaca,* it is just emotional, people are lying. There are some people who name you because they are falling down and they would prefer you to fall with them.[60]

For Jean-Baptiste, despite his early conviction by the national courts, his preference for the national courts was based on what he saw as the failures of the *gacaca* proceedings.

---

[57] Ibid.

[58] Ibid.

[59] Interview with Jean-Baptiste (Participant 10), (Kigali, Rwanda, April 20, 2009) notes on file with author.

[60] Ibid.

For Aloys, the question of a just process turned on the judicial competence of the judges and lawyers. He opened our interview by requesting that we conduct our discussions in English rather than Kinyarwanda. Aloys holds a bachelors degree in Economics from the Netherlands and is serving a life sentence in Kigali Central Prison. Like Michel and Jean-Baptiste, he was similarly critical of the initial work of the national courts: "Nowadays people are more calm than before. Then they were shouting that we were criminals. Nowadays they take time to check the evidence."[61]

Aloys's criticisms of the national court cases related to the judges' legal expertise, and he raised similar concerns regarding *gacaca*: "I started my case in 2000 and it was a problem to get competent judges. Out of the three judges on the bench there were two students still in university!"[62] In stating his preference for his appeal to go before the national courts, Aloys noted, "I would prefer my appeal to go to the national courts because I don't know about the *gacaca* judges' level of handling the law."[63] For Aloys, the post-2004 improvements in the capacity of the national courts provided the basis for his support of the national courts and his scepticism of *gacaca*.

In contrast, for Athanase a just process turned on the question of an appropriate sentence. He had been tried by the national courts in 1998 and sentenced to life in prison:

> I confessed and asked for forgiveness from my heart. I was accused of what happened in the church in Nyange . . . I would have preferred to go to *gacaca* because the people who are transferred from the ordinary court to *gacaca* have their sentence reduced. *Gacaca* has made a great contribution because people who confess have had their sentence reduced. I think that it works if the judges are not taken by their own interests.[64]

Having testified before the ICTR, Athanase evaluated the international court on these same terms: "In the past, those in charge were the ones who would be given life. Now even the common citizens are given life imprisonment . . . it is not equal justice."[65]

Michel, Jean-Baptiste, Aloys, and Athanase were all tried by the national courts and were appealing their cases through *gacaca*. Two of them had testified before the ICTR. Their exposure to the concurrent workings of three post-genocide courts led them to use one process as a means to criticize the other. Each participant articulated a particular version of what constituted a just process and then examined all of the courts against these criteria, challenging one court vis-à-vis the others.

---

[61] Interview with Aloys (Participant 11), (Kigali, Rwanda, April 20, 2009) notes on file with author.

[62] Ibid.

[63] Ibid.

[64] Interview with Athanase (Participant 16), (Rural District, Western Province, Rwanda, April 21, 2009) notes on file with author.

[65] Ibid.

The work of the national courts informally intersects with *gacaca* and the ICTR through the experiences of these common participants. These intersections highlight a perception that the concurrent courts compete with one another. In addition, the national courts have formally interacted with the international and localized courts through the transfer of cases between the jurisdictions. For the suspects who have been subject to the courts' authority, the competition among the three courts is an everyday reality. However, inside the national courts there remained an assumption of compatibility.

The judges and lawyers working in the national court system have focused on their improved legal education and described the work of the ICTR in terms of its ability to assist in developing this domestic capacity. Similarly, the work of *gacaca* was described in terms of how it supported the national courts' work. When criticisms were raised about *gacaca,* the national court participants drew attention to the lack of formal judicial training of the *gacaca* judges. These understandings have impacted the potential transfer of cases between the jurisdictions. The national courts argued for the transfer of cases from the ICTR, in order to assert the current capacity of the Rwandan judges and lawyers. Similarly, when transferring cases to *gacaca,* the national courts assumed that the *inyangamugayo* should have focused on professionalizing *gacaca,* and pressured the localized courts to apply more formal and rigid procedures.

4.2 UNDERSTANDINGS OF THE ICTR

For the national court judges and lawyers, the ICTR was generally evaluated against the perceived major contribution of their own work, namely the development of legal training and capacity building. This interpretation starts to shed light on the institutional culture of the Rwandan courts. Within the empirical study, the work of the ICTR was ascribed a meaning consistent with how the actions of the domestic courts were being assessed. As a senior prosecutor stated,

> The ICTR has attempted to play a supervisory role. If you can go on the record to say that Rwanda cannot be trusted, it is your biggest failure. It was their role to build the system. If they did not meaningfully engage with Rwanda and help our system to grow, then their legacy is meaningless . . . We have done a lot to accommodate the practice of the ICTR, they also need to adapt to the national system. It is a matter of law and legal tradition.[66]

When participants acknowledged the value of the ICTR, reference was made to its role in the judicial capacity building of Rwandan judges and lawyers. As one judge stated,

---

[66] Interview with National Prosecutor (Participant 9) Parquet Général (Kigali, Rwanda, September 5, 2008) notes on file with author.

"Some judges from Rwanda have gone to Arusha and here we have a library and they have given us some of the judgments and tapings."[67] Another prosecutor was more forthright:

> The ICTR has contributed first, I would say, especially to the training. The Rwandan judges and prosecutors have been going to Arusha for training sessions and capacity building, especially in the last year and a half in preparation for the transfer of cases.[68]

Similarly, his colleague evaluated the ICTR in terms of its assistance in training the judges of the High Court and the Supreme Court.[69] Participants routinely argued that their analysis of the ICTR came from the perspective of being a trained lawyer: "As a lawyer I know it was necessary; Rwandans could not get their hands on the big fish."[70] As another private lawyer stated, "As a lawyer, I am not sure that the ICTR has worked on the ground."[71] It was important to the participants that they establish their technical expertise and examine the work of the ICTR on this basis.

The value of international law more broadly was also described within the national courts' cultural context. Participants specifically referred to international law and international legal standards as useful for improving the overall capacity of Rwandan lawyers and judges. As one judge said,

> The High Court will continue improving, especially given the emphasis on judicial training since 2004 . . . We've also conducted trainings on legal procedures and the UN will soon send personnel here to train us in human rights conventions.[72]

The work of the national courts and the ICTR has been understood in a single cultural context, and the courts' actions are ascribed consistent meanings. The work of the national courts is asserted through a focus on the raised educational requirements of the judicial and legal personnel, and the work of ICTR has been assessed on this same basis.

---

[67] Interview with National Court Judge (Participant 16) High Court (Regional, Rwanda, April 23, 2009) notes on file with author.

[68] Interview with National Prosecutor (Participant 4) Parquet Général (Kigali, Rwanda, August 13, 2008) notes and recording on file with author.

[69] Interview with National Prosecutor (Participant 5) Parquet Général (Kigali, Rwanda, August 13, 2008) notes on file with author.

[70] Ibid.

[71] Interview with Private Lawyer (Participant 13) Rwandan Bar (Regional, Rwanda, August 28, 2008) notes on file with author.

[72] P. Clark, Interview with National Court Judge (Participant 3), Supreme Court (Kigali, Rwanda, April 12, 2010) notes on file with author.

4.2.1 Interpreting the Rule 11 *bis* Decisions

The national courts' focus on legal expertise and capacity building has influenced the courts' interactions with the ICTR. The affects of the divergent objectives of the ICTR and the national courts are apparent in their approach to the potential transfer of suspects to Rwanda under Rule 11 *bis*. Before the ICTR Prosecutor's application for the transfer of Munyakazi's case, the Rwandan government invested enormous time and energy in the Rule 11 *bis* applications. The government built the Mpanga prison near Nyanza in southwestern Rwanda, which contains a "UN block" designed to meet standards equivalent to the UN Detention Facility in Arusha.[73] In 2007, Rwanda abolished the death penalty, in line with the requirements laid out in Rule 11 *bis*[74] and, as noted at the start of this chapter, the Rwanda parliament passed specific legislation to govern the transferred cases. These legal changes were enacted to ensure that Rwanda has an adequate legal framework to receive cases from the ICTR.

However, the Rule 11 *bis* decisions have played a very different role for the national courts than they have for the ICTR. The national courts pursued the transfer of cases to Rwanda because they wanted to affirm, to an external audience, their domestic legal capacity. The national courts have not pursued the transfer of cases because it would enable them to apply the procedural standards and legal definitions of international crimes developed through the ICTR's case law. In discussions with current Rwandan judges and lawyers regarding the transfer decisions, the emphasis was not on the national courts' prior application of international criminal law, but rather on the current legal expertise of Rwandan practitioners. In the words of one of the prosecutors involved in the Rule 11 *bis* application, "It is important that the cases are transferred. It is important for the image of the country, of our judges and prosecutors, to show that we are meeting international standards."[75]

The divergent objectives of the ICTR and the national courts have meant that at points of interaction between the courts, such as in relation to the Rule 11 *bis* cases, each court has assumed that the other is pursuing a complementary objective. In the words of the then-Prosecutor General Martin Ngoga during the oral hearings of the Munyakazi transfer application:

> Rwanda is working very hard to secure cooperation of national jurisdictions in which we find fugitives of genocide. And the decision of this Chamber will either

[73] "Mpanga, a Stronghold for the UN in Rwanda" *International Justice Tribune* (5 May 2008) http://www.rnw.nl/international-justice/article/mpanga-stronghold-un-rwanda accessed July 10, 2011.

[74] Rule 11 *bis* states explicitly that the Trial Chamber must be satisfied that "the accused will receive a fair trial in the courts of the State and that the death penalty will not be imposed or carried out."

[75] Interview with National Prosecutor (Participant 5) Parquet Général (Kigali, Rwanda, August 13, 2008) notes on file with author.

complement those efforts or cripple them. And this forms the very basis of the legacy of this Court.[76]

The national courts expected the ICTR to be oriented toward developing Rwandan legal expertise and supporting domestic trials. However, as shown in Chapter 2, very few ICTR personnel thought it was the role of an international court to directly develop domestic capacity. The ICTR's focus has been on developing a robust body of international case law. Recalling one of the earlier statements by an ICTR lawyer, "If the issue had been about strengthening the Rwandan judiciary, then the trials should have happened in Rwanda . . . in this instance there was a need for an international response."[77] The international court has operated on the assumption that the domestic courts are, or should be, pursuing the ICTR's objective of developing the application of international criminal law.

If the Rwandan prosecutors had argued the Rule 11 *bis* decisions through detailed reference to genocide-related domestic litigation and case law with a particular focus on the domestic application of international criminal law, the ICTR Trial Chambers may have found their arguments more persuasive. As one ICTR judge stated explicitly, "Much comes from practice and Rwanda was not able to supply examples of when they had tried genocide."[78] Following the transfer for Jean Uwinkindi, the national courts have encountered practical constraints in their efforts to use international criminal cases in their legal arguments. In the prosecutor's opening statement at Uwinkindi's trial, he articulated an intention to draw on ICTR case law. However, this was met with an immediate objection from the defense, who argued that they did not have access to these cases. The prosecutor then photocopied and provided the defense with these cases during the recess, but did not have Kinyarwanda translations available. The outcome was that the Chamber ruled that they would "not hear arguments on the jurisprudence that day."[79]

At points of interaction between the courts, such as during the transfer of cases between the jurisdictions, both the ICTR and the national courts have attempted to pressure the other institution to pursue objectives in line with their own understood contributions. However, the research inside the courts shows how the objectives of the courts have diverged. The impact of the differing understandings of transitional justice inside the ICTR and the national courts is that, rather than complementing one another, the courts have often competed.

---

[76] *Prosecutor v Yussuf Munyakazi* (Oral Hearing on Rule 11 *bis*) ICTR-97-36-A, T Ch III (24 April 2008). Transcript on file with author.

[77] Interview with Legal Officer (Participant 3), Chambers, UN ICTR (Arusha, Tanzania, July 7, 2008) notes on file with author.

[78] Interview with Trial Chamber Judge (Participant 4), Chambers, UN ICTR (Arusha, Tanzania, July 9, 2008) notes on file with author.

[79] *Prosecutor v. Jean Uwinkindi* (Monitoring Report May 2014) MICT-12-25, (4 July 2014) para. 27.

4.3 UNDERSTANDINGS OF THE *GACACA* COURTS

Inside the national courts, the explanation of *gacaca's* work cohered with the national courts' focus on judicial reform and domestic legal capacity building. The participants in the national courts were broadly supportive of *gacaca*, describing how it had provided a means of dealing with the justice systems' caseload. "We think that *gacaca* did a splendid job in handling the cases at the rate that they did," said one senior judge. "That is why we have sent most of the cases that we have in our courts to *gacaca*. We think that the process is faster and, on the whole, we are satisfied that justice is being done."[80] For this judge, the *gacaca* courts were understood in terms of how they had supported the national courts' activities.

When participants criticized *gacaca*, the critiques related to the legal expertise of the judicial staff and the professional integrity of the local judges. As one lawyer stated, "With the *inyangamugayo*, it is an issue of capacity."[81] Another judge said,

> One of the major challenges facing *gacaca* has been the acceptability of the process to the legal fraternity. Lawyers are arrogant people who think that they know better than other people. They think that justice is their exclusive right. They might have had exclusive access to law, the legal text, but this is separate from justice.[82]

As discussed in detail in the next chapter, the *gacaca* courts have been heavily criticized by a number of international NGOs and external commentators, initially in relation to their standards of due process and the absense of legally trained judges. The national courts' focus on judicial expertise meant that the Rwandan judges and lawyers were generally willing to accept criticism of the *gacaca* courts. As Martin Ngoga stated,

> There is a long list of deficiencies in the *gacaca* courts and I can see them and would be one of the first to identify them, but I will not say it was a bad idea. It is the best we have for the time being and there have been continued improvements in the level of the judges and these judges are now dealing with fewer cases.[83]

The willingness of many of the national court personnel to accept a degree of criticism of *gacaca*, particularly regarding the need to improve the expertise of the *gacaca* judges, is consistent with how personnel in the national courts interpret their own work. At

---

[80] Ibid.

[81] Interview with National Prosecutor (Participant 4) Parquet Général (Kigali, Rwanda, August 13, 2008) conducted in conjunction with P. Clark, recording and notes on file with author.

[82] Interview with former National Court Judge (Participant 7), Ministry of Justice (Kigali, Rwanda, September 3, 2008) conducted in conjunction with P. Clark, notes on file with author.

[83] Interview with Martin Ngoga (Participant 9) Prosecutor General for Rwanda, Parquet Général (Kigali, Rwanda, September 5, 2008) notes on file with author.

points of formal interaction between the national courts and *gacaca,* such as the transfer of Category 1 cases to *gacaca,* the national courts' interpretations affected the work of the localized courts, manifesting in pressure on these courts to move toward increasingly formal procedures.

4.3.1 A Pressure toward Formalism

In May 2008, the majority of Category 1 cases, previously before the national courts, were transferred to the *gacaca* courts. The local courts were empowered to try suspects charged with the planning and leadership of the Rwandan genocide at *sub-prefecture* and *commune* levels, and those accused of sexual violence.[84] At this point of transfer, the internal objectives of the national courts have come to the fore as the Rwandan judges and lawyers have exerted pressure on the *gacaca* courts to follow more formal procedures.

The Category 1 cases before the *gacaca* courts have increasingly attempted to mirror processes before the national courts. At the hearings attended between February and April 2009, all of the Category 1 cases started with the *gacaca* judges reading extracts of the 2008 Organic Law relating to the laws governing confession, participation, and the penalties for false testimony. There was a strong emphasis by the *gacaca* judges on adhering to the correct order of proceedings.[85] As Phil Clark notes, in discussion of a Category 1 trial in Nyamirambo district of Kigali Ville in August 2008,

> The key characteristics of this hearing were the singular focus on discovering the legal facts about the events under consideration, with almost no discussion of their personal, emotional impact on the individuals concerned, and little communal interaction among the participants.[86]

For Clark, this challenges one of the key strengths of *gacaca,* that of providing a dialogical space to create the potential for real engagement between perpetrators and victims.[87] Inside the national courts, the transfer of Category 1 cases to *gacaca* was described by one of the lawyers as the conclusion of a logical trend:

> Why should you have two jurisdictions trying the same crimes? Why should you have *gacaca* and the ordinary courts both trying genocide? The solution is to take

84 Article 7 of the Organic Law no. 13/2008 of 19th May 2008 modifying and complementing the Organic Law no. 16/2004 of 19th June 2004 establishing the organization, competence and functioning of Gacaca Courts charged with prosecuting and trying the perpetrators of genocide and other crimes against humanity, committed between October 1, 1990 and 31st December 1994.

85 Authors research notes, Kigali, Northern Province and Western Province Research cites Rwanda, February–April 2009. Notes on file with author.

86 Clark 215.

87 Ibid. 165–168.

> them to *gacaca* and reinforce the *gacaca*... The challenge is that in the first category, these guys are very intelligent, they may know the law better than the judges.[88]

In practice, "reinforcing *gacaca*" has meant an increasing focus on the order of procedures leading to an increased formalism in *gacaca* hearings. In the Category 1 cases, the *gacaca* judges exercised tighter control over who could speak, and the bench was solely responsible for calling witnesses to provide oral testimony. *Gacaca's* formalism increased the active role of the *inyangamugayo,* placing a greater emphasis on their knowledge of the law and the "correct" structure of a *gacaca* hearing, but simultaneously restricting the role of general participants in the discussions.

Consistent with their own focus on improved legal education, the national judges and lawyers emphasized the need to improve the training of the *gacaca* judges to handle the Category 1 cases. As was often noted, "There will be extra training for the *gacaca* judges."[89] This position inside the national courts coincided with continued criticisms by international NGOs of *gacaca's* failure to adhere to international standards of due process because of, among other things, the legal expertise of the *gacaca* judges.[90] Avocats Sans Frontières made an explicit plea for the importance of "procedural formalism,"[91] noting in 2010 that the *gacaca* judges had "not yet totally understood"[92] the importance of this.

The national courts' willingness to accept criticisms of the *gacaca* courts, particularly in relation to the judges' legal training and their own position on the need to "reinforce" *gacaca,* manifested in an increasing pressure on the *gacaca* judges to formalize their proceedings. This formalism was evident in the *gacaca* courts' increased adherence to a prescribed order of events rather than more careful attention to the judges' interpretations and application of the law.

The national courts' understandings of the ICTR and *gacaca* have been shaped by what the national courts themselves purport to have achieved. How the actions of domestic courts are assessed affects how the concurrent work of the international criminal tribunal and the *gacaca* courts are viewed and understood. This contextual approach suggests that these understandings have significantly shaped the national courts' formal interactions with the ICTR and *gacaca.*

---

[88] Interview with National Prosecutor (Participant 4) Parquet Général (Kigali, Rwanda, August 13, 2008). Interview conducted in conjunction with P. Clark, recording and notes on file with author.

[89] Interview with National Prosecutor (Participant 5) Parquet Général (Kigali, Rwanda, August 13, 2008) notes on file with author.

[90] Penal Reform International, "Eight Years on ... A Record of Gacaca Monitoring in Rwanda" (Final Research and Monitoring Summary) March 2010, 31.

[91] Avocats Sans Frontières, "Monitoring of the Gacaca Courts—Judgment Phase" (Analytical Report 3) October 2006–April 2007, 49.

[92] Ibid.

5. Conclusion

Improvements in judicial expertise and training are understood as the dominant contributions of the national courts to Rwanda's transitional period. The Rwandan judges and lawyers routinely focused on the post-2004 reforms, highlighting the increased educational requirements of the judges and prosecutors and the improvements in criminal proceedings and pretrial detention. This focus on the post-2004 period meant that the judges and lawyers could assert their capacity to receive cases from the ICTR, while distancing themselves from the acknowledged practical and political constraints on the earlier prosecution of international crimes in Rwanda. This interpretation of the courts' own actions has influenced its engagement with the ICTR and the *gacaca* courts.

Among a group of suspects convicted by the national courts, the competition among the three courts is readily apparent. The actions of one court provide the basis for critiquing the others. However, inside the national courts there remains an assumption that the courts will work together. The national courts' own actions and those of the ICTR and *gacaca* are understood within a specific legal cultural context. The Rwandan judges' and lawyers' assessments of the concurrent work of the ICTR and *gacaca* are consistent with how they have valued their own work, and these practitioners have assumed that their work will be supported by the actions of the ICTR and *gacaca*.

However, the empirical work inside the ICTR suggests that this is not the case. Although all three courts are complementary in law, it becomes apparent that the international and national courts have diverged substantially. The ICTR practitioners draw attention to their contribution to international criminal case law, and have expected the Rwanda national courts to do the same. In contrast, the domestic judges and lawyers have focused on legal education and have expected the ICTR to support this endeavor, while pressuring the *gacaca* courts to aspire to similar ends. The next question raised by these interactions is: What role has *gacaca* played in this increasingly competitive concurrent structure?

4 Inside the *Gacaca* Courts

1. Introduction

During this study I interviewed two judges with starkly opposing views. Both were women of great stature, highly regarded in their domestic jurisdictions. Each had played a significant part in the adjudication of the crimes of war and genocide that tore Rwandan society apart. Yet, eloquent as their words were, they spoke past one another. As the first stated, in the wood-paneled judicial chambers of the ICTR, "*Gacaca*, firstly I would not consider *gacaca* a court. It is a gathering of people speaking about events and recycling them. They have been set up many years after the events and they do not contribute any fresher recollection."[1] The second, in a crammed office in a rural district in Rwanda, said

> In Arusha the big fish are there. The victims travel there, but in *gacaca*, everyone is already here: survivors, perpetrators, judges, they are all here in the community. That is the difference . . . Those in Arusha haven't asked for forgiveness yet they have committed many crimes here. They should face us, the Rwandan family, but they avoid us by being there.[2]

[1] Interview with Trial Chamber Judge (Participant 4), Chambers, UN ICTR (Arusha, Tanzania, July 9, 2008) notes on file with author.

[2] Interview with *Inyangamugayo* (Participant 7) (Rural District, Rwanda, August 29, 2008) conducted with P. Clark, notes on file with author.

Despite being compatible in law, through the eyes of these two judges, the ICTR and *gacaca* have competed with one another, either muddying the evidentiary waters of the ICTR judgments or preventing key actors from being accountable to their immediate community. The previous two chapters showed a divergence in what the ICTR and the Rwandan national courts have been understood to achieve, militating against the courts' ability to effectively complement each another. In line with an interpretive examination of how actions are ascribed meaning,[3] this chapter discusses the understandings of the work of the localized *gacaca* courts.

Building on a large body of work on legal pluralism, an interpretive approach provides one route to assess a multitude of legal orders operating in a single social sphere.[4] In this chapter, qualitative interviewing teases out the collection of ideas that give meaning to the work of *gacaca* judges and coordinators.[5] A focus on the "internal rationality of the organization . . . the idiosyncrasies of personal interaction, and the intrinsic logics of diverse public and 'private' legal orders"[6] enables us to identify the "distorted communications"[7] evident in a plural context and to better interpret the interactions among these justice processes.

The *gacaca* courts are certainly not a classical example of plural ordering. As noted in Chapter 1, *gacaca* is a state-implemented but locally administrated set of transitional justice processes that draw their name and some of their procedural aspects from a traditional Rwandan dispute resolution process.[8] As a result, in some respects *gacaca* draws strongly on state authority and, as will be discussed below, in others its power relates much more closely to the immediate social sphere. Established by law in 2001, since 2005 over eleven thousand courts have operated across Rwanda, co-ordinated by the NSGJ as a centralized government body. Procedurally, the courts function very differently from the national courts and the ICTR, as lawyers do not play any formal role in the hearings, and the trials are presided over by popularly elected lay-members of the local community, the *inyangamugayo*.[9]

---

[3] Clifford Geertz, "Thick Description: Toward an Interpretive Theory of Culture" in Clifford Geertz (ed), *The Interpretation of Cultures: Selected Essays* (Fontana Press 1993) 6.

[4] Sally Engle Merry, "Legal Pluralism" (1988) 22 Law & Social Review 869, 886; Sally Falk Moore, "Law and Social Change: The Semi-autonomous Social Field as an Appropriate Subject of Study" (1973) 7 Law and Society Review 70; and Peter Fitzpatrick, "Law and Societies" (1984) 22 Osgoode Hall Law Journal 115.

[5] As noted in the Introduction, this interpretive cultural account draws strongly on David Garland's notion of the constituent elements of penal culture, and is in line with David Nelken's position that the concepts used by the judicial actors to describe what the courts are trying to achieve both reflect and constitute the culture of the institution.

[6] G. Teuber, "The Two Faces of Janus: Rethinking Legal Pluralism" (1991) 13 Cardozo Law Review 1443, 1456.

[7] Ibid. 1455.

[8] The Kinyarwanda translation of *gacaca* is "grass." The customary courts from which post-genocide *gacaca* derives its name were most routinely characterized by the meeting of concerned parties on the grass.

[9] In 2001, these *inyangamugayo*, identified as persons of integrity within the community, were elected by popular vote across the country. Formal schooling was required only for the president and the secretary

In line with the analysis of the international and national courts, this chapter is structured around three sections. It opens with a discussion of the mandate of the *gacaca* courts and the current appraisals of their practice, arguing for the importance of taking specific account of the agency of the *inyangamugayo*, while recognizing competing claims about the efficacy and value of the courts. In the second section, the criticisms raised against the courts are taken inside the institution through detailed qualitative research that responds to and deepens the current literature on transitional justice. What emerges from the qualitative interviewing of *inyangamugayo* and *gacaca* administrators is that these localized courts are principally understood to have contributed to finding the "truth" about the genocide and determining individual accountability. However, consistent with the historical exercise of state power in Rwanda, there are marked differences between what these objectives mean to personnel working in the central offices of the NSGJ in Kigali and to the *inyangamugayo* who adjudicate the cases in the communities. At the national level, there is a stronger emphasis on providing an overall macro-account of the genocide, while inside of specific *gacaca* jurisdictions there is a more complex and constrained examination of particular individuals' conduct and the locations of the bodies of the victims. Such an analysis, by taking *gacaca* on the terms identified by its personnel, emphasizes the courts' intimate and inseparable connection with the Rwandan conflict.

The third and final section analyzes the implications of these grounded understandings of *gacaca's* work for the concurrent operation of post-genocide criminal justice in Rwanda. The *gacaca* courts have prioritized their own local objectives. The outcome has been that the practices of both the national courts and the ICTR have been criticized, and specific *gacaca* courts have pursued trials that are in direct conflict with proceedings already initiated at a national and international level. Overall, this interpretive analysis shows that the ICTR, the national courts, and *gacaca* have pursued very different objectives, leading to competition among the courts. To better explain why this competition has occurred, and its implications, Chapter 5 then pursues a comparative examination of the legitimacy of Rwanda's concurrent justice processes.

---

of the court, and all of the judges received basic training over a three-week period. The elections were government-run and generally considered to be free and fair. Simon Gasibirege, "L'élection des Juges Inyangamugayo: Rupture ou Continuité?," in De La Paix À La Justice: Les Enjeux De La Réconciliation Nationale 93–127 (E. Ntaganda ed, 2002) referred to in Phil Clark, "Hybridity, Holism, and 'Traditional' Justice: The Case of the *Gacaca* Courts in Post-Genocide Rwanda" (2007) 39 The George Washington International Law Review 765. PRI provides a similar position on the success of the elections, although it articulates some concerns that the high voter turnout was due to a perceived obligation rather than support of the justice initiative, and that there had been insufficient information provided to the communities prior to voting. Penal Reform International, "*Gacaca* Jurisdictions and Its Preparations" (Research on Gacaca Report 1) July–December 2001 at 34.

2. The Establishment and Mandate of the *Gacaca* Courts

From as early as 1995, *gacaca* was discussed as a potential post-genocide justice process.[10] However, it was only in the face of a floundering national court system and as a result of a strong internal political debate that the localized courts gained real political traction.[11] The final decision to pursue a national justice program through *gacaca* emerged from a series of "reflection meetings" at the Office of the President in Urugwiro between May 1998 and March 1999. At these meetings, attended by Rwandan political actors, including ministers, members of parliament, opposition leaders, broader civil society members, and lawyers, there was serious contestation over the structure and operation of post-genocide *gacaca*.

Then-president Pasteur Bizimungu opened the meetings by identifying "fighting the culture of revenge"[12] through the domestic enactment of law and "punishing the crime of genocide and massacres"[13] as two of the main achievements of the Unity Government. However, as discussed in the preceding chapter, while demanding justice resulted in mass arrests that were central to the RPF securing control over the territory, the national courts were unable to deal with the resultant caseload of over 120,000 suspects. As a result, the initial debates at the reflection meetings framed *gacaca* as a response to these challenges faced by "classical justice."[14] At this early stage, despite reference to the historically conciliatory processes of earlier iterations of *gacaca*,[15] the

---

10 Clark 781.

11 Ibid. 781–783.

12 Republic of Rwanda Office of the President, "Report on the Reflection Meetings Held in the Office of the President of the Republic from May 1998 to March 1999" (August 1999) 3 (hereafter the "Report on the Reflection Meetings"); document on file with author. It must be noted that this report was not readily available to researchers, although it was requested from 2003. The current document was found in the archives of the National Unity and Reconciliation Commission in July 2008.

13 Ibid. 3.

14 Participants inside Rwanda used the term "classical justice" when referring to courts whose procedure and practice are drawn from civil or common law legal traditions.

15 Although little has been written about the operation of these courts before the Belgian colonial period, it is generally agreed that *gacaca* was organized around the family unit and presided over by male heads of households with the objective of re-establishing social cohesion between families within the group. See Bert Ingelaere, "The Gacaca Courts in Rwanda" in Luc Huyse and Mark Salter (eds), *Traditional Justice and Reconciliation after Violent Conflict: Learning from African Experiences* (International Institute for Democracy and Electoral Assistance 2008) 33–34. However, Reyntjens and Ntampaka note a shift in *gacaca* during the middle and second half of the twentieth century as the practices altered from a local dispute resolution toward a more formalized means of administrative control. Nonetheless, despite the increasingly closer alignment of *gacaca* with the state throughout the twentieth century, *gacaca's* procedures and decisions remained unwritten and never dealt with serious violent crimes. See Charles Ntampaka, "Le Gacaca Devenu une Justice aux Mains des Victimes" [1999] Umubano and Filip Reyntjens, "Le Gacaca ou la Justice du Gazon au Rwanda" [1990] Politique Africaine quoted in Clark, 779–780.

objectives of the new post-genocide *gacaca* courts were oriented toward punitive sanctions. The stated expectations of the court were:

> To punish criminals and eradicate the culture of impunity; to re-establish unity and harmony among Rwandans; to rebuild Rwanda without sectarianism; to give penalties aimed at correcting one who pleaded guilty, but which also helped developing Rwanda.[16]

Following these recommendations, a 2001 Organic Law established the *gacaca* courts.[17] Highlighting how the objectives of *gacaca* have shifted over the course of the courts' formation and operation, in law, *gacaca's* mandate was extended to include a focus on truth-telling, reconciliation. and the reintegration of prisoners. This dynamism continued through the courts' operation as repeated amendments were adopted to respond to specific challenges. Nonetheless, throughout these amendments, the courts retained the *modus operandi* of popular dialogue. Through a General Assembly, organized at the *cellule* and sector level, members of the local community participated in collecting information about the crimes and those accused of committing them, and later, in providing exculpatory and accusatory evidence at the trials. However, there remained important continuities with the earlier approach to genocide trials, with *gacaca's* mandate including punishing criminals and eradicating the culture of impunity. In addition, in written law the post-genocide *gacaca* courts were to deal exclusively with crimes of genocide and crimes against humanity and the courts retained the categorization of accused used by the national courts. The failure to include war crimes among these international offenses meant that any allegations of crimes committed by RPF soldiers during the civil war and the genocide were excluded from *gacaca's* jurisdiction. In addition, the courts were to remain heavily dependent on the established plea-bargaining system, by which the maximum possible sentence could be reduced through the provision of a complete confession, an apology, and, following the 2008 amendments to the law, a request for forgiveness.[18]

From the outset it is clear that the *gacaca* courts were introduced as a response to the severe constraints on national criminal prosecution, and they retained important

---

[16] Report on the Reflection Meetings, 60. The phrasing of this quote is taken directly from the original document.

[17] Organic Law No. 40/2000 of 26/01/2001 Setting Up *Gacaca* Jurisdictions and Organizing Prosecutions for Offences Constituting the Crime of Genocide or Crimes against Humanity Committed between 1 October 1990 and 31 December 1994, Official Gazette of the Republic of Rwanda, March 2001 (*Gacaca* Law 2001).

[18] As was the case in the national courts, incentives to confess have been heavily built into the process. Confession prior to appearance on the list can commute the sentencing range in Category 3 from 5–7 years down to 1–3 years and in Category 2 down from 25–30 years to 7–12 years. Reduction in sentence also occurs after accusations are made, although these are less pronounced. In March 2007, further incentives for confession were introduced as the sentencing structure increasingly shifted toward community service. For those who confessed, part of their prison term was provisionally suspended, leaving community service as the only requirement for the completion of the sentence.

features of this initial approach to post-genocide justice. Unsurprisingly, the initial concerns about the process related to the crucial discrepancies between the proposed *gacaca* process and the criminal justice procedures that underpinned the ICTR and the national courts. While these criticisms are most commonly associated with external legal commentators on *gacaca*, Rwandan legal practitioners participating in the initial reflection meetings held at Urugwiro noted similar concerns.

At the reflection meetings, participants specifically raised queries around the lack of education and legal training of the proposed *inyangamugayo* and the impact of this on the lay-judges' capacity to manage the trials and adjudicate them impartially. The participants also expressed concerns that *gacaca* would "not be in conformity with international law,"[19] and suggested that *gacaca* should only be used to carry out investigations rather than trials.[20] These criticisms from the Rwandan participants present at the early discussions are mirrored in the initial writings on *gacaca* by both international academics and NGOs.

Based on Rwanda's ratification of the ICCPR and the African Charter on Human and Peoples' Rights (ACHPR),[21] external observers initially challenged *gacaca's* adherence to due process. Taking the courts as a "centrally-organized state initiative,"[22] *gacaca's* structure was critiqued as a violation of equality of arms, the right to be presumed innocent, and the right to impartial judges.[23] The focus of this body of literature is on the failure of the state to provide sufficient legal safeguards, resulting in a process that favors the prosecution and is open to distortions by local political interests and personal bias.[24] As noted in the preceding chapter, until this point, the trials before the national courts had been criticized for the limited number of defense counsel available and the inexperience of the judicial personnel. *Gacaca* was seen to remove the few existing safeguards offered to the innocent.[25] These critiques focus on the written law governing *gacaca* and examine the courts' work in terms of the punitive orientation of their mandate and the rights of the accused. Such critiques have also been extended to challenge *gacaca's* ability to meet the Rwandan state's international legal obligations to provide reparation to the victims of the violence.[26]

---

[19] Report on the Reflection Meetings 63.

[20] Report on the Reflection Meetings 62–63.

[21] African Charter on Human and Peoples' Rights (adopted June 27, 1981, entered into force October 21, 1986) 21 ILM 58 (ACHPR).

[22] Alison Des Forges and Kenneth Roth, "Justice or Therapy?" (2002) 27 Boston Review http://bostonreview.net/BR27.3/rothdesForges.html accessed March 10, 2011.

[23] Jeremy Sarkin, "The Tension between Justice and Reconciliation in Rwanda: Politics, Human Rights, Due Process and the Role of the *Gacaca* Courts in Dealing with the Genocide" (2001) 45 Journal of African Law 143, 162–164.

[24] Allison Corey and Sandra F. Joireman, "Retributive Justice: The *Gacaca* Courts in Rwanda" (2004) 103 African Affairs 73, 85.

[25] Amnesty International, "*Gacaca*: A Question of Justice" (Report) (December 2002) AI-Index AFR 47/007/2002, 34.

[26] Paul Christoph Bornkamm, *Rwanda's* Gacaca *Courts: Between Retribution and Reparation* (Oxford University Press 2012).

More recently, the criticisms of the courts have centered on the mandated objectives of revealing the truth about the genocide and reconciling Rwandans. In what now constitutes the majority of scholarship on the localized courts, *gacaca* is examined as a means of coercive state control. The widespread participation of everyday Rwandans in *gacaca* and the sheer number of localized courts makes *gacaca* centrally important to gaining an understanding the informal interactions among the post-genocide courts and the legitimacy of transitional justice in Rwanda more broadly. As a result it is necessary to outline these more detailed political and sociological criticisms of the localized courts. Responding to this existing work, it is important to take account of how criticisms of, and support for, *gacaca* can be coherently read together. An examination of this literature supports the need to pay particular attention to the devolved structure of *gacaca* and the agency of the *inyangamugayo* when assessing the interpretations of the courts' work offered inside of the institution.

In the current critical literature, *gacaca* is examined as a nontraditional and state-imposed institution.[27] From this starting point, authors argue that the local courts provide the current Rwandan government with an effective, highly coercive, and unconstrained means of social control.[28] At the national level, through a "state-imposed informalism,"[29] *gacaca*'s mandate of establishing the truth of genocide is interpreted as re-enforcing the RPF's preferred historical account. According to Bert Ingelaere, within *gacaca's* "truth," the colonial powers created ethnic groups out of a harmonious and equal society, laying the basis for the genocide. The RPF altered this division through military "liberation," and challenged the "negative forces" that furthered the long-standing genocidal tendencies both inside and outside of the country.[30] This meta-narrative is reinforced through *gacaca's* failure to deal with RPF-related killings, leaving the ruling party to affirm the moral integrity of its actions through its chosen transitional justice mechanism.

---

[27] Waldorf argues that by 1994, the traditional practice of *gacaca* was "moribund" and that the features of post-genocide *gacaca* are better understood as a current political move to effectively extend state control into local communities. Similarly, Ingelaere argues that the post-genocide and traditional *gacaca* are "different in kind," as traditional *gacaca* was designed to "readjust power relations between families" rather than to determine a set of facts or the "truth" about the offense. Lars Waldorf, "Mass Justice for Mass Atrocity: Rethinking Local Justice as Transitional Justice" (2006) 79 Temple Law Review 88; and Bert Ingelaere, "'Does the Truth Pass across the Fire without Burning?' Locating the Short Circuit in Rwanda's *Gacaca* Courts" (2009) 47 Journal of Modern African Studies 507, 516.

[28] The leading scholarship in this area has been conducted by Lars Waldorf and Bert Ingelaere and will be discussed in detail in this section. In addition, similar positions are argued by Susan M. Thomson and Rosemary Nagy, "Law, Power and Justice: What Legalism Fails to Address in the Functioning of Rwanda's *Gacaca* Courts" (2011) 5 The International Journal of Transitional Justice 11; Timothy Longman, "An Assessment of Rwanda's *Gacaca* Courts" (2009) 21 Peace Review: A Journal of Social Justice 304; and Alana Erin Tiemessen, "After Arusha: *Gacaca* Justice in Post-Genocide Rwanda" (2004) 8 African Studies Quarterly 57.

[29] Waldorf 91.

[30] Ingelaere, "'Does the Truth Pass across the Fire without Burning?' Locating the Short Circuit in Rwanda's *Gacaca* Courts" 521–522.

At the local level, scholars argue that in both process and outcome, *gacaca* is culturally incompatible with Rwandan social practices, exacerbating ethnic cleavages, fueling local-level conflicts, and increasing perceived insecurity. Ingelaere contends that the historical and cultural basis of communication in Rwanda is intrinsically linked to power politics. This plays out through strategies of "accusing" and "conspiring in silence" to ensure or prevent conviction.[31] The cleavages between ethnic groups and local power balances play out on the stage of *gacaca*. "Truth" is not in the individual's interests to divulge, and is further hidden in what Lars Waldorf describes as "a pervasive culture of secrecy in rural Rwanda."[32] The spoken words at *gacaca* are viewed as a mixture of top-down coercive memory-making and local political opportunism. These critiques of illegitimate state extension and cultural incongruence must be taken seriously. However, they also need to be read in light of the broader objectives of *gacaca* and the nuanced support and criticism of the process indicated in a series of fieldwork studies.

Early survey research conducted before the start of *gacaca* indicated strong initial support for the courts.[33] Such support was, in part, explained by the perceived need for a response to the overcrowded prisons, which severely undermined the livelihoods of the largely agrarian rural population. Both Waldorf and Ingelaere argue that, before the start of *gacaca,* "a shaky peace"[34] or cohabitation out of necessity[35] was occurring. For these commentators, this silent social healing was disturbed by the *gacaca* hearings, creating further insecurity at the local level. Yet the work of Simon Gasibirege and Stella Babalola find that before *gacaca,* within their sample group, the major concern, second only to poverty, was the perceived insecurity and distrust among members of the same community. This is wholly understandable, given the nature of the genocide. As discussed in the historical overview of the conflict provided in Chapter 1, *gacaca* did not create the mistrust and insecurity but, as becomes clear in the discussion of its understood objectives, its operation has undoubtedly both affected and been affected by these perceptions and experiences of insecurity.

While this initial survey work was conducted before the trial phase of *gacaca*, Max Rettig undertook a similarly designed smaller study in 2006 and 2007 in Sovu near the

---

31 Bert Ingelaere, "'Does the Truth Pass across the Fire without Burning?' Transitional Justice and Its Discontents in Rwanda's *Gacaca* Courts" [2007] Institute for Development Policy and Management University of Antwerp Discussion Paper, 33.

32 Waldorf 109.

33 Timothy Longman, "Justice at the Grassroots? *Gacaca* Trials in Rwanda" in Naomi Roht-Arriaza and Javier Mariezcurrena (eds), *Transitional Justice in the Twenty-First Century* (Cambridge University Press 2006) 210–213 and Simon Gasibirege and Stella Babalola, *Perceptions about the* Gacaca *Law in Rwanda: Evidence from a Multi-Method Study* (Johns Hopkins University School of Public Health, Center for Communication Programs 2001) 13.

34 Waldorf 111.

35 Ingelaere, "'Does the Truth Pass across the Fire without Burning?' Transitional Justice and Its Discontents in Rwanda's *Gacaca* Courts" 24.

town of Butare. He too records in his survey work broad support for the process.[36] This echoes the survey research conducted by the International Rescue Committee (IRC) on behalf of the National Unity and Reconciliation Commission (NURC) in 2002, 2005, and 2007, which shows agreement with the supportive statements of *gacaca's* activities. However, Rettig raises concerns that such support is induced through direct government sensitisation and that, in practice, *gacaca* participants experienced both fear and insecurity when attending *gacaca* and giving testimony. Ingelaere has interpreted the NURC data in a similar manner, particularly noting a decline in the popular support during the course of *gacaca's* operation, and arguing that any empirical research gathered prior to the courts' nationwide implementation is of limited interpretative value when assessing the overall impact of the courts' activities on its participants.[37]

Rather than exploring how support for the process may coexist with criticism and concern about the courts' work, the interpretation of the data appears to be geared towards explaining why the evidence of popular support is not an accurate depiction of reality. There is a strong tendency toward similar readings in a large amount of the current scholarship on Rwanda, where accounts of positive opinions on *gacaca* are explained as politically imposed.[38] In these accounts, the truth only emerges in quieter moments within trusting relationships and is invariably critical. As discussed in the Introduction, the expression of different views at different times by participants does not necessarily mean that one position is imposed and the other honest. Divergent views on *gacaca* can and do coexist for individuals and within larger groups.

Supporting this position on individuals holding both positive and critical readings of *gacaca*, recent survey work on perceptions of the localized courts, following the completion of the trial process, shows similarly strong overall support for *gacaca* coupled with ongoing concerns around physical security before and after giving testimony. Joanna Pozen, Richard Neugebauery, and Joseph Ntaganira suggest that while "the political climate in Rwanda may have influenced primarily positive responses to global questions about *gacaca*, the literature may overly discount other potential explanations for this trend."[39] They go on to explain the concurrent support and criticism of the courts as an indication of a popular desire for some form of judicial or quasi-judicial response to

---

36 Max Rettig, "*Gacaca*: Truth, Justice, and Reconciliation in Postconflict Rwanda?" (2008) 51 African Studies Review 25.

37 Ingelaere, "'Does the Truth Pass across the Fire without Burning?' Transitional Justice and Its Discontents in Rwanda's *Gacaca* Courts" 14–20.

38 Susan M. Thomson, "Whispering Truth to Power: The Everyday Resistance of Rwandan Peasants to Post-Genocide Reconciliation" [2011] African Affairs 1; and Jennie E. Burnet, "The Injustice of Local Justice: Truth, Reconciliation, and Revenge in Rwanda" (2014) 3 Genocide Studies and Prevention: An International Journal 173.

39 Joanna Pozen, Richard Neugebauery, and Joseph Ntaganira, "Assessing the Rwanda Experiment: Popular Perceptions of *Gacaca* in Its Final Phase" (2014) 8 International Journal for Transitional Justice 22, 20.

genocide-related atrocities, coupled with dissatisfaction with the operation of trials and ensuing secondary effects such as security concerns.[40]

In line with these findings but offering a different explanation, further survey work looking at the psychosocial impact of participating in *gacaca* hearings provides a valuable explanation of the simultaneous rise in perceived insecurity and the general popular support for the process. Bernard Rimé *et al* contrast perception surveys conducted before and after the operation of *gacaca* with those in a sector in which *gacaca* had not yet occurred. They argue that the survey responses are in line with Émile Durkheim's model on collective ritual. The theory suggests that, on the one hand, collective rituals triggered a strong reactivation of the emotions associated with the commemorated event. On the other hand, they contributed to the reconstruction of participants' collective identity by boosting group cohesion and social integration. The study noted a significant increase in fear, anxiety, and sadness after giving testimony among both victims and perpetrators included in the study, and a simultaneous decrease in perceived homogeneity of the victim and perpetrator group, while the opposite trend was evident in the control group where *gacaca* had not yet commenced.[41] Unfortunately, the general framing of their data does not take adequate account of the punitive nature of *gacaca*. However, these more recent studies do support the position that positive readings of *gacaca* in survey work should not automatically be read as a further example of Rwandan state coercion, and can be coherently read alongside criticisms of *gacaca*.

Qualitative work on the courts offers further guidance on how criticism and support for *gacaca* can be internally consistent. Phil Clark's qualitative research argues that *gacaca* is a "kinetic social institution that is shaped heavily by the population's perceptions and actions."[42] The dynamic nature of *gacaca* is reflected in participants' identification of a wider set of "profound objectives" of the process, identified by Clark as reconciliation, forgiveness, healing, peace, justice, and truth.[43] For Clark, it is the dialogical space offered by *gacaca* that creates the potential for transformative engagements between genocide victims and perpetrators. The focus of his work is on the agency of the general Rwandan population in interpreting and directing *gacaca*. However, he acknowledges that there is a "fine balance required between popular ownership over gacaca and the need, in select instances, for gacaca judges to mediate communal discussions."[44] Clark notes that state officials and *gacaca* judges have played "a vital role in mediating the dialogical space at gacaca, often in order to maintain a sense of order and security and to

---

40 Ibid.

41 Bernard Rimé, Patrick Kanyangara, Vincent Yzerbyt, and Dario Paez, "The Impact of *Gacaca* Tribunals in Rwanda: Psychosocial Effects of Participation in a Truth and Reconciliation Process after a Genocide" (2011) 41 European Journal of Social Psychology 695.

42 Phil Clark, *The* Gacaca *Courts, Post-Genocide Justice and Reconciliation in Rwanda: Justice without Lawyers* (Cambridge University Press 2010) 7.

43 Ibid. 31–32.

44 Clark, *The* Gacaca *Courts, Post-Genocide Justice and Reconciliation in Rwanda: Justice without Lawyers* 189.

ensure that gacaca pursues the objectives for which it is designed." At the same time, he warns against "unjustified interventions"[45] by judges and community leaders in the hearings. However, Clark does not examine how the judges' own understandings of *gacaca's* objectives may have shaped the direction and operation of the courts. Nor does he explore whether there is a distinction between the approach of state officials and that of the *gacaca* judges themselves.

Similarly drawing on extended periods of qualitative research in Rwanda, Jennie E. Burnett argues that at an interpersonal level *gacaca* has provided an opportunity to settle personal scores. She provides valuable personalized accounts of the experiences of false accusation before the courts and how, at times, such false accusations have been successfully challenged through the participation of the General Assembly and through the *inyangamugayo*. While generally critical of the courts, she goes on to argue that "in the places where *inyangamugayo* have legitimacy and power within the community, and the will to carry out trials according to legal procedure, *Gacaca* is working well."[46] However, she neither provides specific examples of when this has been the case, nor does she explore how the judges themselves have understood their role. Building on this existing work and the need to take account of co-existence of very serious critique and support for *gacaca*, this chapter argues that the devolved structure of *gacaca* and the agency of the *inyangamugayo* is of central importance when assessing the interaction among the law, the state, and the popular experiences of the courts.

In practice, the functioning of *gacaca* depends heavily on the *inyangamugayo*. Under the 2001 Organic Law, the structure of *gacaca* devolved more power to the *cellule* and sector level than was initially envisaged in the Urugwiro reflection meetings. The *gacaca* courts have heard the majority of cases relating to the genocide, which have been adjudicated, appealed, and reviewed at the local level. In addition, through the course of various amendments to the law, the *inyangamugayo* have been empowered to summon witnesses to testify at hearings, issue search warrants, fine those found guilty of perjury, and, having reached a verdict, impose a sentence of up to life imprisonment.

What is clear is that through their decisions and management of the courts, the *inyangamugayo* have shaped how *gacaca* has operated in each community. This provides an important point of entry into researching the work of the courts. How the personnel working for the NSGJ in Kigali and the *inyangamugayo* have ascribed meaning to their work shapes the objectives of the process, its engagement with the Rwandan state, and its concurrent operation with the national courts and the ICTR.

The qualitative research reflected in this chapter asserts that there remains substantial popular support for *gacaca*, but both the *gacaca* judges and participants attending the hearings were openly critical of aspects of the courts' work. Rather than popular support

---

[45] Ibid. 216.

[46] Jennie E. Burnet, *Genocide Lives in Us* (The University of Wisconsin Press 2012) 210–211.

being explained as a response to centralized state coercion, this critical engagement with the localized courts suggests a complex set of domestic evaluations of the role of *gacaca* in the post-genocide period. As with the ICTR and the national courts, this chapter suggests that *gacaca* is credited with achieving some of its objectives more readily than others. Having reflected on a number of practical constraints identified by participants, this chapter argues that the dominant interpretations of the activities of *gacaca* illuminate the institution's specific legal culture. Going deep inside the institution to unravel the socially constructed meanings attached to *gacaca*'s work enables greater understanding of the interactions between the concurrent systems of post-genocide criminal justice. Inside *gacaca,* participants emphasized the courts' contribution to gaining an understanding of the conflict over other stated objectives, and it is on these terms that assessments were made of the other concurrent transitional justice processes, which explains how and why the courts have competed with one another.

3. Inside the Institution

Empirical research was conducted within the NSGJ in Kigali, coupled with observations at *gacaca* hearings and a series of focus groups and individual interviews. Fifty participants were interviewed in total, and the coding of this material took into account two tiers of engagement with *gacaca*: first the senior leadership and the legal officers based within the NSGJ in Kigali, and the local coordinators who are based in the districts and report to the legal officers. These participants equate broadly to the actors Clark identifies as "state officials" in the *gacaca* context.

The second group of interviewees were the *inyangamugayo,* who carry the weight of the trials at the local level. In gauging the perspectives of this group, the empirical work focused on the same districts as the regional work on the national courts. The objective of the site selection in the Northern and Western Provinces was to take account of rural and urban divides in the practice of *gacaca* and to include insights from areas with different experiences of the Rwandan civil war and genocide. The coding of these tiers shows important differences between how *gacaca* is being understood centrally and implemented locally. In Kigali, the work of the courts is explained in terms of a broad national account of the genocide, whereas locally, the attention is on information about the location of bodies and specific individuals' involvement in the violence.

3.1 A DETERMINATION OF TRUTH

Inside *gacaca,* the pursuit of "truth" emerged as the dominant justification of the courts' activities. In response to the open question, equivalent to that asked of the lawyers and judges at the ICTR and the national courts, "What do you see as the major contribution of the process?," the majority of respondents identified *gacaca's* contribution to gaining information about the crimes committed during the genocide. As one *inyangamugayo,* an elderly Hutu man and long-term resident in Kigali, articulated,

> Basic information was needed. It was helpful to the victims and survivors to know what happened. Many survivors didn't know what happened because as a survivor you were not outside to see, but as a perpetrator you know you killed. This is helpful from a national and a family perspective.[47]

At both the national and family levels, the understandings of truth were nuanced, viewed as both a challenge and contribution to *gacaca's* activities. In the words of one of the NSGJ legal officers, "It is difficult to say what *gacaca* has contributed. I suppose I would say the most important part of the process has been the pursuit of truth . . . but it has been difficult."[48]

Notably, the focus on the determination of "truth" differed across the tiers of respondents. For the legally trained officers based in the central office of the NSGJ in Kigali, particularly those who were outside of the country at the time of the genocide, there was a strong emphasis on *gacaca's* overall contribution to "finding out what happened."[49] As one legal officer in an informal discussion articulated, "I came to work here because I was interested in having more information about what happened in the genocide, in the planning and the action of it. I was not inside the country at the time and I wanted to understand what happened."[50]

On first reading, these understandings could support the criticism of a top-down narrative of the conflict, in which, as Ingelaere suggests, the state's meta-narrative of a "truth" that exonerates the RPF is reinforced through *gacaca*. However, there are crucial differences in the understandings across the different tiers of respondents. Among the *inyangamugayo,* the understanding of truth, rather than relating to a broad narrative of the conflict, was closely connected with how the conflict played out in particular communities. Examining how the objective of "truth" was interpreted at the local level calls into question whether *gacaca* has been wholly co-opted by the central government to communicate its meta-narrative of the genocide.

At the local level there was a very personal emphasis in the attainment of truth: information about where the remains of the dead were buried. This perspective emerged strongly from the focus group with the *inyangamugayo* in the Western Province. As

---

47 Interview with *Inyangamugayo* (Participant 15), (Kigali, Rwanda, March 10, 2009) notes on file with author.

48 Interview with National Service for Gacaca Courts Personnel (Participant 22) (Kigali, Rwanda, March 11, 2009) notes on file with author.

49 Interview with National Service for Gacaca Courts Personnel (Participant 1) (Kigali, Rwanda, August 14, 2008) recording and notes on file with author.

50 Informal discussion with National Service for Gacaca Courts Legal Officer (Participant 20) (Kigali, Rwanda, March 9, 2009) notes on file with author.

one of the judges stated, "Before *gacaca,* the genocide perpetrators could not reveal the information together with the victims. Now they are providing full information to the victims about where the bodies are buried."[51] Similarly in follow-up research undertaken in 2012 in the Southern Province, an *inyangamugayo,* herself a genocide survivor, said,

> My main motivation was to uncover the truth. If the person was innocent, justice should be done and he should be released and for me, personally, I wanted to know information about who died.[52]

In the localized articulation of "truth," *gacaca* provides a means for people to determine information about their community's own experience of the conflict. This was consistent with my observations at the *gacaca* hearings in the rural research sites. I attended nineteen hearings and in each, the members of the three communities struggled to fully understand the crimes committed in their specific locales. The objective of truth was evidenced in my field notes and interviews from the opening of the trial of a former mayor in the Northern Province in late March and early April 2009:

> The case begins as the others have. There is a minute of silence in commemoration. With a strong emphasis on adherence to the procedure, extracts of the 2008 Organic Law are read out to all present. Three procedural aspects are explicitly articulated: the laws governing confession, participation and the penalties for false testimony. On reflection, the events that transpire will turn around the understandings, application and implementation of these three central tenants. The articulated driving force here is the pursuit of truth. The discussion is not framed by an understanding of fair trial rights or the presumption of innocence; it is better understood as a community, still divided, trying to come to terms with the fact that one person killed another, and that many community members remain silent. The issue is what happened, who was there, and how did one man die? This understanding is intimately tied to the communities' efforts to account for their own history, of which this death and many others are an intricate part.[53]

As these observations indicate, in *gacaca* the localized pursuit of "truth" rests on three requirements: first, the active participation of the General Assembly; second, dialogue within a divided communities; and, third, confession. Although the constraints on all three of these dimensions will be discussed in the next section, it is initially important to examine how they are understood as components of *gacaca's* pursuit of truth. As with

---

[51] Focus group with *Inyangamugayo* (Rural District, Western Province, Rwanda, April 24, 2009) notes on file with author.

[52] Focus group with *Inyangamugayo* and *gacaca* witnesses (Rural District, Southern Province, Rwanda, April 13, 2012) notes on file with author.

[53] Author's field notes, Rural District, Northern Province, Rwanda, March 31, 2009.

the analysis of the ICTR and the national courts, this process of sense-making of *gacaca's* work illuminates the legal culture of the institution and enables a better understanding of the interactions among the post-genocide courts.

3.1.1 Obtaining the Truth through Dialogue

The requirement of public dialogue in understanding *gacaca's* contribution to "truth" was articulated most strongly by the *inyangamugayo*. *Gacaca* was explained through its provision of a space in which the truth of the conflict could be established through open discussion. In the words of participants across the three districts:

> One of the major problems after the genocide was that there was a huge amount of silence. After 1994, it was particularly difficult for people to communicate with one another. *Gacaca* has improved communication. At *gacaca*, people could speak what was in their heart, they could speak of their wounds.[54]
>
> Another problem was that people who killed were very separate from the community. Now *gacaca* has meant that they have had to sit down in the same place.[55]
>
> *Gacaca* is very wide and broad so people have been able to sit down and talk.[56]
>
> The truth came out because people were able to speak out.[57]

The *inyangamugayo*'s interpretation of *gacaca*, as a way to obtain "truth" through a process of discussion, supports Clark's analysis of the dialogical function of the courts.[58] The importance of *gacaca* providing this space for dialogue was reiterated through the research process. As discussed in the Introduction, participants were most comfortable and willing to be interviewed on issues of the genocide and post-conflict justice when they were at the *gacaca* hearings themselves. At hearings, I would often find myself engaging with General Asembly participants on their thoughts on *gacaca* in the breaks between proceedings or during the deliberations of the *inyangamugayo*. *Gacaca* has operated as a place to offer opinions and to talk on these sensitive issues through providing an official process in response to the violence of the genocide. However, as laid out in the final chapter of this book, among the general Rwandan citizens who attend the *gacaca* hearings, there remains deep contestation over what issues are discussed.

---

[54] Interview with *Inyangamugayo* (Participant 6) (Rural District, Northern Province, Rwanda, August 29, 2008) conducted in conjunction with P. Clark notes on file with author.

[55] Interview with *Inyangamugayo* (Participant 36) (Rural District, Northern Province, Rwanda, March 20, 2009) notes on file with author.

[56] Interview with *Inyangamugayo* (Participant 43) (Rural District, Western Province, Rwanda, March 21, 2009) notes on file with author.

[57] Interview with *Inyangamugayo* (Participant 39) (Kigali, Rwanda, March 26, 2009) notes on file with author.

[58] Clark, *The* Gacaca *Courts, Post-Genocide Justice and Reconciliation in Rwanda: Justice without Lawyers* 132.

3.1.2 Obtaining the Truth through Public Participation and Confession

The dialogical function of *gacaca* depends heavily on the engaged participation of victims, perpetrators, members of the General Assembly, and the *inyangamugayo*. Participation at the hearings I attended differred enormously, ranging from fifteen directly affected parties to over two hundred people across all age groups. At one hearing in the Northern Province, the number of people present at the trial was notably high, fluctuating between eighty to one hundred people. I asked the participants why they had come, and the responses varied. One woman said that she was just passing by and had been drawn by the crowd. Another participant had thought about it more deeply: "Rwandans are patient," he said.

> The war went on for a long time and it was very bad. Now that there is peace we are happy to come here. The process can go on as long as it needs to but the truth will be told in the end and then it will be done.[59]

This same participant went on to describe his understanding of dialogue in *gacaca*. He argued that the willingness of genocide suspects to confess and the provision of information by other prisoners who have been convicted or accused were key for effective dialogue at *gacaca*.[60] Many of the personnel within *gacaca* held a similar position. At both the national and local level, dialogue before *gacaca* was understood to rely on the active participation of perpetrators in the truth-telling process. This dependence on the oral testimony of genocide suspects is common across the procedures before the ICTR, the national courts, and *gacaca*. The result, as discussed in the previous chapters, is that a number of Rwandan detainees have participated in all three of the post-genocide justice processes, highlighting an important informal interaction throughout the courts' actions.

The heavy reliance of the *gacaca* process on confession was routinely identified by the *inyangamugayo*:

> Confession has been the main way of getting the truth. It is much better if the one being charged confesses then he gives information about where the weapons were distributed, where people were . . . thrown.[61]

Truth-telling in *gacaca* has depended on the engaged participation of genocide suspects more than any other participants. However, truth-telling through confession is both complex and compromised. Perceptions on why a large number of perpetrators had confessed differed among the interviewed participants.

---

[59] Informal discussion with *gacaca* participant (Participant 12) (Rural District, Northern Province, Rwanda, April 1, 2009) notes on file with author.

[60] Ibid.

[61] Interview with *Inyangamugayo* (Participant 34) (Rural District, Northern Province, Rwanda, March 20, 2009) notes on file with author.

The dominant interpretation offered by the NSGJ legal officers in Kigali was that prisoners were aware that confession triggered a reduced sentence, and therefore they confessed. Self-interest was understood to prompt confession. Less common, but nonetheless articulated at both the national and local level, was the idea that the choice to confess connected with the choice to participate in the genocide. One NSGJ legal officer, who had been involved in *gacaca* since its inception, stressed that confessions had occurred before the enactment of the 1996 Genocide Law through which the plea-bargaining system was implemented. He argued that confessions should be understood in the context of Rwanda's specific conflict:

> Even before the law was introduced, people confessed, they came back to Rwanda and they entered into a guilty plea. It was after this that it was included in the law. The confessions started first. I think this has to do with the nature of the genocide because confession for normal crimes is not so common. You could say that the people confess for the same reasons that they participated: they were conforming to what was wrong, and now they conform to what is right, so they confess.[62]

At the local level, among the *inyangamugayo,* confession was similarly connected with the incentives that drove the killings, reflecting a community trying to understand how and why people killed one another:

> Before, people went and confessed to their crimes . . . Because they were the people in the village, because of the history, they were taught to kill. They were taught, "I will get what you have. You will take what I have." Now they have been taught something different.[63]

In these statements, confessions as a means of obtaining the "truth" and the choice to confess were explained in terms of the popular understandings of the causes of the genocide. Failure to confess, particularly among those in more senior government positions, was also viewed by a number of *inyangamugayo* as consistent with the role that political leaders played during the genocide. This was explicitly discussed in a focus group in the Northern Province:

> *Inyangamugayo 1*: Those people who were educated, they are the ones who won't confess. They had to have the people believe in the [ethnic] difference, they had to make them inhuman.

[62] Informal discussion with National Service for Gacaca Courts Legal Officer (Participant 23) (Kigali, Rwanda, March 16, 2009) notes on file with author.

[63] Interview with *Inyangamugayo* (Participant 30) (Rural District, Northern Province, Rwanda, March 20, 2009) notes on file with author.

Inyangamugayo 2: The reason they will not confess is that they lost the war the first time. It is out of greed, now they don't want to lose for a second time.

Inyangamugayo 3: Yes, if they confess to their crimes they lose for a second time.[64]

These understandings of confession as a means to obtain the "truth" about the genocide are deeply and consistently linked to how people have tried to make sense of the genocide itself. In a transitional period in Rwanda, the interpretation of the actions of these legal processes are inseparable from the explanations of the conflict itself.

The third understanding of obtaining truth through confession was expressed at the local rather than the national level. Some *inyangamugayo* identified the personalized need to confess. In the words of one local judge, "with the people who were able to confess, they were able to free their hearts."[65] This position on personal atonement was rarely voiced within *gacaca,* although it was more readily acknowledged by some of the prisoners. As noted in the previous chapter, both Michel and Athanase described their confession as a request for forgiveness.

Showing some of the breadth of interpretation of the localized courts' work, there is significant variation in explanations of the reasons for and role of confession. Nonetheless, it is notable that "truth," with all of its attendant challenges and caveats, was identified as the principal contribution of *gacaca* by those at the different tiers of authority inside the NSGJ and in the local communities. *Gacaca's* contribution to truth-telling through dialogue and the active participation of the people affected by the genocide seems in line with a restorative perspective on transitional justice.[66] However, an interpretive approach highlights how the personnel inside *gacaca* emphasized the role of perpetrators' confessions in driving both the dialogue and the truth-telling. Rather than focusing on restoration or individual healing, the attention is on the use of *gacaca* as a communal means of determining how and why the genocide occurred. As Ariel Meyerstein writes in relation to the structure of the courts, "[T]he gacaca's model mirrors the mass participation of the genocide itself."[67] The operation of *gacaca,* its pursuit of "truth," and the role of popular dialogue and confession in obtaining this truth, coheres with its principal agents' attempts to make sense of how and why the genocide occurred.

---

[64] Focus group with *Inyangamugayo* (Rural District, Northern Province, Rwanda, March 20, 2009) notes on file with author.

[65] Interview with *Inyangamugayo* (Participant 37) (Rural District, Northern Province, Rwanda, March 20, 2009) notes on file with author.

[66] Charles Villa-Vicencio, "Transitional Justice, Restoration, and Prosecution" in Dennis Sullivan and Larry Tifft (eds), *Handbook of Restorative Justice: A Global Perspective* (Routledge 2006) 387; and Kieran McEvoy and Anna Eriksson, "Restorative Justice in Transition: Ownership, Leadership and 'Bottom-Up' Human Rights" in Dennis Sullivan and Larry Tifft (eds), *Handbook of Restorative Justice: A Global Perspective* (Routledge 2006) 322.

[67] Ariel Meyerstein, "Between Law and Culture: Rwanda's *Gacaca* and Postcolonial Legality" (2007) 32 Law & Social Inquiry 467, 476.

At the national and local levels, among both the *inyangamugayo* and the legal officers interviewed in Kigali, there was an emphasis on the specific applicability of *gacaca* to the genocide and the violence that characterized it. As one employee at the National Service stated,

> It would be difficult to apply it [*gacaca*] to other countries. Often these countries are fighting one another or regions are fighting. It was a response because here, in Rwanda, neighbours were killing each other. We were fighting each other.[68]

The reality of interethnic relations was described in similar terms by an *inyangamugayo,*

> Here we have a TRC and *gacaca*. . . for Apartheid it was about blacks and whites; here we were of the same country, the same language. We had many relationships, in very many cases it is inside the family, a nephew who has killed an uncle, that is why we have this process.[69]

This reading is supported by recent research on popular accounts of the genocide among rural Hutu citizens who similarly highlight this fratricidal reading of the violence.[70] *Gacaca's* primary objective of "truth" drives the work of the judges and legal officers at both a local and national level. This "truth" is inextricably linked to the nature of the conflict itself; however, there is a difference between how the truth is understood centrally and locally. At the local level, the work of *gacaca* is more strongly influenced by the immediate experience of the conflict than it is by a national meta-narrative of ethnic relations in Rwanda. While the *inyangamugayo* in the Western Province emphasized the importance of locating bodies, in the Northern Province, as discussed in the next section, there was a greater emphasis on determining the guilt or innocence of particular accused.

At this juncture in the empirical study, the divergent objectives of the three levels of courts are starkly evident. The ICTR has focused on building an international legal order. The national courts have been most concerned with judicial education, while the personnel in *gacaca* articulate a focus on determining the "truth" of the genocide. At the national level, this truth was focused on a macro account of the conflict, while at a local level, it has been more variable. As noted in the Introduction, at first reading this might appear an ideal case of a holistic response to the Rwandan genocide. However, the courts' actions are interpreted in divergent cultural contexts. Inside the ICTR, the

---

68 Informal discussion with National Service for Gacaca Courts Personnel (Participant 22) (Kigali, Rwanda, March 21, 2009) notes on file with author.

69 Interview with *Inyangamugayo* (Participant 39) (Kigali, Rwanda, March 21, 2009) notes on file with author.

70 Aruradha Chakravarty, "Navigating the Middle Ground: The Political Values of Ordinary Hutu in Post-Genocide Rwanda" (2014) 451 African Affairs 232, 244.

national courts and *gacaca,* how one process is justified affects how the actions of the others are viewed and understood. The notably different interpretations of post-genocide criminal justice offered by the judges, lawyers, and *inyangamugayo* have influenced the courts' ability to complement one another and to respond to the atrocities perpetrated in Rwanda.

3.2 ACCOUNTABILITY

The second dominant justification for *gacaca* offered by its personnel was accountability. In the legalist writings on transitional justice, accountability generally refers to the criminal prosecution and punishment of perpetrators of serious human rights violations.[71] However, recent criminological research has argued for a broader deployment of the term, in which accountability refers to the obligation, on individuals or institutions, to justify decisions made.[72] Inside the *gacaca* courts, there was variation between the perspectives on accountability at the different levels of the NSGJ.

Among the *inyangamugayo,* there was a general focus on identifying the particular individuals who should account for their actions during the genocide. As one local judge in Kigali stated, "We share many things and the suspicion whether he is innocent or guilty needed to be removed."[73] This search for individual guilt or innocence is consistent with the formulation of *gacaca* as a means of better understanding the conflict at the local level. The focus of the *gacaca* court studied in the Western Province was on the location of bodies, while in the Northern Province there was a greater emphasis on the "truth" about individual involvement in the genocide. As one *inyangamugayo,* in this instance a Hutu woman with no formal schooling but an intimate understanding of the conflict, stated,

> To me, *gacaca* was very crucial. I was one of the people who saved people, helped them with their lives, that's why I was elected. It is not as easy as people think, there were people who were killed for helping others, there were those who killed actively and those who did not kill. It has helped a lot with unity of these people.[74]

---

[71] This understanding has most recently been applied in Francesca Lessa and Leigh A. Payne, *Amnesty in the Age of Human Rights Accountability* (Cambridge University Press 2012).

[72] Louise Mallinder and Kieran McEvoy, "Rethinking Amnesties: Atrocity, Accountability and Impunity in Post-conflict Societies" (2011) 6 Contemporary Social Science: Journal of the Academy of Social Science 107, 109–111. The authors draw on an interdisciplinary collection of writings on accountability to create a broader set of characteristics that moves beyond the narrow deployment of the term as synonymous with criminal trials.

[73] Interview with *Inyangamugayo* (Participant 15) (Kigali, Rwanda, March 10, 2009) notes on file with author.

[74] Interview with *Inyangamugayo* (Participant 32) (Rural District, Northern Province, Rwanda, March 20, 2009) notes on file with author.

Particularly important in this statement is the judge's reference to intra-Hutu accountability and unity. For this *inyangamugayo, gacaca* has not resulted in the collective guilt of all Hutu, as argued in some appraisals of the courts' work,[75] but rather has allowed for crucial differentiation between individuals' involvement in the genocide. In Scott Straus's account of the genocide, the contest for power following the downing of President Habyarimana's plane was initially an *intra*-Hutu struggle for dominance and authority in a period of acute crisis, in which the Hutus promoting violence won.[76] If this position is accepted, as this particular *inyangamugayo* articulated, intra-Hutu accountability is a crucial component of post-genocide justice.

To some extent these interpretations of the courts' work are formulated in terms of a broader notion of accountability, namely the differentiation between people who are obliged to explain the decisions they made during the genocide and those who are not. At the higher tiers of the NSGJ in Kigali, the understandings of accountability were more clearly punitive. There was a general perception that sentences through *gacaca* had been low, especially in light of the use of community service, and the impact of sentencing was emphasized on a national rather than an individual level. In the words of one senior participant, "It has had an effect on the consciousness of people, on the culture, the understanding that criminal actions will be punished. People are now aware that they will be held responsible for their actions."[77] The contribution of such punishment was explained as a means of challenging "the culture of impunity" and given priority by those in the leadership structure at the NSGJ:

> You can't talk about reconciliation when you are not punishing the crime. It is impossible. Who is reconciled with who? You are giving them amnesty. Punishment is one of the tools to eradicate impunity, to say enough is enough.[78]

The role of punishment was not as readily emphasized at the local level. The *inyangamugayo* focused more on the determination of guilt than sentencing. However, this must be read against a backdrop in which the majority of suspects had already been incarcerated for over ten years, and the bulk of an individual's remaining sentence could be commuted to community service. As one judge in the Western Province stated, "Because of this, [*gacaca*] prisoners were able to be released, people who were innocent are out, and those who were guilty are in jail."[79]

---

75 Waldorf 98.

76 Scott Straus, *The Order of Genocide: Race. Power, and War in Rwanda* (Cornell University Press 2006) 89.

77 Interview with National Service Personnel (Participant 3) (Kigali, Rwanda, February 25, 2009) notes on file with author.

78 Ibid.

79 Interview with *Inyangamugayo* (Participant 44) (Rural District, Western Province, Rwanda, March 26, 2009) notes on file with author.

The differences in understandings of accountability between, on the one hand, the NSGJ leadership and legal officers, and, on the other, the *inyangamugayo,* could explain some of the local variance in the practice of the *gacaca* courts. For example, in the Category 1 cases I observed, which concerned higher-profile suspects that drew the attention of the central officers in Kigali, there is a greater focus on the punitive aspect of the process and, as discussed in Chapter 3, a push toward more procedural formalism. In addition, due to the devolved structures of the courts, different districts have focused on slightly different interpretations of the work and role of the courts, with the judges interviewed in the Western and Northern Provinces differing in the emphasis they placed on their work.

Within this study, the actions of the *gacaca* courts were most routinely identified as contributing to determining truth and establishing individual accountability. There were differences between the central understandings of the *gacaca* courts' work in Kigali and the *inyangamugayo's* interpretations outside of the capital. In the center, the focus was on the meta-narrative of the genocide and the punitive function of the courts. On the margins, the truth was explained in terms of the location of bodies and the accountability of particular individuals for their involvement in the crimes. At the local level, truth and accountability were explicitly connected with how the genocide itself is being understood.

However, if we accept variation in how *gacaca* is conceived of centrally and implemented locally, this does not mean that the local implementation is automatically constructive or positive; in fact it can be highly divisive. If the *inyangamugayo* are competent mediators and are responsive to the articulated needs and interests of their immediate community, then the pursuit of truth through *gacaca* can be very constructive. If these same judges pursue other political or social interests, their involvement in the highly volatile adjudication of genocide crimes may exacerbate community tensions and mistrust. As discussed later in this chapter, the variance in the work of *gacaca* is identified as both a strength and a point of critique by a selection of prisoners tried by *gacaca* and, as detailed in Chapter 5, all of the post-genocide courts have been interpreted in a context of continued division and mistrust. Nevertheless, the final chapter of this book argues that the general participants, who have engaged with *gacaca,* the national courts, and the ICTR, all emphasized the importance of Rwandan transitional justice contributing to establishing truth about the genocide, and *gacaca's* endeavor to do this has strengthened its legitimacy.

3.3 EXPEDITIOUS JUSTICE

The contribution identified third most frequently by participants inside *gacaca* was the localized courts' ability to expedite the justice process. As noted at the start of this chapter, post-genocide *gacaca* was initially implemented as a response to the inability of the national courts to handle the genocide caseload. Nine years after the start of *gacaca's* nationwide operation, the ability of *gacaca* to process a large number of cases remained one of the key contributions identified by actors inside the institution.

The speed of the *gacaca* trials and their acceleration after 2007 have been criticized by some international NGOs monitoring the courts.[80] The staff within the institution generally dismissed this critique. As one *gacaca* coordinator said, "Some feel that *gacaca* has been too fast, but there was no reason for it to be slow because after the information stage, the truth was out there. The witnesses lived on the hills and saw everything."[81] In articulating *gacaca's* contribution to expeditious justice, as with the understood contribution of truth-telling, there was a recognition that the speed of trials depended heavily on confession. In the words of one *inyangamugayo* in the Northern Province, "Confession helped those who survived find the truth that they were looking for and it has helped the process to go faster."[82] *Gacaca* has consistently been understood to provide a pragmatic solution to the practice of indefinite detention that characterized the initial post-genocide period.

Throughout this chapter, it has been argued that *gacaca* is a process that has altered over the course of its operation, and its understood objectives have shifted over time. Opinions and understandings of *gacaca* have changed through the different phases of the courts' operation, from the pre-*gacaca* trials, through the pilot stage, followed by the nationwide information stage, and, finally, during the trials, appeals, and reviews. *Gacaca* has been understood throughout its operation as a feasible response to the challenges facing Rwandan criminal justice that were articulated in the early reflection meetings in the Office of the President, and the speed of the process has remained one of the contributions attributed to the courts. In contrast, *gacaca's* perceived contribution to reconciliation has altered far more during the course of its operation.

3.4 RECONCILIATION

Jeremy Sarkin[83] and Bert Ingeleare[84] both emphasize that, as an objective of transitional justice, reconciliation only emerged in Rwandan government discourse around 2000. Nonetheless, by the start of *gacaca's* nationwide information phase in 2005, reconciliation was regularly articulated by participants as a central aspiration of the *gacaca* process. In the empirical research conducted in 2008–2009, there were divergent opinions over

---

[80] Avocats Sans Frontières, "Monitoring of the *Gacaca* Courts—Judgment Phase" (Analytical Report 3) October 2006–April 2007.

[81] Interview with National Service for Gacaca Courts Personnel (Participant 5) (Rwanda, April 28, 2008) conducted in conjunction with P. Clark, notes on file with author.

[82] Interview with *Inyangamugayo* (Participant 34) (Rural District, Northern Province, Rwanda, March 20, 2009) notes on file with author.

[83] Sarkin 154.

[84] Bert Ingelaere, "Living the Transition: A Bottom-Up Perspective on Rwanda's Political Transition" [2007] Institute for Development Policy and Management University of Antwerp Discussion Paper, 32.

whether *gacaca* had contributed to reconciliation. As with the ICTR, some respondents argued that there had been instances of reconciliation to date, while others interpreted this objective only as a possibility in the future.

Among the legal officers, reconciliation was most strongly connected with the property crimes in Category 3 that had been dealt with through *gacaca*. In the words of one senior lawyer,

> If you look at Category 3, this is an instance of reconciliation; if the accused and the survivors want to resolve it without going to the court, then they can and it will be over. They will go to *gacaca* and have an official document signed to say that it is resolved. In the ordinary courts, you would be condemned to five or more years.[85]

This interpretation of reconciliation was similarly seen in the structure and wording of the information that the NSGJ has collected from each of the *gacaca* courts at both a *cellule* and sector level. During the 2009 research period, the NSGJ was writing its final *gacaca* report. As part of their completion program, all *gacaca* courts had to fill in a series of fact sheets documenting details of the cases heard, including the gender of the accused; whether they had confessed, and, if so, at what stage in the process; and the verdict. The outcome of reaching a settlement in relation to Category 3 property crimes was described in this document as "reconciliation" and directly translated as a "certification of forgiveness." The National Service viewed the determination of Category 3 crimes, where the agreement occurs outside of the *gacaca*, as the principal reflection of reconciliation. The understanding that reconciliation has occurred when a *gacaca* court hearing has been successfully avoided is consistent with the more punitive understanding of the *gacaca* trials articulated within the central administrative structures.

In contrast, in both the rural research sites, participants referred to the practice of exchanging livestock as the key indicator of reconciliation. As the Director of Good Governance and Unity, a government position outside of the NSGJ, in the Northern Province stated, "people on the hills are now giving cows to one another again, this is a sign of reconciliation."[86] This was similarly mentioned in the focus groups with *inyangamugayo* in the Western Province:

> It has made a good contribution to the reconciliation process. The criminals of genocide are now living with the victims, some of them have started inter-marrying and giving each other cows as it was before.[87]

---

[85] Interview with National Service for Gacaca Courts Personnel (Participant 14) (Kigali, Rwanda, March 2, 2009) notes on file with author.

[86] Interview with Director of Good Governance and Unity (Rural District, Northern Province, Rwanda, August 27, 2009) conducted in conjunction with P. Clark, notes on file with author.

[87] Interview with *Inyangamugayo* (Participant 41) (Rural District, Western Province, Rwanda, March 26, 2009) notes on file with author.

However, individual experiences of victims and perpetrators being reconciled were not generally provided in discussion with the local judges, with the majority of participants viewing reconciliation as a potential future outcome of *gacaca.* Within the NSGJ, the local courts' work was described as "the beginning of reconciliation"[88] and by one *inyangamugayo,* as "a step towards reconciliation."[89] Outside of the *gacaca* setting, this reading was further explained by Fatuma Ndangiza, the Executive Secretary of the NURC:

> There is the challenge of dealing with the past and not being stuck in the past. Balancing truth-telling, justice and reconciliation is difficult ... We will really only experience reconciliation after *gacaca.* It has opened the wound, because truth-telling is not comfortable.[90]

Within *gacaca,* there has been a shift away from more adamantly advocating reconciliation as an objective of the process, to a clearer focus on the courts' role in determining truth.

As was the case with the ICTR and the national courts, the emergent understandings of *gacaca's* actions show a more restrained conception of the courts' contributions. *Gacaca's* initial mandate included the broad goals of ending impunity, establishing the truth of the genocide, reconciling Rwandans, and creating a basis for the reintegration of former prisoners. The process itself has shaped how the contributions of transitional justice are understood. For the *inyangamugayo*, the interpretations of *gacaca's* work have increasingly oriented toward a localized account of the conflict.

Gacaca's responsiveness to the immediate local context is driven by both the involvement of the General Assembly participants and the *inyangamugayo's* own interpretations of the direction of the courts. The latter's views were influenced by the NSGJ's conception of the objectives of *gacaca,* but there was also local-level variation in the interpretations of the courts' actions. The *inyangamugayo* have played a dynamic mediating role in the operation of *gacaca.* In part, the more modest contributions of *gacaca,* articulated by both the *inyangamugayo* and the lawyers working in the NSGJ, are due to a number of practical constraints on the operation of the court. The constraints identified by participants, both within the NSGJ in Kigali and in the district research sites, related to participation, silence, and corruption.

---

88 Interview with National Service for Gacaca Courts Personnel (Participant 22) (Kigali, Rwanda, March 11, 2009) notes on file with author.

89 Interview with *Inyangamugayo* (Participant 15) (Kigali, Rwanda, March 10, 2009) notes on file with author.

90 Interview with Fatuma Ndangiza, Executive Secretary, National Unity and Reconciliation Commission (Kigali, Rwanda, August 6, 2008) conducted with P. Clark, notes and recording on file with author.

4. Practical Constraints

Gacaca has operated in a very challenging and charged environment. If actors inside the NSGJ and the *gacaca* judges adjudicating the cases on the hills see *gacaca* as contributing to a better understanding of the conflict, these same actors acknowledge very real constraints on the process.

4.1 PARTICIPATION

The popular nature of *gacaca* means that the process depends on participation from a broad range of Rwandan citizens. As with the requirement of confession, the legal officers inside the NSGJ connected the importance of participatory justice to the nature of the conflict itself:

> Justice is important and in this process all the people participate. This is important because so many people participated at the time of the genocide, it was not just the authorities. At the district level, there is only one authority, yet there were many, many people involved in the killing.[91]
>
> It is the people who know and they can say what happened, only they can say what happened. Participation is important because the information about the genocide is with the people.[92]

At the local level, the *inyangamugayo* similarly described the dependence of the process on participation:

> At times, the cases have been more difficult than at other times. It depends on how many people come. If there are a lot of people it becomes easier. When there are one or two and we find that their tongues are different and then it is difficult.[93]

As reflected in these accounts, popular participation is the major procedural safeguard against false accusations or partial confessions, further highlighting the interconnection between confession and participation in the "truth-telling" claims of the courts, discussed in Section 3.1.2.

---

[91] Informal Interview with National Service for Gacaca Courts Legal Officer (Participant 20) (Kigali, Rwanda, March 9, 2009) notes on file with author.

[92] Informal Interview with National Service for Gacaca Courts Legal Officer (Participant 16) (Kigali, Rwanda, February 27, 2009) notes on file with author.

[93] Interview with *Inyangamugayo* (Participant 34) (Rural District, Rwanda, March 20, 2009) notes on file with author.

Both external commentators and actors inside the institution have identified challenges with participation, and highlighted that participation has fluctuated at different phases of the *gacaca* process.[94] However, inside of the institution, this challenge is interpreted in light of what the courts have contributed to truth-telling and accountability, and is not viewed as insurmountable. On the first research trip in 2008, the *inyangamugayo* in a rural area of the Northern Province noted a decline in participation during the *gacaca* trials after high participation at the initial information-collecting stage. However, by April 2009 in that same area, the change in the Organic Law transferring Category 1 cases to *gacaca* saw a rise in participation. The prominence in the community of those accused in Category 1 fueled greater interest in the process. The role of elites in the genocide is articulated in both the official and popular understandings of the history of the genocide. On the ground, people have wanted to understand the role that these more senior leaders played in the violence in their community.

Reflecting a similar social structure, the participation of current elites in *gacaca* was identified as crucial to the success of the courts' practice, and articulated in interviews with the *inyangamugayo*. In Kigali, a Hutu man who was university educated, reflected on his motivation to be a local judge, saying that it came as a response to the lack of elite participation during the trials: "Many people did not participate, especially the elite from the local population, so the better way for me to give my contribution was not only to attend, but to be involved."[95] He identified another reason for low participation as the fear of being required to talk, of breaking the silence,

> Some of the people who attended, we suspected them or their close relatives to have been involved. It was not easy for them to talk. That is why participation was not as active as was needed. One way not to talk about the people involved was not to come.[96]

This illuminates the other major practical constraint on the attainment of truth and accountability, namely silence. Alongside the fluctuating levels of participation, silence and false testimony were identified as the major practical constraints on the functioning of *gacaca*. These challenges to participation and testimony are similarly reflected in the critical literature on *gacaca,* and have been explained as instances of resistance to the *gacaca* system as a whole.[97] Inside of *gacaca*, among both the NSGJ staff and the *inyangamugayo*, these criticisms were similarly acknowledged but expressed along with the courts' positive contributions to truth-telling and accountability.

---

[94] Clark, *The* Gacaca *Courts, Post-Genocide Justice and Reconciliation in Rwanda: Justice without Lawyers* 148.
[95] Interview with *Inyangamugayo* (Participant 15) (Kigali, Rwanda, March 10, 2009) notes on file with author.
[96] Ibid.
[97] Thomson 14 and Waldorf 154.

4.2 SILENCE AND FALSE TESTIMONY

As an elderly woman at one of the hearings articulated,

> There is a big problem because people are not telling the truth, because they do not want to accuse their neighbours. Maybe you will accuse them and then that person will be jailed and the family will be against you. They saw, these people here, they saw what happened and the criminals they also don't tell the truth. The Banyarwanda especially in this area, they do not tell the truth. Banyarwanda can't tell the truth.[98]

The level of agitation and discomfort of this particular participant was very clear. As will be discussed in the next chapter, many of the general participants' understandings of *gacaca* were directed toward the courts' contributions to truth-telling, but were profoundly influenced by the reality of continued division and mistrust in the country. Adopting an opposing view at the same hearing, another participant stated, "Some of them choose just to stay silent because they do not know how they will be able to present themselves and they will not be able to answer the questions that are asked of them."[99]

Silence or a reluctance to speak were explained by a number of separate but reinforcing phenomena: First, participants spoke of *cekeke*[100] in which *gacaca* participants would not provide accusatory evidence against people with whom they have personal ties. Second, people identified a fear to speak for reasons of personal security or reprimand from the state. *Cekeke* was identified as a problem for *gacaca* by both the legal officers and *inyangamugayo*. In an informal discussion at the NSGJ, one participant said,

> [*Gacaca*] has obtained maybe 60% of the truth. This is important, but it is difficult. There is what they call *cekeke*, that is, for people to stay silent. Even if they know, when they were asked, they would just stay silent, but now, slowly, more people are willing to talk.[101]

This aspect of the local courts work links closely with recent studies on how the genocide unfolded. Lee Ann Fujii argues that in many cases it was the strength of local family ties that led to people joining in the violence.[102] In some cases these same ties are drawn on to ensure that people do not speak out against these crimes. *Inyangamugayo* in the

---

[98] Informal discussion with *gacaca* participant (Participant 6) (Rural District, Northern Province, Rwanda, April 1, 2009) notes on file with author.

[99] Informal discussion with *gacaca* participant (Participant 11) (Rural District, Northern Province, Rwanda, April 1, 2009) notes on file with author.

[100] *Cekeke* can be translated from Kinyarwanda as to "hold your tongue."

[101] Interview with National Service for Gacaca Courts Personnel (Participant 22) (Rwanda, March 11, 2009) notes on file with author.

[102] Lee Ann Fujii, *Killing Neighbors: Webs of Violence in Rwanda* (Cornell University Press 2009) 153.

Northern Province identified one of the responses to the challenge of *ceceke* as persuasion and working within the community:

> There have been problems with testimony because people lie. The *inyangamugayo* have tried to guide people, especially within families, to tell the truth. It is important to ask people to ask each other to tell the truth.[103]

Once again mobilization through face-to-face interactions emerges as key to encouraging active participation in *gacaca*. This was also coupled with a concern that "in the cases where the whole family was wiped out, there was no one to talk so then there is a problem of telling lies because there is no one to tell the truth."[104] Again, the importance of challenging this silence was connected with the nature of the genocide and the crimes themselves:

> At times you find that relatives, or people who stayed together or their children played together, then they don't want to show the truth. In other countries this might be normal, but here the truth relates to the death of people.[105]

As indicated earlier, the *inyangamugayo* have had various responses to the practical constraint of silence. As already mentioned, one response was to persuade the members of their community to engage with *gacaca*. The second response has been coercive, as was explicitly discussed during a focus group:

> *Inyangamugayo 1*: When people are not speaking, under Article 29 we have power to arrest them. We try to convince people to speak, but if they don't, we have the right to put them in jail for three months, then they speak.
>
> *Inyangamugayo 2*: When you don't speak the truth and we know that you don't speak the truth, or we find that you are not telling the truth, under Article 32, we can call you before the court.[106]

In resorting to a more coercive means of ensuring participation, these judges make reference to the written law. Under the 2004 Organic Law, Article 29 establishes that participation in *gacaca* is mandatory, and determines that omission of information,

---

[103] Interview with *Inyangamugayo* (Participant 6) (Rural District, Northern Province, Rwanda, August 29, 2008) conducted in conjunction with P. Clark, notes on file with author.

[104] Interview with *Inyangamugayo* (Participant 39) (Kigali, Rwanda, March 21, 2009) notes on file with author.

[105] Interview with *Inyangamugayo* (Participant 34) (Rural District, Northern Province, Rwanda, March 20, 2009) notes on file with author.

[106] Focus group with *Inyangamugayo* (Rural District, Northern Province, Rwanda, March 20, 2009) notes on file with author.

provision of false testimony, "slanderous denunciation,"[107] or refusal to testify are subject to three to six months' incarceration. The maximum sentence for repeat offenders is increased to one year. Similarly, under Article 30, any individual who "exercises pressures or attempts to exercise pressure"[108] on a witness or judge can incur a prison sentence of between three months and one year, and, in the case of a repeat offense, up to two years. Articles 29 to 32 are a revision of the powers outlined in the 2001 law where omission or refusal to testify was subject to one to three years' imprisonment, with half the sentence commutable through community service.[109] The inclusion of both denunciation and false testimony, in 2004, as additional offenses suggests an increasing reliance of the judges on these powers, and highlights some of the constraints on truth-telling in *gacaca*.

Amendments to the Organic Law have been used as a means to respond to the practical constraints on *gacaca*, particularly concerning participation. The *inyangamugayo* were given increasing powers to call witnesses and prosecute for perjury. However, this resort to coercion has in some instances exacerbated the fear of testifying. Although not identified by the *inyangamugayo*, this did emerge among participants in attendance at the hearings. As one woman sitting next to me at the back of a hearing in a rural district argued,

> People keep quiet, they are scared to speak but I do not think that it is *ceceke*. Like that old man, when he said that the genocide happened "only a little" here, maybe he just does not understand that killing even ten people can be part of genocide. So people don't talk because they might not be understood . . . The community has been sensitised here for a long time, they know they have to talk, but they fear that if they say the wrong thing, or are not able to say it right, they will be in trouble or locked up.[110]

The judges saw silence as a hindrance to obtaining both exculpatory and accusatory evidence. After attending a *gacaca* hearing in a rural sector, I was offered a lift back into town with the *inyangamugayo*. While in the car, one of the judges expressed frustration over the unwillingness of people to speak, articulating the impact that this has had on the objective of individual accountability:

> It is a problem that they do not talk. There was a man, he had been in prison for eleven years and no one said anything. He could have been sentenced to thirty years. It would be like taking his life and he was innocent![111]

The practical challenges raised by silence and false testimony must be assessed against the reality that people have spoken, at length, particularly during the first information

[107] *Gacaca* Law Modified 2004 art. 29.

[108] Ibid. art. 30.

[109] *Gacaca* Law 2001 art. 32.

[110] Informal discussion with *gacaca* participant (Participant 15) (Rural District, Northern Province, Rwanda, April 15, 2009) notes on file with author.

[111] Informal discussion with *Inyangamugayo* (Participant 48) (Rural District, Northern Province, Rwanda, April 15, 2009) notes on file with author.

phase of *gacaca*. Rather than silence undermining the value of *gacaca* as a whole, inside the institution it was viewed as a constraint on the process that had changed over time and led to various responses from the *gacaca* personnel. The majority of evidence was initially supplied during the nationwide information stage of *gacaca,* which ran from January 2005 until June 2006. However, the trial phase, which ran from July 2006 and officially concluded on June 18, 2012, demanded a recapitulation of this information amid, at times, declining participation.

In 2009, the *inyangamugayo* acknowledged the challenge with *gacaca's* dependence on continued participation over a sustained period:

> Some people did not want to say what they had said before. They felt that after the information stage, they had told their story and then it should be finished . . . Three of the cases I have heard were very hard because witnesses refused to say what they had said before.[112]

As this discussion and the Organic Law itself indicate, the challenge of silence is coupled with the problem of false testimony. This was an issue in the provision of both accusatory and exculpatory evidence. Silence and false testimony emerged as the major practical constraints identified at the local level among the *inyangamugayo*. In contrast, in the NSGJ in Kigali, there was a stronger emphasis on corruption and security as major practical challenges to the achievement of *gacaca's* objectives.

4.3 CORRUPTION AND WITNESS SECURITY

The legal officers in Kigali identified corruption as one of the main challenges faced by *gacaca*. Some of the responses also noted that the incidents of corruption had increased toward the end of *gacaca's* operation:

> One of the challenges has been corruption. It is funny—somehow this has got worse as we are coming to the end of process. It is as if the people are saying *gacaca* is winding up and I have not got anything out of the process, now I have to.[113]

Corruption, or as the 2004 Organic Law reads in Article 30, "attempts to exercise pressure or threaten the witnesses or the Seat members of the Gacaca Court," is punishable with a sentence of up to one year imprisonment, increased to as much as three in cases of repeat offenders. As with refusal to testify, this was only introduced in 2004. As the wording of the Article indicates, this is also connected with the challenge of security

---

[112] Interview with *Inyangamugayo* (Participant 10) (Rural District, Northern Province, Rwanda, September 2, 2009) notes on file with author.

[113] Informal Interview with National Service for Gacaca Courts Legal Officer (Participant 23) (Kigali, Rwanda, March 16, 2009) notes on file with author.

for both judges and witnesses. Concerns over security emerged as the major practical constraint identified within the leadership structures of the NSGJ. As one senior staff member stated, "The first challenge was insecurity, witnesses feeling that they were not secure. We dealt with this through security organs and we have devised strategies with the national police."[114] As discussed in Section 2.3, increased feelings of insecurity in the immediate aftermath of testifying at *gacaca* emerged strongly in recent survey work on the courts, and it was these concerns that initially prompted the introduction of domestic witness protections programs in Rwanda, which would shift toward an increasing use of anonymous testimony following the Rule 11 *bis* decisions of the ICTR.[115]

The opening section of this chapter outlined how the current analyses of the *gacaca* courts have not taken full account of the role of the *gacaca* judges in this devolved transitional justice process. This empirical research shows that in the interpretations of *gacaca's* contributions and the identified practical constraints there is a distinction between understandings at the national and local level. This shows the importance of the agency of the *inyangamugayo* while highlighting both vertical and horizontal variation between the courts in different *cellules* and sectors. In order to explore the differences between central and marginal examinations of *gacaca,* it is necessary to explore how the judges have understood their role. What emerges is a picture of transitional justice inside Rwanda as highly context-specific.

4.4 THE ROLE OF THE *INYANGAMUGAYO*

As discussed, the initial criticisms of *gacaca,* both at the Urugwiro reflection meetings and in the early academic literature, focused on the lack of judicial impartiality of the *gacaca* judges. Similarly, more recent work on *gacaca* suggests that the judges have acted opportunistically in a given local context, deepening community distrust and leading to increased conflict over *gacaca* decisions.[116] In contrast, Domiltilla Mukantaganzwa, the Executive Secretary of the NSGJ, saw the devolution of control down to the *inyangamugayo* as one of the strengths of the process:

> There is also ownership. People have been able to be in charge of their problems. Of course we have offered people to help them but they have been in charge. This is what has made *gacaca* so important to people.[117]

---

[114] Interview with National Service for Gacaca Courts Personnel (Participant 1) (Kigali, Rwanda, August 14, 2009); interview conducted in conjunction with P. Clark, notes on file with author.

[115] Redress, "Testifying to Genocide: Victim and Witness Protection in Rwanda" Redress (October 2012) by P. Clark and N. Palmer http://www.redress.org/africa/rwanda accessed August 28, 2014.

[116] Bert Ingelaere, *The Rise of Meta-conflict during Rwanda's* Gacaca *Process,* L'afrique Des Grands Lacs. Annuaire 2010–2011 (Filip Reyntjens, Stefaan Marysse, and Stef Vandeginste eds, L'Harmattan 2011).

[117] Domiltilla Mukantaganzwa, Executive Secretary, National Service for Gacaca Courts, (Kigali, Rwanda, February 25, 2009) notes on file with author.

Coming from the affected community, the *inyangamugayo* do bring what Timothy Longman terms "contextual competence"[118] to the courts. The judges interviewed within this study generally had a rich understanding of their role in the process. A number of them articulated their educational contribution, seeing their first job as explaining the process of *gacaca* to people, while others focused on their role in interpreting the law, or undertaking investigations and encouraging participation. Some judges framed their choice to take up the position in terms of service to the country:

> It is our job to do all of this. We do a lot for the community and for rebuilding the state. It has been a lot of work, but this is the same for all Rwandans. During the week we work for our family, but we consider *gacaca* as part of this work for rebuilding the family and the country.[119]

Yet judging their own community has proven to be costly. In all of the interviews and focus groups in the three research sites, judges expressed concerns about personal isolation:

> The major challenge has been that there are two parties and those that the judgment favoured see themselves as your friend and those it was against are your enemies. We [*inyangamugayo*] can be hated.[120]
>
> For certain *inyangamugayo,* within their communities, even people they were friends with started distancing themselves and being rude because they were scared.[121]

The *inyangamugayo* provide a very human face to the trials of genocide in Rwanda. Those judges who were interviewed acknowledged the impact of their own experience of the conflict. As one Hutu judge reflected, "the *inyangamugayo* are members of the Rwandan society. They are as divided as Rwandan society."[122]

To describe *gacaca* as predominantly a top-down means of social control fails to fully acknowledge the dynamic role played by the *gacaca* judges and other local actors. The ability of both the judges and the General Assembly participants to shape the direction and objectives of a particular *gacaca* court helps to explain the variance in what the courts have been understood to achieve and how they have operated in practice. The

---

118 Longman, "Justice at the Grassroots? *Gacaca* trials in Rwanda" 215.

119 Interview with *Inyangamugayo* (Participant 6) (Rural District, Northern Province, Rwanda, August 29, 2008); interview conducted with P Clark, notes on file with author.

120 Interview with *Inyangamugayo* (Participant 47) (Rural District, Western Province, Rwanda, April 24, 2009) notes on file with author.

121 Interview with *Inyangamugayo* (Participant 33) (Rural District, Northern Province, Rwanda, March 20, 2009) notes on file with author.

122 Interview with *Inyangamugayo* (Participant 15) (Kigali, Rwanda, March 10, 2009) notes on file with author.

gacaca judges have critically engaged with the process; however, there remain social and political constraints on their work. The success of *gacaca* in a particular local area is heavily dependent on the strength of character of the judges.

The *gacaca* judges' agency in directing the objectives and actions of the courts has also impacted upon the concurrent work of the ICTR and the national courts. The local specificity of the *gacaca* is seen as both a strength and a weakness by a group of prisoners subject to the authority of more than one of the post-genocide courts. Inside *gacaca,* the judges' interpretation of their own work has led to the local courts pursuing their own objectives despite national or international interests pulling in a different direction.

5. Concurrent Transitional Justice

The previous chapters have shown the complicated intersections among the ICTR, the national courts, and *gacaca.* The courts' concurrent practice has been examined from the vantage point of the ICTR and national court practitioners and a group of prison participants subject to these courts' authority. The empirical study shows a divergence in the interpretations of the courts' work, illuminating an increasingly competitive system of transitional justice.

For a selection of prisoners who have appeared before more than one of the Rwandan post-genocide courts, there are tensions between the courts' practice. The judges and lawyers inside the ICTR see the international orientation of their actions as a strength. Inside the prisons, the external nature of the ICTR's laws and procedures is a point of critique. However, in formal interaction among the courts, it is the ICTR's interpretation of transitional justice that prevails, seen in the reasoning of the Rule 11 *bis* decisions and the ICTR's use of *gacaca* documents.

The prisoners who were tried by the national courts, some of whom have testified before the ICTR and are appealing their cases through *gacaca,* are not unanimously supportive of one set of proceedings over another. The practice of one court is routinely used as the basis to critique the others. These prisoners did not view the courts as complementary, but rather in direct competition. Inside the national courts, however, the judges and lawyers have assumed that the actions of the ICTR and *gacaca* should complement their own practices, which are oriented toward improving legal capacity. The result is a mismatch of expectations between the international court and its domestic counterparts, seen in the tensions over the transfer of cases between the courts.

This section on concurrent transitional justice examines similar tensions evident in the practice of the *gacaca* courts. It explores the points of interaction among the three courts from the perspective of prison participants tried before *gacaca,* and the legal practitioners and the *inyangamugayo* inside the *gacaca* courts. In practice, the highly localized nature of the *gacaca* proceedings, seen as a strength by the *gacaca* judges, has challenged the concurrent practice of international and national transitional justice.

5.1 INFORMAL INTERACTIONS: A COMMON GROUP OF PARTICIPANTS

Inside the Rwandan prisons, there were points of commonality between the prisoners' and the *inyangamugayo*'s interpretations of *gacaca*, highlighting the importance of a local understanding of the conflict and the provision of some legal process for the thousands of incarcerated suspects. However, the localization of the *gacaca* courts made them more vulnerable to the local political interests, and a number of prisoners raised criticisms of *gacaca's* variability.

As outlined, the *inyangamugayo* emphasized how the localized character of the *gacaca* courts has allowed them to better determine the "truth" about the genocide, locate the remains of the deceased, and enable them to hold specific individuals accountable for their actions. This differs from the position held by the NSGJ, where the emphasis is on the macro account of the genocide rather than on the specific details of the violence. The strength of the localized process offered by specific *gacaca* courts was acknowledged by some of the prison participants. André, who had confessed and was sentenced to twenty-four years by a *gacaca* court, was broadly supportive of the courts' probative value and the role of the General Assembly as a procedural safeguard:

> Going before *gacaca* is better because it ends the problem . . . It really happens, if you are charged with the crimes you did not commit then others will stand up and say. In 1995, 96 and 97, people were arrested, but there was no proof . . . then if you are released, you go back into the community and you may be accused again for other crimes and have to go back. With *gacaca* it is finished.[123]

Céléstin was similarly supportive. At the time of the interview in 2009, his case was ongoing, having been transferred from the national courts to *gacaca*. He noted, "*Gacaca* has tried many cases which would not have been the case with ordinary courts. Although I am still in prison, I accept that *gacaca* has solved problems and people have been released."[124]

As was seen with Jean-Baptiste's and Aloys's testimony in Chapter 4, Céléstin also used one court's proceedings, in this case *gacaca,* to raise criticism against another. Both André and Céléstin, with varying exposure to *gacaca*'s work, support *gacaca's* pragmatic contribution to the overcrowded prisons and its potential for gathering more information about the crimes at the local level. However, as discussed, the localization of the *gacaca* courts, articulated as a strength inside the institution, has caused variation between the courts. It was this variation that was most readily identified as a criticism of the process inside the Rwandan prisons.

---

[123] Interview with André (Participant 8) (Kigali, Rwanda, April 20, 2009) notes on file with author.

[124] Interview with Céléstin (Participant 7) (Kigali, Rwanda, April 16, 2009) notes on file with author.

According to Silvestre, who confessed, was tried by *gacaca,* was rearrested on addition charges, and is now still awaiting trial, "To a big extent it depends on the court. If the court wants the truth found, they can find it, but if the court doesn't want the truth, it can't."[125] For Evaliste who was arrested as late as 2009 and stated that his arrest was as a result of his refusal to resign as secretary of his sector,

> One of the challenges is that the *gacaca* courts are politically influenced and the local leaders decide. Even the President of the court he said to me, "We have been together and drink together but this is just what had to happen."[126]

For Evaliste, the General Assembly did not provide a mechanism to challenge what he understood to be false accusations against him, motivated by local political opportunism that the *inyangamugayo* were not able to resist. The strength of a local examination of the genocide, asserted within *gacaca,* also emerges as one of its points of critique. As noted in the earlier discussion of the role of the *inyangamugayo* and the place of confession and public participation in providing an accurate account of the violence, the value of the *gacaca* proceedings has depended on the ability of these judges to facilitate the proceedings and the willingness of individuals to provide testimony.

In *gacaca's* formal interactions with the ICTR and the national courts, the views of the *gacaca* personnel have shaped the practice of concurrent transitional justice. Among both the centrally based lawyers within the NSGJ and the local lay judges, the work of the ICTR and the national courts was interpreted in terms of the principal contributions of *gacaca*: the pursuit of local "truth" and accountability to a community. *Gacaca's* own understanding of transitional justice has led to criticisms of the ICTR and the national courts, and has impacted upon the *gacaca's* formal interactions with the concurrent post-genocide courts.

5.2 UNDERSTANDINGS OF THE RWANDAN NATIONAL COURTS

The *gacaca* personnel's discussions of the national courts were consistent with what they saw the local courts as having achieved. The national courts' actions were interpreted within *gacaca's* "socially established structures of meaning."[127] The national courts were most readily evaluated against *gacaca's* ability to expedite the genocide trials:

> *Gacaca* really has been appreciated by the community, because within *gacaca,* they have seen justice done. They are not sure of how the prosecutions in the ordinary

---

[125] Interview with Silvestre (Participant 14) (Rural District, Western Province, Rwanda, April 21, 2009) notes on file with author.

[126] Interview with Evaliste (Participant 12) (Rural District, Western Province, Rwanda, April 21, 2009) notes on file with author.

[127] Geert 12–13.

courts were going to do this because it takes a lot of time and it is going to take money.[128]

At the NSGJ in Kigali, participants explained the achievements of *gacaca* in direct contrast to the work of the national courts:

> Those who plead guilty and even those who don't confess, they are getting out of jail . . . *Gacaca* has been able to show the truth about the genocide. In the ordinary courts, the case is heard in the headquarters of the province. If you don't have the money to pay for transport then you will not bring your evidence to that court, and they will not hear the truth. That is why *gacaca's* decentralised justice has been important.[129]

Although this was a particular focus at the national level of the NSGJ, it was also acknowledged by the *inyangamugayo.* In the words of one judge, "*Gacaca* has worked well in a short time, while classical justice has taken a long time."[130]

In addition to expediting trials, at this local level the national courts were criticized for failing to "hear the cases in the location where the crimes happened."[131] As was apparent in the prisons, the practice of *gacaca* was used as a means to critique the work of the national courts. At the local level, there were even stronger criticisms raised against the ICTR, similarly based on how the *gacaca* personnel, particularly the local judges, understood their own work.

5.3 UNDERSTANDINGS OF THE ICTR

The criticisms of the ICTR were deeply embedded in the local processes of justice. Among the respondents in both the Northern and Western provinces, the ICTR was measured against what was understood as the principal contributions of *gacaca*, namely, the pursuit of truth and accountability to a specific community. As a sector coordinator articulated, in his challenge to the ICTR's contribution to truth,

> When travelling to Arusha, some people have changed their testimony there and this creates problems. The reason for this is sometimes about corruption.

---

128 Interview with National Service for Gacaca Courts Personnel (Participant 3), National Service for Gacaca Courts (Kigali, Rwanda, February 25, 2009) notes on file with author.

129 Interview with National Service for Gacaca Courts Personnel (Participant 14) (Rwanda, March 2, 2009) notes on file with author.

130 Interview with *Inyangamugayo* (Participant 6) (Rural District, Northern Province, Rwanda, August 29, 2008); interview conducted in conjunction with P. Clark, notes on file with author.

131 Interview with *Inyangamugayo* (Participant 7) (Rural District, Northern Province, Rwanda, August 29, 2008); interview conducted in conjunction with P. Clark, notes on file with author.

> Sometimes it is about loyalty, giving false testimony to protect people. It goes back to the war.[132]

Echoing a similar perspective, one *inyangamugayo* said, "The ICTR, they choose people to come from here and then they call only those who they want to speak. It is not like here where everyone, whether they are for or against, must speak."[133] The judges' understandings of the ICTR place its activities in direct tension with what they perceive as the central objective of their own process, specifically that of verbalizing an account of the truth of the conflict. The *inyangamugayo* criticized the ICTR for what they have found the most challenging and important in their own experience of dealing with the genocide.

The second emergent criticism of the ICTR, routinely identified by the *inyangamugayo,* was the failure of the Tribunal to ensure accountability of the most senior accused to the affected community. Here the removal of key figures, an identified contribution within the ICTR, sits in tension with *gacaca's* pursuit of accountability to the local population. As the same judge quoted in the previous paragraph said,

> Having the people in Arusha has limited the process of reconciliation. Those who committed the crimes are still outside the country. They did not commit the crimes internationally. If they were to be brought here and present here, they would be able to answer to us. When people know that the masterminds are still out there, it unsettles their hearts. The ICTR was not for the Rwandan people.[134]

This was consistent with the interpretation of the work of the ICTR offered by the *inyangamugayo* in the opening of this chapter. Participants across the country consistently articulated these views and challenged the mutual compatibility of the concurrent processes. As another judge said,

> I want to know why some human beings are being valued more than others. From a human perspective, who is more valuable? In front of the court, all people are equal. Why do those courts make some people more equal than others?[135]

These testimonies underscore that the practice of domestic transitional justice directly affects how international criminal justice is viewed and understood in the local context.

---

[132] Interview with *Inyangamugayo* (Participant 5) (Rural District, Northern Province, Rwanda, August 28, 2008) notes on file with author.

[133] Interview with *Inyangamugayo* (Participant 36) (Rural District, Northern Province, Rwanda, March 20, 2009) notes on file with author.

[134] Interview with *Inyangamugayo* (Participant 35) (Rural District, Northern Province, Rwanda, March 20, 2009) notes on file with author.

[135] Interview with *Inyangamugayo* (Participant 28) (Rural District, Northern Province, Rwanda, March 20, 2009) notes on file with author.

The divergence between how the judges and lawyers at the ICTR, the national courts, and *gacaca* have understood transitional justice has led to severe criticism among the courts. The reasons for the divergence and its implications for the legitimacy of all three of the courts will be discussed in more detail in the next chapter. What this research starts to show is that concurrent transitional justice processes should, at the very least, be assessed and ideally formulated, in conversation with one another, because how one process is understood affects how the others are interpreted.

5.3.1 Interpreting the Role of *Gacaca* in the Brown et al[136] decision

The potential for competition among the courts is evident in the critiques of the concurrent courts provided by participants working inside *gacaca*. The previous chapters on the ICTR and the national courts showed how the hermeneutical tensions among the courts are most apparent at the points of formal contact and transfer of cases. In line with this finding, the *gacaca* courts' prioritization of their own understood objectives, over and above those of the national courts, is clearly seen in a recent extradition case concerning four genocide suspects currently living in the UK.

In April 2009, the UK High Court concluded that Rwandan genocide suspects Vincent Brown, Charles Munyaneza, Emmanuel Nteziryayo, and Celestin Ugirashebuja would "suffer a real risk of a flagrant denial of justice by reason of their likely inability to adduce evidence of supporting witnesses"[137] if they stood trial in Rwanda, and upheld an appeal against their extradition. This reasoning followed the earlier decision by the ICTR refusing the transfer of cases to Rwanda and relied heavily on an amicus curiae brief submitted by HRW. During the case, it was brought to the attention of the defense counsel that two of the suspects, Emmanuel Nteziryayo and Celestin Ugirashebuja, had, in fact, been tried in absentia by the *gacaca* courts.

At the time the Rwandan national prosecutors involved in the extradition request did not know that the two accused had been tried by *gacaca*, and as a result pursued independent investigations, interviewing the local *gacaca* judges involved in the decisions. Ugirashebuja's case is of particular interest as he had been acquitted of all charges by a *gacaca* appeals court in the Ruhango sector in the Southern Province. An examination of the *inyangamugayo* statements and the trial transcripts as they related to Ugirashebuja's case provide a remarkable insight into how the *gacaca* courts have asserted their own objectives at points of formal interaction between the courts. The case shows the impact of the divergent interpretations of the work of the courts, illustrating how, at a local level, the *gacaca* courts have asserted the validity of their own actions.

---

136 Brown, Munyaneza, Nteziryayo, and Ugirashebuja v The Government of Rwanda and the Secretary of State for the Home Department, [2009] EWHC 770 (Admin).

137 Ibid. para. 66.

In the UK decision, the judges stated that, given their broader finding on the willingness of witnesses to testify in defense and their concerns around the independence and impartiality of the national courts, they did not need to deal with the *gacaca* cases in much detail, noting only that, "It is not clear whether this surprising turn of events was simply a case of the left hand not knowing what the right was doing, or an indication of something more sinister."[138] An analysis of the record of the *gacaca* interviews conducted by a Rwandan national prosecutor challenges both of these readings, showing that the localized courts were well aware of what they were doing and actively chose to pursue what they understood to be a principled position.

The composition of the *gacaca* appeals court that heard Ugirashebuja's case is, in many ways, typical of the structure of *gacaca* across the country. The bench comprised three men and three women between the ages of thirty to forty-eight, all of whom are subsistence farmers with basic primary school education. As he was a Category 1 suspect, in 2008 Ugirashebuja's case had been transferred from the national courts to be tried by *gacaca*. When interviewed, all of the judges affirmed that they were aware that Ugirashebuja had been arrested in the UK and faced extradition to Rwanda. One of the judges specifically articulated her support for the local adjudication of the case,

> I remember that we even mentioned it [the extradition] while we were chatting, wondering whether he will be extradited and be judged here. We were wondering how the case would be judged here, face to face. It was a hot debate topic.[139]

In addition, all of the judges affirmed what they saw as the robust nature of the *gacaca* process in determining individual involvement in the genocide. In the words of the President of the *inyangamugayo*:

> There were several witnesses on the side of the defence. Witnesses on the side of the defence included four prisoners and other local residents. Those prisoners had been summoned at the request of Moise [a witness testifying against the accused], allegedly because they were the ones who implemented the orders given by Ugirashebuja. When they were questioned they said they were not incited into killing by Ugirashebuja . . . After hearing testimonies from all the witnesses, we retired and concluded the case. We reached the conclusion on a consensus that the defendant was not guilty of any offences he was accused of and he was acquitted of all the offences accused of in Rwonga sector.[140]

---

[138] Ibid. para. 146.

[139] Interview with *Inyangamugayo* (Kigali, Rwanda, December 6, 2008). Interview conducted by Odethie Birungi, Prosecutor at the Head Office of the Parquet General of the Republic of Rwanda. Official English translation provided by Oliver Mpumuro on file with author.

[140] Interview with *Inyangamugayo* (Kigali, Rwanda, December 19, 2008). Interview conducted by Odethie Birungi, Prosecutor at the Head Office of the Parquet General of the Republic of Rwanda. Official English translation provided by Justin Nsabimana on file with author.

This statement was made to a Rwandan national prosecutor; it offers a clear and assertive defense of the *gacaca* proceedings, highlighting the role of exculpatory evidence and the specific localized nature of the enquiry. It is not a case of the left hand not knowing what the right is doing: it is a case of the right hand asserting its value and prioritizing its own activities.

As with the application for the transfer of cases from the ICTR to Rwanda, the extradition of four suspects from the UK would have signaled a vote of confidence in the capacity of the Rwandan domestic judges. As discussed in the previous chapter, the current professional capacity of the Rwandan judges and lawyers is central to how the courts have tried to assert their own contribution during the transitional period. The *gacaca* courts' trial of the suspects jeopardized the possibility of this extradition. However, the decision by the *gacaca* judges to try Nteziryayo and Ugirashebuja in absentia was in line with one of the central objectives of *gacaca*: to better understand the conflict through providing full information about the genocide-related events in the specific location where the violence occurred and where those involved in the trial live.

When the *gacaca* trial proceedings were brought to the national courts' attention, the *inyangamugayo* took the opportunity to assert the value of their own work to the national prosecutors. Based on the jurisdictional primacy of the national courts and the claim that if the location of the accused was known, he should not have been tried in absentia, the *gacaca* decisions were nullified. But the conflict between the national court proceedings and *gacaca* shows the impact of the divergent understandings of Rwanda's transitional justice processes on the actions of the local and national courts. At points of interaction between the ICTR, the national courts *gacaca,* and, in this instance, a further foreign jurisdiction, the courts have not automatically complemented one another, but often directly been in conflict. Each court has consistently prioritized its own objectives and evaluated the other courts in light of this orientation, resulting in conflicting proceedings and direct criticisms among the post-genocide courts.

6. Conclusion

This chapter firmly embeds *gacaca* within its local context. To understand *gacaca* exclusively as a top-down, culturally inconsistent form of state coercion, as various commentators do, neglects the devolved structure of the process and the agency of those involved in the adjudication of the crimes. When taken on its terms—and those of its personnel—*gacaca* was established as a response to the failures of "classical justice." Despite a myriad of initial objectives, by 2009, *gacaca* was principally understood to aid in establishing the truth about the genocide. However, how *gacaca* was explained at the center differs from how it has been implemented at the margins.

In Kigali, at the central offices of the NSGJ there was a focus on the macro account of the genocide, an account that tended toward the official reading of history that favors the current ruling party. In contrast, at the lower levels among the *inyangamugayo, gacaca* has been used more specifically as a means to respond to, acknowledge, and explore particular crimes. At this level, where the trials are adjudicated, there is a shift in the interpretation of transitional justice away from the broader objectives of establishing an overall understanding of the conflict, fighting impunity, and reconciling Rwandans, to a more specific discussion of particular violent events in specific locations. This suggests that the practice of *gacaca* itself has shaped how the contributions of transitional justice are understood within the local courts. However, the determination of this "truth" has relied heavily on the active participation of the General Assembly and on confessions offered by particular accused. Consistent with the historical exercise of power in Rwanda, local ties have been drawn on to both restrict and encourage testimony, and the weight of the fair adjudication of a particular case has rested heavily on the shoulders of the *inyangamugayo*.

As with the ICTR and the national courts, there are acknowledged practical constraints on *gacaca*. These constraints were readily articulated by all involved in the process, including those based centrally in the NSGJ, and those determining the cases at the local level. In the discussions of the courts' contributions and challenges, what is most apparent is that the operation of *gacaca* is intimately connected with the genocide itself and with a widely supported need to have some formal response to the violence of the genocide.

There was some variation in the understood objectives and the practice of the courts in the different research sites. This variation illuminates the agency of the *gacaca* judges in directing the activities of specific courts. However, the variation among the courts has also led to criticisms of *gacaca's* work and has impacted upon *gacaca's* engagement with the concurrent justice processes. Inside the Rwandan prisons, although the localization of the courts was seen as a strength, the variability among their practice was criticized.

Within the *gacaca* courts, the critiques against the ICTR and the national courts were based on *gacaca's* own understood objectives. This is a similar phenomenon to that found inside the ICTR and the national courts. At points of formal interaction between the courts, each court has focused on its own understood objectives, leading to competition among the ICTR, the national courts, and *gacaca*. If, as the current literature and legal practice of the ICC suggests, international, national, and local transitional justice processes are to effectively complement one another, this research suggests it is necessary to have an ongoing dialogue regarding the objectives of these concurrent processes. In addition, an examination of how the courts have interacted with one another must be grounded in a deep contextual understanding of what each justice process has been understood to achieve. Having established this basis, the next chapter explores why the three Rwandan courts have been understood to pursue such distinct objectives, and the implications of these competing conceptions for the legitimacy of the courts' activities.

5 Legitimating Transitional Justice in Rwanda

1. Introduction

The previous three chapters have given a detailed account of how the legal actors of Rwanda's post-genocide courts have ascribed meaning to their practices. What emerges from the empirical data is that, internally, the courts have been understood to pursue very different objectives. The ICTR, the national courts, and *gacaca* do not exercise jurisdictional challenges to one another, and purport to pursue complementary objectives. However, the courts' practice has led to a divergence in their objectives and increased competition among the courts. The ICTR has been principally concerned with the development of international jurisprudence. The national courts have focused on domestic legal reform, while the personnel inside *gacaca* have viewed their central contribution as obtaining a better local understanding of the conflict. Within each system, how one process is justified affects how the others are viewed and understood, resulting in the courts raising severe criticisms against one another and impacting their interactions.

Why have the judges and lawyers inside the judicial institutions all articulated a narrower set of objectives than those initially envisaged in the courts' founding documents? Part of the answer is given by the practical constraints identified by these participants and laid out in the earlier chapters. Transitional justice processes are difficult to implement, and all three courts have faced numerous challenges that have constrained participants' understandings of what can be achieved. This, however, takes us only halfway. The aggregated empirical data shows that within the institutions, certain attainable contributions are given priority over others; for example, the ICTR has focused on the development of international case law above its understood contribution to removing key players from the political arena. It will be argued in this final chapter that the courts' dominant ascriptions of meaning can usefully be understood as a means of legitimation.

Throughout the transitional period, the ICTR, the Rwandan national courts and *gacaca* have been attempting to establish their legitimacy to exercise power over the Rwandan population. This chapter argues that the courts have attempted to legitimate their work in different ways. These different means of self-legitimation explain the divergent interpretations of the courts' actions, apparent in the empirical research.[1] Yet, all three concurrent courts respond to a single conflict. Inside the prisons and among a group of general Rwandan participants, the legitimacy of all three of the courts has been based on their perceived ability to meet the needs of everyday citizens, and has been challenged by the popular practice of criticizing one court through reference to the actions of the concurrent institutions. In trying to establish their own legitimacy, the ICTR, the national courts, and *gacaca* have simultaneously challenged the legitimacy of the concurrent institutions.

In a transitional period, the legitimacy of the courts is often in question, and Rwanda is no exception. The authority of the Rwandan state to exercise power over the population was fractured during the genocide. Since the RPF gained effective control of Rwanda in July 1994, the government has embarked on a process of establishing its authority to rule. The courts have played a key role in this process. As discussed from the outset of this book, the RPF gained power through a military victory. As it was an unelected ruling force, this immediately raised questions over the legitimacy of its power.[2]

Delegitimation of the previous regime has been crucial in establishing the current government's political control. The brutal crimes of the genocide and the involvement of the previous ruling elite in these crimes provided one basis for such an exercise. As a result, since 1994, criminal law has been central to the Rwandan state's exercise of power. The legitimacy of these legal institutions is therefore of central importance to the exercise of power during the transition following the genocide. In addition, as highlighted in Chapter 2, the establishment of the ICTR responded to the legitimacy deficit of those exercising authority. Following the UN's failure to protect civilians in the lead-up to and during the genocide, the Security Council similarly turned to a legal institution to re-establish the authority of the international community, in this instance, principally a moral authority requiring condemnation of human rights abuse.

The grounded empirical research laid out in this book can be used to explain how the ICTR, the national courts, and *gacaca* have attempted to legitimize themselves. This explanation is structured around three points. First, it is established that David Beetham's

---

[1] As discussed below, the term "self-legitimation" is drawn from Rodney Barker, *Legitimating Identities: The Self-Preservation of Rulers and Subjects* (Cambridge University Press 2001).

[2] Filip Reyntjens, "Rwanda, Ten Years On: From Genocide to Dictatorship" (2004) 103 African Affairs 177.

theory of legitimacy is useful in interpreting the work of the post-genocide courts. Second, in the application of Beetham's theory, the different objectives emphasized inside the three courts can be explained as three alternative means of legitimation. This analysis provides initial insights into how and where the legitimacy of the ICTR, the national courts, and *gacaca* has been eroded. Third, it is argued that the legitimacy of all three of the courts could have been strengthened if the courts had focused on, and supported one another in, providing evidence about the genocide and civil war to the affected population.

2. Legitimacy and Transitional Justice

Rodney Barker argues that while legitimacy is an ascribed attribute, legitimation is the action of ascribing. For Barker self-legitimation consists of the actions that those in power take "to insist on or demonstrate, as much to themselves as to others, that they are justified in the pattern of actions that they follow."[3] While Barker usefully draws attention to the value of describing the action of legitimation that aids in interpreting how the ICTR, national court, and *gacaca's* judges and lawyers have made sense of their own work, Beetham's work attempts not only to discuss legitimacy empirically but also normatively. Beetham's theory of legitimacy helps to illuminate how the courts have embarked on the activities of legitimating their authority while also bringing attention to where the courts' authority has been challenged or eroded.

Drawing strongly on Max Weber, Beetham argues that legitimacy comprises three distinct elements. To be legitimate, the exercise of power must (1) conform to established rules, (2) the rules must be justified by reference to beliefs shared by both dominant and subordinate parties in the power relation, and (3) there must be evidence of consent by the subordinate to that particular relationship.[4] As Kieran McEvoy succinctly summarizes, these elements delineate the legal, moral, and sociological dimensions of the legitimate exercise of power.[5]

This multidimensional structure provides "a guide to identifying the specificity of particular historical forms of legitimation, and to making judgments about legitimacy-in-context, as part of the explanatory enterprise."[6] The use of this guide allows for a determination of how transitional justice institutions have attempted to establish their legitimacy, and how and where it has been eroded. As Clifford Geertz's interpretive concept of culture guided the explanation of the social data collected inside the ICTR, the national courts, and *gacaca*, so Beetham's understanding of legitimacy provides a means to better describe the data's theoretical importance.

---

[3] Barker 30.

[4] David Beetham, *The Legitimation of Power* (Peter Jones and Albert Weale eds, MacMillan 1991) 15–16.

[5] Kieran McEvoy, "A Commentary on Locality and Legitimacy" in Oxford Transitional Justice Research (ed), *Critical Perspectives in Transitional Justice* (Intersentia 2011).

[6] Beetham 245.

This is central to the exercise of socially grounded legal research. The empirical data illuminating the legal cultures of the courts provides the descriptive basis from which normative judgments about the legitimacy of post-genocide justice in Rwanda can be drawn.[7] As Denis J. Galligan writes,

> Theoretical concepts can be the basis for classifying and making sense of social data . . . The process is reflexive, for it may be that the particular case shows up something new that has not been accounted for in the general theory, or that aspects of the theory are based on mistakes or misunderstandings.[8]

The use of Beetham's theory of legitimacy in this examination of transitional justice in Rwanda allows for a grounded theoretical contribution to the literature on the role and actions of legal institutions during transitions. The research shows why the cultures of legal institutions matter. Legal institutions are central to understanding the legitimation of power during transitional periods. The objectives of a set of legal rules shape and are shaped by their practice inside the legal cultures of particular judicial institutions, influencing the capacity of multiple concurrent or sequenced transitional justice processes to operate concurrently.

In a transitional context, courts engage in an active process of self-legitimation but continue to be evaluated against the interests and beliefs of the people subordinate to their authority. The legitimacy of the courts can and should be reinforced through more effective debate and criticism among the international, national, and local systems to avoid one court's objectives militating against what another court is trying to achieve. However, for these processes to be legitimate, they must be consistent with the beliefs and interests of the people who are subordinate to the courts' authority. The empirical understandings of transitional justice in Rwanda, laid out in the next section, form the basis of these theoretical insights into the legitimate exercise of power during a transition.

3. Legitimating the ICTR

According to Beetham, the first condition of legitimacy is that power should be acquired and exercised in accordance with established rules. The rules relating to the ICTR are drawn from its Statute, the Rules of Evidence and Procedure, and the resultant case law. Conformity with these rules has provided the touchstone for the institution's legitimacy. In Beetham's view, a generalized respect for the rules allows for the functioning of the institution, as they establish a degree of "social order or settled expectation."[9]

---

[7] David Garland, *Punishment and Modern Society: A Study in Social Theory* (Oxford University Press 1990) 10.

[8] Denis J. Galligan, *Law in Modern Society* (Oxford University Press 2007).

[9] Beetham 69.

Security Council Resolution 955 and the resultant rules provide the first ground for the ICTR's legitimate exercise of power, and empirically, these rules emerge as central to the judges and lawyers working inside the institution.

When the ICTY and the ICTR were established, it was not universally accepted that they had legitimate authority over citizens of Rwanda and the former Yugoslavia, respectively. The courts' authority was not based on treaty law, but rather on the shakier ground of Security Council Resolutions. They were ad hoc in nature and did not have a body of case law to draw on for either the definition or application of war crimes, crimes against humanity, or genocide. The Nuremberg trials had taken place many years before and, with the particularities of history, they offered only very limited guidance.[10] Yet, there was a growing call for the exercise of legal authority over the individuals involved in the horrific acts in the Balkans, and an even louder iteration following the Rwandan tragedy. As a result, there was a clear need for a set of rules through which to exercise authority over these individuals. The establishment of these rules, through the Statute and the Rules of Evidence and Procedure, and the gradual development of international case law, was of huge initial significance to the legitimacy of the ICTR. The important empirical observation is that twenty years later they have remained so.

As established in Chapter 2, most participants within the ICTR identified the development of international case law as the court's central contribution. The establishment of the rules and their consistent application are of principal importance to the actors inside this institution. They provide the court with a means of legitimating their authority. In the words of one of the ICTR participants,

> Apart from the specific function of adjudicating on the cases that are before the court, we have developed a broad body of jurisprudence and practice in the prosecution of international crimes of this nature.[11]

There was a focus not only on the development of the case law, but within this, the careful application of the relevant procedural rules. However, conformity to a set of rules is only the first step in Beetham's construction of the legitimate exercise of power: "Rules cannot justify themselves simply by being rules, but require justification by reference to considerations which lie beyond them."[12]

If it is accepted that the rules have to be justifiable, the first question is: Justifiable to whom? In any power relation, there is a dominant and subordinate actor or group: one who exercises authority over another. However, in the case of the ICTR as a supranational

---

[10] Kevin Jon Heller, *The Nuremberg Military Tribunals and the Origins of International Criminal Law* (Oxford University Press 2011) 3.

[11] Interview with Member of Chambers (Participant 21), Chambers, UN ICTR (Arusha, Tanzania, July 25, 2008) notes on file with author.

[12] Beetham 69.

institution, the position of subordinate and dominant is not entirely clear. The intuitive answer is that if the ICTR is dominant, then the subordinate party refers to those people within the personal jurisdiction of the court, and those who can be summoned to come before it. However, this group also includes the states, which, under Article 28 of the Tribunal's Statute, must offer the court full cooperation. This means that for the action of the ICTR to be legitimate, the rules must be justified in terms of a shared belief, and serve a common interest of the Rwandan citizenry, the Rwandan state (which is the principal body from which cooperation is needed), and the UN. Further complicating the issue, this shared belief and common interest must extend to citizens of other states and the states themselves, which, at a given moment, may be required to cooperate with the international court. Finally, all of these parties must demonstrate their acceptance of the authority of the ICTR through their express consent to its power.

A global shared belief and the universal interest in the prevention of genocide could be drawn on to establish the moral legitimacy of the ICTR; however, these assertions are fragile. As Paul Roberts and Nesam McMillan note in their discussion of the juristic paradigm of international criminal justice, "A global community of penal sentiment is elusive and probably, at this time, illusory."[13] In addition, an articulation of the universal interest in the prevention of genocide did not emerge through the empirical study. Instead there was a strong focus on the establishment and development of international case law, suggesting that the ICTR has principally tried to establish its authority through Beetham's first criterion, that the institution's power is acquired and exercised according to established rules.

If legitimacy is principally derived from the rules, the dominant power, in this case assumed to be the ICTR, can be less concerned with the subordinate party. It provides an internal means of legitimating the court's power. As Beetham argues,

> The much readier access of the powerful to the law, and the fact that it provides both the source and protection of their power, makes appeal to the law as the ground of legitimacy a particularly favoured strategy for the dominant group.[14]

However,

> The more that the powerful appeal to the law as a self-sufficient justification of their power, the more they [the dominant] have to respect it themselves for their legitimacy to be sustained.[15]

---

[13] Paul Roberts and Nesam McMillan, "For Criminology in International Criminal Justice" (2003) 1 Journal of International Criminal Justice 315, 330.

[14] Beetham 67.

[15] Ibid. 68.

This plays out in the action of the ICTR, which, as Robinson notes, has been "scrupulously generous"[16] in upholding procedural rights. In this way, Beetham's evaluation of legitimacy provides an important theoretical insight into the empirical focus by participants at the ICTR on the establishment of the rules and on the court's careful adherence to due process. Beetham's theory helps to explain the social data and suggests that during periods of rapid domestic change, international criminal courts will engage in an active process of legitimation through focusing on the application and development of legal rules.

4. Legitimating the National Courts

Some commentators would argue that the Rwandan national courts fall at the first legitimacy hurdle, failing to meet the criterion of conformity to a set of rules. There have been allegations of executive involvement in politically sensitive cases, most recently with the arrest of opposition leader, Victoire Ingabire, and her American counsel, Peter Erlinder. International NGOs and academics have questioned the independence of the Rwandan judiciary[17] and its ability to provide an effective balance to executive power. At a fundamental level these arguments center on the consolidation of power in the position of the president, allowing Kagame to exert significant sway and political pressure on all arms of government.[18]

Yet, as established in Chapter 3, clear rules for the national prosecution of international crimes were laid out, and were supported both inside and outside of the country. Despite initial criticism, the resultant rules of the 1996 Organic Law were applied with increasing conformity.[19] Inside Rwanda, power over those accused of participation in genocide-related crimes has been "acquired and exercised in accordance with established rules."[20] This does not mean, though, that such power is legitimate, but suggests that there is potential for a deeper analysis of the courts' justification of their authority. The national courts currently exert significant authority over the Rwandan citizens and have actively attempted to assert their legitimate use of this power. As a result, it is important to understand how such legitimation has happened, and if and where it has been eroded.

The national courts' judges and lawyers most often identified the 2004 reforms requiring higher standards of education in the legal profession as the

[16] Darryl Robinson, "The Identity Crisis of International Criminal Law" (2008) 21 Leiden Journal of International Law 925, 927.

[17] Human Rights Watch, "Law and Reality: Progress on Judicial Reform in Rwanda" (Report) (July 2008).

[18] Filip Reyntjens, "Constructing the Truth, Dealing with Dissent, Domesticating the World: Governance in Post-Genocide Rwanda" (2011) 110 African Affairs 1.

[19] M. Moussalli, "Report on the Situation of Human Rights in Rwanda" (Report) (25 February 2000) Economic and Social Council E/CN.4/2000/41, 27.

[20] Beetham 64.

central contribution of the courts to the transitional period. In practice there have been extensive judicial reforms during that time. The most notable of these reforms, not regularly mentioned by participants, is the promulgation of the new Constitution in May 2003.[21] The Constitution formed the basis for many of the reforms introduced the following year. It is therefore of particular analytical interest that the participants within the national courts focused on improved judicial training as the principal reform. Why is there not more direct reference to the new Constitution and the compliance of Rwandan law with international legal standards? In Chapter 3, it was argued that the courts' focus on judicial education could, in part, be explained as a means of circumventing the earlier critiques raised against their work. In addition, this empirical finding can be usefully examined in terms of legitimacy and how the national courts have attempted to establish their authority.

Unlike the ICTR, conformity with the newly established legal rules did not emerge empirically as the principal contribution of the national courts to the transitional period. The national courts' clear focus on improved legal education is better explained through the justifiability of these rules in terms of Beetham's second criterion, a shared belief between the dominant and subordinate parties. In this instance, the subordinate group clearly relates to all persons in the territory of Rwanda who are subject to domestic law. A strong focus by participants on the new Constitution and the adherence of the Rwandan legislative framework to international law would have suggested that the courts relied heavily on the first criterion of legitimacy, derived from rules, as seen in the ICTR's continued focus on these rules. But as demonstrated, this was not the dominant understanding inside the national courts. The improvement in the courts' practice was asserted through a focus on the development of judicial capacity. This suggests a different means of legitimating the courts' power. It draws attention to an understanding of legitimacy through a shared belief between the dominant and subordinate group. The Rwandan judges and lawyers appeal to the high social value attached to education in Rwanda.

The empirical data indicates a strong reference among the national courts' judges and lawyers to the importance of legal education and training. This is what Beetham would term an "external belief" in "scientific doctrine."[22] Based on their legal expertise and required education level, participants within the courts argued that they are able to exercise legitimate power over people in the territory of Rwanda. However, as Beetham identifies, external technocratic expertise "works in an anti-democratic direction, by assigning the power of decision-making to the expert at the expense of the citizen, and to the professional at the expense of the lay person"[23] Within Beetham's normative construct of what constitutes legitimate power, this moral justification of the courts' authority requires the application of merit-based principles in the selection of those who

[21] Constitution of the Republic of Rwanda, Law No. Special of 2/05/2003.

[22] Beetham 64.

[23] Ibid.

participate in the training. This would need to be coupled with a consultative determination of the applicable legal rules, freely open to all citizens.[24]

Initially, a remarkable characteristic among the newly trained magistrates in national courts was that, in the first few years, the candidates came forward from both ethnic groups, initially resulting in ethnic diversity on the bench and broad access to the educational opportunities this position held.[25] However, it is unclear if there was a continuation of this trend, and such an observation was made before both the start of *gacaca* and the major 2004 judicial reforms. The use of Beetham's theoretical framework shows that "in-context," there remain challenges to the legitimacy of the Rwandan judiciary. The major challenge is the potential limitation of education and training to a narrow part of the population, that of an RPF-aligned, predominantly Tutsi elite, many of whom were outside the country at the time of the genocide. If educational and technical expertise continues to be drawn on as a means of legitimation, access to legal educational opportunities must be broadly available, and advancement through the legal profession must be based on merit.

At first glance, the *gacaca* courts could be seen to respond to the weakness in or erosion of the legitimacy of the national courts through their introduction of locally elected lay judges. The national courts, relying on technical expertise, move in an antidemocratic direction. Given the social context of Rwanda, where power has generally remained in the hands of a small elite, there is the potential for weaknesses in the equal access to such educational opportunities, challenging this means of legitimation. *Gacaca* claims to open up these opportunities through the popular election of the *inyangamugayo*. However, *gacaca* too requires a more careful evaluation of the institution's process of legitimation.

5. Legitimating the *Gacaca* Courts

The post-genocide *gacaca* courts were established by domestic legislation, amended several times after promulgation. The law itself has played an important role in establishing a degree of "social order or settled expectation"[26] in the process of trying genocide suspects. As one elderly *inyangamugayo* articulated, "Having the laws was important because then they were understood by everyone. Even the *gacaca* before, it had clear laws but they were

[24] In establishing his theory of legitimacy, Beetham identifies a spectrum of rule characteristics that he argues move in a legitimating direction. Central to this normative hierarchy of characteristics is the position that the more open the rules are to "criticism and revision by the decision of equal citizens," the more legitimate the exercise of power through these rules. Beetham, at the time, was writing at the end of the Cold War and arguing for a global democratic order.

[25] International Crisis Group, "Five Years after the Genocide in Rwanda: Justice in Question" (Report) (7 April 1999) 8.

[26] Beetham 69.

just not written."[27] The judges at all the hearings I attended used a copy of the most recent Organic Law, and the later *gacaca* trials have seen an increasing reference to the legislation itself. As noted in Chapter 4, the transfer of Category 1 cases from the national courts to *gacaca* saw an increase in the formalism of the courts with a more uniform set of proceedings. In part, this was a response to the national courts' own focus on legal professionalism. However, the amendments to the Organic Law have resulted in some legal uncertainty, and there has been extensive discretion in the interpretation of these laws. One of the *gacaca* personnel I interviewed discussed the implications of this uncertainty:

> It was a challenge to understand the reason for the special laws. There were some opportunities to train the *inyangamugayo,* but the law has been revised. Very often it was difficult to understand the detail of these modifications. Collectively, as *inyangamugayo,* we would discuss to try and have a common understanding, what does the law say exactly? What is the meaning of this added fact? This was discussed in the meetings for the *inyangamugayo.*[28]

Bert Ingelaere similarly notes the openness of the government to adjusting *gacaca's* rules over the course of its operation, although he concludes that, "All in all, however, the modifications have come about rather slowly and are relatively minor."[29] The rules have remained clear and relatively settled. This, however, does not make them legitimate.

Despite the *gacaca* courts' move toward legal formalism, empirically, the written law was not the means of legitimation articulated by either the personnel working inside the NSGJ or the *gacaca* judges adjudicating the hearings. As with the national courts, the focus of the *gacaca* judges and lawyers is better explained through Beetham's second criterion, namely, the justifiability of the rule content through reference to beliefs and interests shared by those exercising power and those subject to it. The *gacaca* personnel identified two dominant contributions: *gacaca* has been understood to aid in obtaining a better understanding of the "truth" of the conflict and in the provision of a legal process for those accused of genocide. As one legal officer articulated this common interest, "*Gacaca* has contributed to a process, a process for those accused."[30]

The personnel exercising the authority of the courts have drawn on what they understand as a common interest among Rwandans in having a legal process that provides further information about the conflict at a local level. The strength of this claim depends

---

[27] Interview with *Inyangamugayo* (Participant 30) (Rural District, Northern Province, Rwanda, March 20, 2009) notes on file with author.

[28] Interview with *Inyangamugayo* (Participant 15) (Kigali, Rwanda, March 10, 2009) notes on file with author.

[29] Bert Ingelaere, "The Gacaca Courts in Rwanda" in Luc Huyse and Mark Salter (eds), *Traditional Justice and Reconciliation after Violent Conflict: Learning from African Experiences* (International Institute for Democracy and Electoral Assistance 2008) 52.

[30] Informal discussion with National Service for Gacaca Courts Legal Officer (Participant 21) (Kigali, Rwanda, March 11, 2009) notes on file with author.

on whether the people subject to the courts' authority identify a similar common interest. The next section of this chapter examines a broader set of popular views on the ICTR, the national courts, and *gacaca*. As will be discussed, the coding of this interview material showed a popular understanding that Rwandan transitional justice needed to provide a full and truthful account of the genocide and civil war. To some extent this maps onto the objectives articulated inside of *gacaca,* and where the localized courts were understood to meet this need their legitimacy was significantly strengthened. First, however, understanding the attempted legitimation of *gacaca's* power within the legal institution explains the state's response to everyday Rwandans' engagement with *gacaca,* and highlights where *gacaca's* authority has been challenged.

The erosion of, or weakness in, *gacaca's* legitimating process turns on Beetham's final requirement: express consent. Specific actions "confer legitimacy because they constitute public expression by the subordinate of their consent to the power relationship, and their subordinate position within it."[31] Within Beetham's theoretical framework, the legitimacy of *gacaca* relies on continued expressive consent. The modus operandi of the courts requires that people show their acceptance of the courts' authority through attending and actively participating in the hearings. However, both of these activities are potentially costly.

In the predominantly subsistence farming communities of rural Rwanda, one day every week spent at *gacaca* reduces potential productivity. In addition, speaking out at a hearing may have local repercussions. As one participant quoted earlier said at a hearing,

> People keep quiet, they are scared to speak . . . people don't talk because they might not be understood.[32]

A weakness in *gacaca's* legitimating process is highlighted by the stringent requirement of weekly attendance and active participation as the means of expressive consent. This has implications for the work of those inside the *gacaca* court structures. As detailed in Chapter 4, the major practical challenges, readily identified by those working for the courts, related to both participation and silence. In the final stages of *gacaca,* I attended hearings in which only the affected parties and their direct family members were present. At another hearing, although attendance was high, few General Assembly members were willing to speak.

The failure to attend *gacaca* or the choice not to actively participate in the hearings every week challenges the legitimacy of the courts. People may have attended and spoken at the cases that pertained to their personal experience of the genocide, but then chose not to attend the other cases. One genocide survivor I interviewed related this

---

[31] Beetham 91.

[32] Informal discussion with *gacaca* participant (Participant 15) (Rural District, Northern Province, Rwanda, April 15, 2009) notes on file with author.

particular experience.[33] In addition, people may have provided information at the lowest administrative level during the information stage of *gacaca* and then been reluctant to repeat this evidence during the more formal trial stage because of the continued requirement of weekly participation or the emotional strain and trauma of providing testimony.[34] Regardless of these understandable constraints, the failure of continued express consent remains a problem for the state and the legitimacy of the *gacaca* courts.

This theoretical examination of the legitimation of the *gacaca* process helps to explain the strong stance local authorities have taken when there is either silence or low participation in *gacaca* hearings. Extracts from a hearing I attended illuminate this point, as the NSGJ personnel berated the local population for failing to provide full consent through active participation in the hearing. The local *gacaca* coordinator made the following public speech in which she directly appealed to the common interests of getting information about the conflict and providing those already incarcerated with a legal process:

> You people here have got a big problem. You do not want to tell the truth, and you know almost everything. Many of you, when I look at you, you were mature at that time but you do not want to testify against, or in favour of the accused, basing it on the truth. And even the one who comes to the front says that the genocide just happened a little. This is denying the genocide. You should tell the truth so that if there is anyone in prison who could be innocent, they can be acquitted, and if there is anyone who is guilty, they can ask for forgiveness and be treated accordingly. In this commune, there is a problem: we do not know where the bodies of the dead are, yet many of you know. Why don't you tell us? You should know that the truth will be revealed.[35]

The coordinator makes direct reference to the common interest of providing a legal process to determine the guilt or innocence of the suspects already incarcerated, and the understood importance of gaining information about the remains of the dead. This is done in an effort to try to establish the express consent of the population to the authority of the courts.

The reliance of the *gacaca* process on express weekly consent has led to increasingly coercive means of participation. The 2004 amendments to the Organic Law introduced fines and potential jail terms for failure to attend or give testimony before *gacaca*. This increased coercion, rather than exclusively interpreted as an example of the repressive and far-reaching nature of the Rwandan state, can usefully be understood as a response

[33] Interview with *gacaca* participant (Participant 17), (Kigali, Rwanda, March 10, 2009) notes on file with author.

[34] K. Brounéus, "Truth-Telling as Talking Cure? Insecurity and Retraumatization in the Rwandan Gacaca Courts" (2008) 39 (1) Security Dialogue 55.

[35] Public address by a local *gacaca* coordinator, author's fieldnotes, Rwanda, April 15, 2009. The phrasing of this speech is reproduced as it was simultaneously transcribed from Kinyarwanda to English during the *gacaca* hearing.

to the erosion of *gacaca's* legitimacy as a result of its dependence on express consent. The interpretations of *gacaca* offered by the NSGJ personnel and the local judges show how *gacaca* has tried to establish its legitimacy during the Rwandan transition. Examining these interpretations as a process to legitimate power highlights the areas in which *gacaca's* authority has been eroded, and better explains the behavior of the Rwandan state in relation to *gacaca*.

The empirical data collected inside each of the three courts illuminates different legal cultures, as each court has been understood to pursue different objectives. At points of interaction among the international, national, and local judicial bodies, these differing cultural contexts have led to direct competition between the institutions, seen in both the tensions around the transfer of cases between jurisdictions and one court's use of the documents gathered in the proceedings of another. Beetham's theory of legitimacy helps to better explain the theoretical importance of this social data: the interpretations of the courts' actions are part of a legitimating process, and examining them as such highlights potential areas where this legitimacy has been eroded. As laid out above, all three post-genocide transitional justice institutions have actively engaged in a process of legitimation. This has resulted in the narrowing of the articulated contributions of the courts. The ICTR, the national courts, and *gacaca* have focused on three different means of establishing their authority. Reflexively, the Rwandan case also highlights the theoretical importance of the role of legal institutions in establishing the legitimate exercise of power during a transitional period.

An interpretive analysis inside the courts has shown that they have engaged in an active process of legitimating their authority. However, the effectiveness of any of the courts' legitimation processes depends on the courts' ability to draw on the shared beliefs and common interests of the citizens over whom they exert their power. The next section examines the implications of the popular interpretations of the ICTR, the national courts, and *gacaca* for the legitimacy of concurrent transitional justice. It examines the courts from the vantage point of the people who are subject to the courts' authority and who have participated in one, two, and, in some instances, all three of these criminal justice processes. Do the legal participants' understandings of the courts' actions align with those who are subject to their authority? Applying Geertz's descriptive point drawn from Gilbert Ryle, when the courts wink (the action), we have determined what meaning they ascribe to such an action. The question now is whether the person who is being winked at shares this understanding.

6. Concurrent Transitional Justice inside Rwanda

This book opened with one man, held in detention in Rwanda, reflecting on his personal experience of all three levels of the post-genocide courts. He is not alone in his experience. As discussed in Chapters 2, 3, and 4, inside the Rwandan prisons, informal interactions among the ICTR, the national courts, and *gacaca* have occurred through a group of participants who have engaged with the concurrent courts. These participants repeatedly highlighted the points of competition between the procedures and objectives of the ICTR, the national courts, and *gacaca*. Similarly, Rwandans who are not incarcerated have also experienced the informal interactions between the courts and criticize one justice process through reference to another. This final section examines how the legitimacy of the ICTR, the national courts, and *gacaca* has been influenced by these popular interpretations of concurrent transitional justice.

The structure of the *gacaca* courts has meant that the majority of the adult population has participated in this transitional justice process, most routinely as members of the General Assembly, but also as judges and, in the case of over 300,000 suspects, as the accused. Rwandans have testified in over 7,000 national court cases trying the crime of genocide and, over a period of sixteen years, these citizens have regularly flown to Arusha to give testimony as witnesses before the ICTR. The extensive involvement of Rwandans in the transitional justice processes provides an important point of intersection between the courts. Most Rwandans have engaged with at least one transitional justice process and ascribe meaning to all three institutions. The population's understandings of what transitional justice should have achieved in Rwanda is central to the legitimacy of the ICTR, the national courts, and *gacaca*.

To examine the legitimacy of the post-genocide courts, this chapter includes the views of people both inside and outside of the prisons who are aware of the three courts' activities. In doing so, it explores the broader popular acceptance of the courts. The chapter draws on the views of the seventeen Rwandan prison participants discussed in earlier chapters and examines them in conjunction with the interpretations of forty-five general participants who attended *gacaca* hearings in the three research sites. Rather than discrete discussions of each of the courts, all of these participants generally made broader statements as to their understanding of the role of post-genocide justice, and evaluated the three courts against these criteria. The courts were most routinely measured against their ability to provide a truthful account of the genocide.

The participants did not emphasize the jurisdictional distinctions among the courts, or acknowledge that, for example, the national courts may have contributed something different to that of *gacaca*, or the ICTR. Both inside the Rwandan prisons and in the Rwandan countryside, the separate contributions of the courts, although clearly articulated within the institutions, were not evident in the popular interpretations of the courts' actions. In addition, critical comparisons were often made among the courts. The most regular criticisms used the domestic processes to challenge the ICTR, but the reverse was also evident. If a belief in the legitimacy of a court is evident in people's not opposing a court's ruling and refraining from attacking the institution,[36] the practice in

[36] J.L. Gibson and G.A. Caldeira, "Defenders of Democracy? Legitimacy, Popular Acceptance, and the South African Constitutional Court" (2003) 65(1) The Journal of Politics 1, 5.

Rwanda of using the processes of one court to criticize the others raises challenges for the legitimacy of all three legal institutions.

These empirical findings show that plural approaches to transitional justice can be accommodated if there is continued exchange among the different actors to resolve disputes at points of formal interactions and misunderstandings at the multiple points of informal interaction. However, all three of the courts would still need to be able to draw on a robust legal, moral, and sociological legitimacy. In Rwanda, the ICTR needed to identify all Rwandans as the Tribunal's clear and relevant population and to actively respond to the beliefs and interests of that community. The national courts needed to provide a means of truth-telling in addition to their strong focus on professionalizing the judiciary, whereas *gacaca* was required to examine as full a set of violations as possible.

The perceived legitimacy of the ICTR, the national courts, and *gacaca* would have been reinforced if all three of the courts took seriously the need for truth-telling articulated by the affected population, although the means of responding to this need could have varied. This research shows that a concurrent system of international, national, and localized justice must be carefully integrated in a particular country's context to holistically respond to the harms committed. If courts fail to do this at points of formal interaction, the courts will compete with one another, and at points of informal interaction, the legitimacy of the whole system will be called into question.

6.1 A REALITY OF CONTINUED DIVISION

Before discussing the broader popular interpretations of the ICTR, the national courts, and *gacaca*, is it is important to note that Rwandans' understandings of the transitional justice processes are influenced by the reality of continued divisions within post-genocide Rwanda. As one participant, a decommissioned-RPF soldier whose family was killed in the genocide, explained,

> When you look around people are smiling, doing their work, but if you get them on their own, there in the back of a house, they will tell you they are suffering . . . Sometimes I see a Hutu and a Tutsi at the same table and they are talking together and I think, "You talked together and then you killed, now you talk again. Will it happen again?"[37]

Among some of the prisoners, the social divisions in Rwanda were articulated in terms of the categories of "survivor" and "accused" rather than through direct reference to any ethnic group. According to Michel, whose views on the courts were discussed in

---

[37] Informal discussion with *gacaca* participant (Participant 17) (Kigali, Rwanda, March 10, 2009) notes on file with author.

Chapter 2, "The problem I am seeing is that if you are released, the survivors find another way of getting you back into jail because some people don't want to let it go."[38] At the same time, Michel described his decision to confess as a request for forgiveness from God. This expression is in tension with the views of some participants who survived the genocide and live with that everyday reality. As one man, a prominent member of the survivor group, *Ibuka,* articulated,

> Forgiveness, peace, reconciliation, the words are very nice. It is like medication for a headache. I am going to survive and it reduces the tension, but it does not cure the problem. My only hope is that we are going to die and the next generation will go forward. They are trying to say good things, but there are no roots to this forgiveness. It is not a bad thing but it is just justice words . . . while for me it is like a headache to just continue to live.[39]

For Ascel, the elderly ICTR witness who in Chapter 2 challenged the external nature of the Tribunal's rules, the divisions in Rwanda were still apparent: "People are still lying to each other," he said. "Is there reconciliation here in Rwanda? No, not the emotional side of it."[40] Acknowledging this division, fear, and scepticism are important in understanding the continued challenges posed by daily interactions in Rwanda. It also means that it is particularly important to see where and how the post-genocide courts' exercise of power over the population has been considered legitimate.

6.2 A CONTRIBUTION TO "TRUTH"

Among the general participants, all three transitional justice institutions were most routinely discussed in terms of their contribution to establishing the "truth" about the conflict. Truth was identified as an objective that all three of the post-genocide courts should have pursued. This differs from the institutional understanding of transitional justice provided inside of the international and domestic courts as discussed in the earlier chapters. Among the judges and lawyer working inside both the ICTR and the national courts, the term "truth" was not invoked in the descriptions of the courts' contributions to the Rwandan transitional period. Among the ICTR judges and lawyers, it was implied that the legal findings in an individual case were the most accurate and truthful account of these events. However, the ICTR's contribution to establishing a

---

[38] Interview with Michel (Participant 4) (Rural District, Northern Province, Rwanda, September 5, 2009) notes on file with author.

[39] Interview with *gacaca* participant (Participant 16) (Kigali, Rwanda, March 19, 2009) notes on file with author.

[40] Interview with Ascel (Participant 2) (Rural District, Northern Province, Rwanda, September 5, 2009) notes on file with author.

broader historical record of the genocide was deeply contested, and some participants argued that it should not have been an objective of the court's work.

Inside the national courts, the focus of the Rwandan judges and lawyers was more forward-looking. The courts were oriented toward current legal capacity building, rather than the backward-looking establishment of facts. Inside *gacaca,* although the NSGJ personnel and the *gacaca* judges explicitly discussed *gacaca's* contribution to "truth-seeking," there were differences at the national and local levels. In the central offices in Kigali, there was a focus on generating a national consensus on how and why the genocide occurred, while in the rural areas, "truth" more specifically related to the naming of individual victims and the perpetrators. Although these different interpretations are very clear inside the institutions and have led to points of competition among the courts in their formal interactions, for the general Rwandan participants, all three of the courts were evaluated in terms of their ability to establish the truth about the conflict.

As one general participant at a *gacaca* hearing stated, "It is important for the victim to hear what has happened, for there to be truth. That can somehow set the victim and the perpetrator free."[41] Similarly, inside the prisons, there was a clear articulation of the importance of truth in a justice process. In Aloys's words, "Justice, as I know it, is a way of getting truth, if it is real justice. If you get truth, you then live with one another correctly."[42] As discussed earlier, Aloys had been tried by the national courts, and stated a strong preference for his case to remain in the jurisdiction of these courts rather than being transferred to *gacaca*.

The majority of respondents emphasized the importance of any transitional justice process establishing the "truth" of the crimes committed during the conflict. In part this is because of the breadth of the concept itself. Pursuing the "truth" can mean many things to different people, allowing for a wide range of interpretations in a society still grappling with real social divisions. The Rwandan participants' understandings of "truth" were often highly subjective, relating to each person's individual experience of the conflict, or his or her personal participation in the post-genocide trials. The ambiguity in the use of the word "truth-seeking" in describing what the Rwandan transitional justice processes should pursue, as Lawrence Rosen notes in his discussion of "creating facts," may allow for uncertainty that "is partly about seeking truth, partly about defusing conflict, partly about maintaining a workable sense of one's experience of the world—and all about stitching together law and culture so that each informs and supports the other."[43]

---

41 Informal discussion with *gacaca* participant (Participant 4) (Kigali, Rwanda, March 14, 2009) notes on file with author.

42 Interview with Aloys (Participant 11) (Kigali, Rwanda, April 20, 2009) notes on file with author.

43 Lawrence Rosen, *Law as Culture: An Invitation* (Princeton University Press 2006) 93.

For some participants, the establishment of truth related to the determination of an individual's involvement in the conflict. As one genocide survivor in Kigali said, "Before [*gacaca*] many people were saying that the people in jail were all innocent, or that they had just committed property crimes. Today, this cannot happen."[44] Another *gacaca* participant in the Northern Province articulated the corollary: "Before there were many people in jail, those who were innocent and just locked up. Now they have been released, and those who were guilty have been locked up."[45]

For the participants who have been subject to the authority of the ICTR, the national courts, and *gacaca*, the focus was clearly on the role that transitional justice processes can, and should, play in delving into the causes and episodes of the civil war and genocide. In 2008–2009, none of the participants, either inside or outside of the prisons, argued that there should not have been any judicial process for trying offenders at both senior and lower levels. *Gacaca*, the national courts, and the ICTR were all evaluated against the perceived need for some sort of justice process. The work of the ICTR, the national courts, and *gacaca* was valued in terms of the participants' common interest in having further information about why and how the conflict happened and who was involved. The legitimacy of transitional justice in Rwanda was bolstered when the courts were perceived as having responded to this commonly articulated need.

In addition, the main challenges to all three of the courts were discussed in terms of truth. Critiques were raised against *gacaca* and its failure to examine all of the harms experienced during the genocide and civil war. Some participants argued that the absence of any trials for war crimes committed by RPF soldiers challenged *gacaca's* contribution to establishing the truth of the conflict. There has been a broad range of harms and losses experienced by Rwandans since 1990, concentrating around the horrors of 1994. The breadth and experience of that loss differs enormously. Together, the ICTR, the national courts, and *gacaca* have addressed a crucial but narrowed spectrum of these losses, constrained by their temporal and subject matter jurisdictions, and at times, by the political climate. The failure of the *gacaca* courts to offer as broad a truth-telling process as possible was challenged by a number of participants. As a young woman at one *gacaca* hearing articulated, "This court [*gacaca*] does not tell the truth, only some of the truth, half of it somehow."[46] From inside the prisons, in the words of Aloys,

> This building of Rwanda while saying you have to pay, but others don't have to pay, is a problem . . . If there is justice for this one, there must be justice for the other.[47]

---

[44] Interview with *gacaca* participant (Participant 16) (Kigali, Rwanda, March 19, 2009) notes on file with author.

[45] Informal discussion with *gacaca* participant (Participant 9) (Rural District, Northern Province, Rwanda, April 1, 2009) notes on file with author.

[46] Informal discussion with *gacaca* participant (Participant 2) (Kigali, Rwanda, March 14, 2009) notes on file with author.

[47] Interview with Aloys (Participant 11) (Kigali, Rwanda, April 20, 2009) notes on file with author.

The criticisms of truth-telling extended to the national courts. As discussed in Chapter 3, inside the prisons, the early trials by the national courts were seen as insufficiently focused on the wide collection of information. In addition, the arrest and removal of key figures to be tried by the ICTR, seen as one of the central contributions inside the international court, was challenged in Rwanda. The removal of leaders to be tried by an international court, and the information their trials may have provided in establishing varied "truths" of the conflict inside Rwanda, led to strong critiques of the ICTR. As Emmanuel, one of the general participants who had testified before all three of the courts, said, "They have information that we need in order to be able understand why Rwandans turned on one another."[48] In the popular interpretations of the ICTR, the national courts, and *gacaca*, general participants were not only making sense of the legal processes, but the processes were understood as a way of making sense of the conflict.

Although critical of the *gacaca* courts, drawing on over a thousand rural-based interviews conducted by his research team, Ingeleare writes, "Ordinary Rwandans prefer the Gacaca courts over the national courts and the ICTR for dealing with the genocide crimes."[49] While Ingelaere speculates that some of the criticisms of the ICTR may be as a result of unfavorable Rwanda government media reports and sensitization campaigns, he concludes that "They sincerely prefer the justice of proximity."[50] This research has taken this position seriously, and having found a similar empirical reality, better explains this behavior. In the face of large-scale incarceration and severe lack of information about who was killed, where, and by whom, all three post-genocide courts were measured against the immediate needs of the courts' general participants to gain more information of how and why the genocide occurred. It was *gacaca's* ability to respond to some of these needs that reinforced its legitimacy, and it is similarly this common interest that the courts have tried to draw on to strengthen their authority. However, the popular practice among the general Rwandan participants of challenging one court in relation to the other courts' actions erodes the legitimacy of concurrent transitional justice in Rwanda as a whole.

6.3 CONFLICTING LEGITIMACY

As discussed, inside the prisons, the concurrent post-genocide courts were directly and routinely compared. As Michel articulated in comparing *gacaca's* and the national courts' contribution to truth-telling, "People like me who went to the classical courts beg to have a chance to go to *gacaca*, because it will reveal the truth . . . In 1997, I feel

---

[48] Interview with *gacaca* participant (Participant 12) (Northern Province, Rwanda, April 1, 2009) notes on file with author.

[49] Ingelaere 51.

[50] Ibid.

that those courts were not seeking for the truth, they were seeking for conviction."[51] In a similar manner, Ascel challenged the ICTR's contribution to truth, comparing the international court's process against the provision of a localized account of the conflict: "People go to Arusha and try to represent the whole village and this is a lie. It is better to go where the problem started from and the people will tell the truth."[52]

Similar direct comparisons were made outside the prisons. After a *gacaca* hearing, two outspoken young men agreed to be interviewed. "Of course we have heard about it [the ICTR]," said Ali, who was in his late twenties and was in Rwanda at the time of the genocide, "but it happens a long way away. We come here [to *gacaca*], this case takes two days but there it takes a very long time."[53] Emmanuel, his companion who had testified before the ICTR, agreed:

> It is a political thing. Perhaps your question is something that you should ask the people at the top, but of course we have our views . . . The leaders they are sitting there in Arusha, they don't want Rwanda to develop, they were leading it so that Rwandans killed one another.[54]

The popular use of one justice process to criticize another suggests that the concurrent work of the post-genocide courts has competed for legitimate authority inside Rwanda. Although the participants' comparisons often favored the domestic process, this was not always the case. As noted in discussion with Alphonse in the Kigali Central Prison,

> *Gacaca* doesn't give you enough flexibility, you are driving but you are between two walls . . . Arusha, I have been there. Arusha is a good answer to the problems with *gacaca*. They are getting real justice because they take time to analyse what happened. If you are guilty there, then you are really guilty.[55]

Transitional justice in Rwanda is not concerned with three different conflicts, but with a single conflict dealt with through three different courts. The institutional separation of the more senior accused and the separation of what the courts are trying to achieve is not a separation that is made in the understandings of transitional justice expressed

---

51 Interview with Michel (Participant 4) (Rural District, Northern Province, Rwanda, September 5, 2009) notes on file with author.

52 Interview with Ascel (Participant 2) (Rural District, Northern Province, Rwanda, September 5, 2008) notes on file with author.

53 Interview with *gacaca* participant (Participant 11) (Northern Province, Rwanda, April 1, 2009) notes on file with author.

54 Interview with *gacaca* participant (Participant 12) (Northern Province, Rwanda, April 1, 2009) notes on file with author.

55 Interview with Alphonse (Participant 9) (Kigali, Rwanda, April 20, 2009) notes on file with author.

by everyday Rwandan interviewees. It is, however, a separation that is made inside the ICTR, the national courts, and *gacaca*.

The divergence between the judges' and lawyers' understandings of transitional justice has led to competition among the concurrent courts at points of formal interaction seen in the tensions over the transfer of cases and the limitations in effective information sharing among the courts. For everyday Rwandans, the legitimacy of all three of the courts has been assessed in terms of a popular need to gain a better understanding of the conflict. Where the ICTR, the national courts, and *gacaca* were able to respond to this need, it reinforced the legitimacy of that particular post-genocide court. In addition, there was a tendency among the participants to criticize one court in terms of the actions of the others, challenging the general acceptance of all three of the courts' work. Formulating plural responses in dialogue with one another that nonetheless took seriously the articulated need for truth-telling could have reduced this competitive tendency.

7. Conclusion

This chapter argues that during transitions, legal institutions actively try to legitimate their authority and ascribe meaning to their actions in support of this process. In post-genocide Rwanda, the objectives of the international, national, and local courts have diverged during the course of their operation. As shown in the previous chapters, within each institution this divergence has often led to one court misunderstanding the work of the concurrent legal institutions. At points of formal interaction between the courts, the different interpretations of transitional justice have led to criticisms of the concurrent institutions and failures in effective collaboration. In short, the different ways in which courts have sought legitimacy simultaneously challenged the legitimacy of the other courts.

In addition, the divergence in what the courts have been trying to achieve, although clearly articulated inside the institutions, was not made by the general Rwandan participants. The group of participants subject to the authority of the post-genocide courts did not independently examine the actions and contributions of the international, national, and local courts. All three courts are assessed against what these participants have understood as important, emphasizing the need to provide information about the conflict.

The concurrent post-genocide courts have tried to independently establish their authority, while inside Rwanda, the processes of one court have led to criticisms of the other concurrent practices. The legitimacy of the ICTR, the national courts, and *gacaca* has depended on their combined ability to respond to the need for truth-telling in post-genocide Rwanda. Recognizing how the courts try to establish their authority can help to reduce the competition among international, national, and localized transitional justice processes through developing complementary processes to support and deepen each of the court's legitimacy in response to the needs of the affected population.

6 Conclusion

THIS CONCLUSION IS structured as follows: first, it provides a summary of the main findings of this study; second, it outlines the contribution of this work to a theory on the role of courts during transitions; and, finally, it discusses the specific policy relevance of this research for the practice of concurrent transitional justice and the ICC's principle of complementarity. This book adopts an interpretive approach in its examination of the multiple layers of justice in post-genocide Rwanda. It opened by mapping the trends, in both the case law and academic literature, toward using a series of concurrent or sequenced justice processes to respond to specific instances of extraordinary violence. With an increasing number of individual and collective objectives attached to these transitional justice practices and pressure to pursue criminal trials, an interpretive approach offers one route to account for the agency of the judges and lawyers involved in the resultant legal institutions. Pursuing a "thick description" of the courts' work enables an examination of which objectives have been prioritized and how the multiple institutions have interacted with one another.

Creating the basis for such a hermeneutical analysis, Chapter 1 examined the social and political context of Rwanda in the lead-up to, during, and after the 1994 genocide. In Rwanda the focus of transitional justice has been on the concurrent local, national, and international criminal courts set up to try those accused of violations of international criminal law during the civil war and genocide. The practice of these courts has been understood in a social context of a highly centralized state with only limited access to power, but the state's control is not as strong at the social margins of the country as it is described at the center.

Chapters 2, 3, and 4 examined the specific meanings attached to the actions of the ICTR, the Rwandan national courts, and *gacaca* within Rwanda's social context, during the transitional period following the genocide. What emerges from this cultural analysis is that inside each of these legal institutions the concurrent transitional justice processes have been ascribed very different and distinct objectives. The ICTR has been understood to contribute to the development of international criminal case law. The national judges and lawyers purport to have contributed to the development of improved legal capacity, and the actors within *gacaca* argue that the local courts have provided a means of gaining more information about the conflict and determining the guilt or innocence of specific individuals.

Crucially, within the courts, how one process is justified affects how the others are viewed and understood. Through empirical research inside the ICTR, the national courts, and *gacaca*, this book argues that how the courts understand their work elucidates aspects of their legal culture. It is through culture that a specific action is ascribed meaning. The actions of the ICTR, the national courts, and *gacaca* have been ascribed particular and different meanings within notably divergent cultural contexts. The interpretive processes of an internationally focused ICTR, a professionalizing national court, and a locally oriented and variable *gacaca* system, have shaped the social practice of law and of the legal institutions. Within each of the post-genocide courts, the personnel interpret the actions of the concurrent courts consistent with their own practice, leading to criticisms of the concurrent legal processes.

The outcome of the cultural incongruence of the three institutions has been direct competition and misunderstandings among the courts at points of formal transfer and information sharing. At points of informal contact, the competition among the ICTR, the national courts, and *gacaca* has challenged the legitimacy of these legal institutions. For a group of participants inside the Rwandan prisons, and those living in the broader post-genocide society, the practices of one court provided the basis for criticism of the other courts, eroding the courts' popular acceptance. In addition, the ICTR, the national courts, and *gacaca* were assessed against common criteria. The three courts were most regularly discussed in terms of their ability to contribute to a process of truth-seeking, including their capacity to determine the involvement of particular individuals in the violence, across social and political hierarchies. The legitimacy of post-genocide justice was understood in terms of all three courts' ability to respond to these needs.

This research shows that transitional justice processes must be designed in response to context-specific societal needs. If multiple processes are implemented in response to the needs of the affected population, it is imperative to try to prevent competing legal cultures developing in the concurrent systems. There is a need to ensure these "concurrent norm-generating communities"[1] engage in greater dialogue in an effort to create a unified culture of complementarity, where the objectives of one institution are understood, supported, and reinforced by the practice of the others. As discussed in the final section, fostering this "culture of complementarity" becomes increasingly important when looked at in light of the policy direction of transitional justice interventions and current practice of international criminal law by the ICC.

1. Developing Theory and the Study of Transitional Justice

While this research has embarked on "an elaborate venture in . . . thick description,"[2] the goal has been to establish a theory to explain the relevant behavior of the courts and their social agents. This conclusion will now provide a preliminary account of the legitimating behavior of courts during transitions and will then apply this theoretical explanation to the actions of Rwanda's post-genocide courts. Based on empirical research into the work of the ICTR, the national courts, and *gacaca*, this book proposes two theoretical contributions to the study of transitional justice.

The first contribution can be simply stated: in evaluating transitional justice "in-context," legal institutions' internal cultures can and should be taken into account. The objectives of transitional justice shape and are shaped by the practice of the legal institutions established to address them. Evaluating the legal culture of transitional justice institutions helps to explain courts' behavior and to assess their impact. Courts, as institutions with distinct cultures, matter, and should be taken seriously.

The second contribution is to highlight that, during transitions, legal institutions will actively try to establish their own legitimate authority. They ascribe meanings to their actions that support this process of legitimation. During transitions, courts play a dynamic role in shaping the objectives of a transitional justice process, and in doing so, actively try to secure their own legitimacy. The ICTR's, the national courts', and *gacaca's* active legitimating behavior helps to explain the formal interactions and points of competition among the concurrent courts. However, the divergence and disagreement among the courts has also challenged the belief in the legitimacy of all three of these legal institutions.

The ICTR has attempted to establish its legitimacy through focusing on the acquisition and exercise of its power in accordance with established rules. This is evident in the ICTR judges' and lawyers' clear and consistent focus on the case law. However, at points of transfer between the jurisdictions, as occurred under Rule 11 *bis*, the ICTR has assumed that the Rwandan national courts should have focused on

---

[1] Paul S. Berman, *Global Legal Pluralism: A Jurisprudence of Law beyond Borders* (Cambridge University Press 2014).

[2] Geertz 6.

the domestic application of international criminal case law. The research inside the national courts suggests that, according to the domestic judges and lawyers, this is not the case. In fact, the actions of the national courts have been oriented in a wholly different direction.

The national courts have endeavored to legitimate their power through focusing on improving legal expertise. The differing legitimating processes of the ICTR and the national courts have created a situation in which the Rwandan judges and lawyers expected that the genocide cases would be transferred from the ICTR, to support their own domestic capacity building. The ICTR personnel were explicit that their role was not to develop domestic capacity, and that the Rwandan national courts needed to demonstrate their previous clear and consistent application of international criminal law. More engagement between the courts' personnel during the operation of the ICTR and the national courts may have allowed a deeper understanding and appreciation of these differing means of legitimating legal authority.

Regarding *gacaca,* the attention of the national courts on legal expertise explains the pressure placed on *gacaca* to move toward increasing formalism, particularly when dealing with the Category 1 cases transferred from the national courts. At the same time, the ICTR's legitimation of its power through case law development resulted in an intentional distancing of the international court's proceedings from the local courts. Despite increasing reference to *gacaca* in the judgments of the ICTR, the international court did not make full and effective use of *gacaca's* capacity to gather information about the death of specific individuals during a period of mass violence.

The large number of *gacaca* courts across the country, each responding to local concerns, has led to substantial variance in *gacaca*'s practice. Inside *gacaca,* the focus of the courts on providing a full local account of the genocide produced continued criticisms of the ICTR for trying senior accused outside of the country. Similarly, the national courts were understood to be inaccessible and distant, impacting *gacaca's* formal interactions with the concurrent courts. As seen in the extradition cases heard in the UK, *gacaca's* process of legitimation, which relies on meeting immediate local needs has, at times, run counter to national or international interests as the local courts have acted independently from and in direct conflict with their national and international counterparts.

When formally interacting with one another, the courts' differing means of legitimation highlight why they have often competed with one another. This also suggests that cooperation could have been strengthened through more continued and equal contact among the differing legal institutions. However, contact between the legal actors within international, national, and local courts is insufficient to ensure complementary legitimating processes. A theory that, during transitions, courts will engage in an active process of trying to establish their legitimacy helps to explain how the ICTR, the national courts, and *gacaca* have interacted with one another. However, this theory does not fully explain the legitimacy of any one of these courts inside Rwanda.

A concurrent system of transitional justice will be assessed against local needs and interests in a particular country context. In Rwanda, the legitimacy of all three of the courts depends on their capacity to establish a full account of how and why the violence occurred. Where the ICTR, the national courts, and *gacaca* were, at least in part, focused on collectively providing this account through plural processes, it re-enforced the legitimacy of all three of the courts' actions and reduced the potential for popular critique of the courts.

2. Policy Implications for Concurrence and Complementarity

As introduced at the start of this book, in the current practice of transitional justice there is an assumption that "if a little is good, a lot must be better." Different transitional justice processes increasingly operate in a single-country context, each designed to respond to myriad needs at different levels of society. The findings of this research have important implications for the increasing use of multi-tiered approaches to transitional justice. The prevalence of international, national, and localized responses to extraordinary violence is particularly prevalent across a number of African states. For example in Sierra Leone, following the implementation of both a hybrid international tribunal and a truth commission, there is now the implementation of localized accountability processes.[3] Similarly, in Kenya, broad constitutional reforms have run in conjunction with a truth commission and the trial of senior officials by the ICC.[4]

Supporting this "holistic" approach to transitional justice, recent large quantitative studies have advocated for a "justice balance," arguing that transitional justice processes positively correlate with advances in human rights and democracy when they combine two sets of mechanisms: amnesties and trials; or amnesties, trials, and truth commissions.[5] What is clear is that there is an increasingly dominant move to institute multiple transitional justice processes within single-country contexts. This preference for a multi-institutional approach to transitional justice is similarly supported by the current structure of international criminal justice, and the implication of this Rwandan research for the work of the ICC warrants discussion.

---

[3] Martien Schotsmans, "'Blow Your Mind and Cool Your Heart': Can Tradition-Based Justice Fill the Transitional Justice Gap in Sierra Leone?" in Nicola Palmer, Phil Clark, and Danielle Granville (eds), *Critical Perspectives in Transitional Justice* (Intersentia 2012); and Andrew R. Iliff, "Root and Branch: Discourses of 'Tradition' in Grassroots Transitional Justice" (2012) 6 International Journal of Transitional Justice.

[4] Stephen Brown and Chandra Lekha Sriram, "The Big Fish Won't Fry Themselves: Criminal Accountability for Post-election Violence in Kenya" (2014) 111 African Affairs 244; Lydiah Kemunto Bosire and Gabrielle Lynch, "Kenya's Search for Truth and Justice: The Role of Civil Society" (2014) 8 International Journal of Transitional Justice 256.

[5] Olsen, Payne, and Reiter.

As noted, within the structure of the ICC, the principle of complementarity is generally understood to establish the Court as a subsidiary to national jurisdictions through Article 17 of the Rome Statute. However, in terms of its legal content, Article 17 is limited to determining whether a case is admissible before the ICC. Insofar as "complementarity" refers to the broader interplay and division of labor between national jurisdictions and the ICC, it is woven through many articles of the Statute, including Articles 1, 17, 18, 19, 20, 89(4), 90, 93(10), and 94.[6] While Antonio Cassese suggests that the principle was adopted to both encourage domestic prosecution of international crimes and to embed within the supra institution a level of respect for state sovereignty,[7] the practice of the Court suggests that neither of these two effects have been fully realized. The major outcome of complementarity has been overlapping prosecutions at the international and national levels.

For a case to be admissible at the international level, the Pre-Trial Chamber of the ICC must first determine whether the same case has been, or is being, investigated or prosecuted by a state with the necessary jurisdiction. In contrast to Cassese's suggestion that complementarity will encourage the domestic prosecution of international crimes, under the current case law, at the national level the conduct need not be charged as an international crime. However, the case must concern the same accused and "the substantially same conduct,"[8] including partial overlap on specific factual incidents. Once the Pre-Trial Chamber has determined that there are domestic proceedings in the same case, the Rome Statute requires an examination of whether the state is either "unwilling or unable"[9] to genuinely undertake these proceedings.

Sarah Nouwen argues that the ICC's reading of what constitutes a case, while sound in terms of the Statute, is underpinned by a broader "anti-impunity" push within the Court itself.[10] The same conduct/same person test means that

> if the ICC prosecutes a person who has been or is being investigated or prosecuted domestically for different conduct, or for the same conduct but [substantially]

---

[6] Darryl Robinson, "Three Theories of Complementarity: Charge, Sentence, or Process" (2012) 53 Harvard International Law Journal 166, 178.

[7] Cassese 351.

[8] *Prosecutor v William Samoei Ruto and Joshua Arap Sang,* (Judgment on the appeal of the Republic of Kenya against the decision of Pre-Trial Chamber II of 30 May 2011 entitled "Decision on the Application by the Government of Kenya Challenging the Admissibility of the Case Pursuant to Article 19(2)(b)) ICC-01/09-01/11, A Ch (30 August 2011): para. 47; *Prosecutor v Saif Al-Islam Gaddafi* (Judgment on the appeal of Libya against the decision of Pre-Trial Chamber I of 31 May 2013 entitled "Decision on the Admissibility of the Case against Saif Al-Islam Gaddafi") ICC-01/11-01/11 A Ch, (21 May 2014) para 72 and *Prosecutor v Abdullah Al-Senussi* (Judgment on the Appeal of Mr. Abdullah Al-Senussi against the decision of Pre-Trial Chamber I of 11 October 2013 entitled, "Decision on the Admissibility of the Case against Abdullah Al-Senussi"), ICC-01/11-01/11-57, A Ch, (24 July 2014) para 75.

[9] Rome Statute of the International Criminal Court (adopted July 17, 1998; entered into force July 1, 2002) 37 ILM 1002 art 17 (a).

[10] Nouwen 70.

different incidents, it does not compete with the national jurisdiction; all it does is to "complement" the national jurisdiction to ensure that there is less impunity.[11]

Darryl Robinson, in supporting the same person/same conduct reading of Article 17, argues that a "conviction for one crime . . . does not and should not legally insulate a person from future proceedings for a completely different crime."[12] When applying this interpretation of the law to instances of mass violence where an individual could be connected to multiple specific violent acts, this reading is strongly in line with the general anti-impunity drive noted by Nouwen.

The practical outcome of this approach is that there are increasing numbers of international and domestic criminal trials running concurrently. In addition, challenging an understanding of complementarity as embedding respect for state sovereignty in the working of the Court, the Court's reading of this aspect of complementarity constrains a state's domestic response to the violence in important ways. The ICC's interpretation of Article 17 establishes the Court as the driver in determining which individuals and which specific conduct will be prosecuted. In the context of wide-scale atrocity, often concerning multiple individuals acting in concert or independently, these prosecutorial choices are of central political and social importance. The current interpretation of Article 17 substantially reduces the exercise of domestic prosecutorial discretion by the state itself. Furthermore, in trying to meet the requirement that "the case that the State is investigating sufficiently mirrors the one that the Prosecutor is investigating,"[13] a state that wants to retain jurisdiction may drag its feet on submitting an admissibility challenge despite the requirement that such a challenge be filed "at the earliest opportunity."[14] This may explain why it took eleven months for the Libyan government to lodge an admissibility challenge in the case concerning Abdullah al-Senussi, allowing Libya an opportunity to ensure that its submission sufficiently mirrored the international institution's work.[15]

In supporting the Court's current reading of complementarity, Robinson suggests that multiple trials of a single individual, if undesirable, could be dealt with through a three-stage process: first, information sharing could occur in line with Articles 89 and 94;[16] second, any disagreement could be addressed through the general consultation

---

11 Ibid.

12 Robinson, "Three Theories of Complementarity: Charge, Sentence, or Process" 179.

13 *Prosecutor v Saif Al-Islam Gaddafi* (Judgment on the appeal of Libya against the decision of Pre-Trial Chamber I of 31 May 2013 entitled "Decision on the Admissibility of the case against Saif Al-Islam Gaddafi") ICC-01/11-01/11 A Ch, (21 May 2014) para. 73

14 Art. 19 (5) Rome Statute.

15 Kevin Jon Heller, "The PTC's Erroneous Decision regarding the Surrender of Al-Senussi" http://opiniojuris.org/2013/06/15/the-ptcs-terrible-decision-regarding-the-surrender-of-al-senussi/ accessed August 31, 2014.

16 Art. 89 (4) reads: "If the person sought is being proceeded against or is serving a sentence in the requested State for a crime different from that for which the Court is sought, the requested State, after making its

provision in Article 97;[17] and, finally, if this consultation is deemed to leave too much discretion in the hands of the ICC, State Parties could amend the Rules of Procedure and Evidence to establish guidelines for consultation and sequencing decisions.[18]

What becomes increasingly clear is that despite a shift from the primacy of the ICTR and the ICTY to complementarity under the ICC, responses to international crime continue to concern overlapping criminal trials conducted at both a domestic and international level, driven by the exercise of prosecutorial discretion at the international level. Continued contact between multiple institutions is a necessary and ongoing reality that has been given legal effect. In the current literature, consultation between the ICC and the state is identified as the major mechanism through which to resolve points of jurisdictional conflict. However, the examination of the Rwandan post-genocide courts suggests that once inside the institutions, the work of the courts is often driven by different objectives, heightening the possibility of misunderstanding and failures in effective cooperation.

Robinson's suggestion of providing guidelines for general consultation between the ICC and national jurisdictions, in an instance where there is an admissible case against a single individual at both the domestic and international level, may offer a legal space in which Drumbl's notion of *qualified deference,* which "creates a rebuttal presumption in favour of local or national institutions,"[19] may be given effect. Such an approach could provide one mechanism for taking more seriously the need to accommodate plural transitional justice objectives when pursing multiple responses to atrocity.

Yet, the cultural clashes evident in this research suggest that such interpretive guidelines would need to be accompanied by efforts to foster pluralism through procedures that enable communication among the different systems of justice. Following Paul Berman's notion of global legal pluralism,[20] and as result perhaps showing "a

---

decision to grant the request, shall *consult* with the Court." (emphasis added). Art. 94 reads: "If the immediate execution of a request interferes with an ongoing investigation or prosecution of a case different from that which the request relates, the requested State may postpone the execution of the request for a period of time agreed upon by the Court."

17 Art. 97 establishes that if a State Party "identifies problems that may impeded the execution of a request or prevent the exection of a request, the State shall consult with the Court."

18 Robinson, "Three Theories of Complementarity: Charge, Sentence, or Process" 181–182.

19 Drumbl, *Atrocity, Punishment and International Law and Policy* 188. According to Drumbl, the guidelines would include but not be limited to the following: an examination of the good faith or motivations of the legislators in determining the domestic law; an assessment of the democratic legitimacy of the process, in which Drumbl appears to describe a process broadly in line with David Beetham's account of legal, normative, and social legitimacy rather than a strict institutional reading of what constitutes a democracy; an assessment of the specific characteristics of the violence and the current political context; an assessment of institutional capacity in the country accompanied by an obligation to provide assistance if needed; an avoidance of gratuitous and iterated punishment; an assessment of the effect of the procedure on the universal substance, allowing for definitional difference up to the point of undermining the universally sanctioned wrong; and, the preclusion of the inflictions of great evils on others.

20 Berman 3.

Habermasian bias in favoring inclusion, participation, and conversation,"[21] formal communication procedures between international criminal justice and domestic accountability processes could allow decision-makers—whether prosecutors, judges, or defense counsel—to be more "uncomfortable in their knowledge of their own power, respectful of the legitimacy of competing legal systems and aware of the possibility that multiple meanings and divergent practices ought sometimes to be tolerated"[22] and better understood. The research conducted inside the Rwandan post-genocide courts shows that if cooperation is to be effective, any change to the law that seeks to realize the full potential of complementarity must actively engage with the legal cultures in which the courts' actions are embedded.

As discussed in this book, Rwanda provides an early example of concurrent criminal justice during a transitional period, with the ICTR exercising primacy over the domestic processes, but operating alongside extensive domestic prosecution before the national courts and *gacaca*. The empirical research into the work of these courts suggests that, at a policy level, it should not be assumed that additional and varied transitional justice processes produce better overall outcomes. The courts will shape the objectives of the process during the course of their operation and will simultaneously seek their own institutional legitimacy. If there is not clear and consistent communication between the different tiers of transitional justice, then the outcome may be that the courts and institutions, rather than complementing one another, will in fact compete.

To mitigate against this potential for competition, this research recommends that if multiple international and domestic justice processes are implemented in the same country, there must be direct, equal, and continued contact between the judicial and legal officers in each of the institutions. It is misguided and potentially damaging to assume that local, national, and international processes, which do not challenge each other jurisdictionally, will automatically complement one another in practice. While supporting the value of developing guidelines for cooperation, it is simultaneously necessary to develop a unified "culture of complementarity" in which different courts are responsive to one another and to the citizens over whom they have authority. A global order of criminal justice can only work if there is more effective debate and criticism among the concurrent legal systems, driven by the needs of affected populations.

---

21 Paul S. Berman, "How Legal Pluralism Is and Is Not Distinct from Liberalism: A Response to Alexis Galán and Dennis Patterson" (2013) 11 International Journal of Constitutional Law 801, 804.

22 Ibid.

APPENDIX I

Interview Schedule

INTERVIEWS AT THE ICTR

- Interview with ICTR Registry Staff (Participant 1), UN ICTR (Arusha, Tanzania, July 3, 2008) notes on file with author.
- Interview with Senior Legal Officer (Participant 2), Chambers, UN ICTR (Arusha, Tanzania, July 4, 2008) notes on file with author.
- Interview with Legal Officer (Participant 3), Chambers, UN ICTR (Arusha, Tanzania, July 7, 2008) notes on file with author.
- Interview with Trial Chamber Judge (Participant 4), Chambers, UN ICTR (Arusha, Tanzania, July 9, 2008) notes on file with author.
- Interview with Prosecutions Investigator (Participant 5), OTP, UN ICTR (Arusha, Tanzania, July 10, 2008) notes on file with author.
- Interview with Appeals Council (Participant 6), OTP, UN ICTR (Arusha, Tanzania, July 11, 2008) notes on file with author.
- Interview with Legal Officer (Participant 7), Chamber, UN ICTR (Arusha, Tanzania, July 15, 2008) notes on file with author.
- Interview with Trial Chamber Judge (Participant 8), Chambers, UN ICTR (Arusha, Tanzania, July 14, 2008) notes and recording on file with author.
- Interview with Senior Defence Council (Participant 9), Defence, UN ICTR (Arusha, Tanzania, July 15, 2008) notes and recording on file with author.
- Interview with Senior Trial Attorney (Participant 10), OTP, UN ICTR (Arusha, Tanzania, July 15, 2008) notes and recording on file with author.
- Interview with Appeals Council (Participant 11), OTP, UN ICTR (Arusha, Tanzania, July 17, 2008) notes on file with author.

- Interview with Appeals Council (Participant 12), OTP, UN ICTR (Arusha, Tanzania, July 17, 2008) notes on file with author.
- Interview with Appeals Council (Participant 13), OTP, UN ICTR (Arusha, Tanzania, July 25, 2008) notes on file with author.
- Interview with Trial Attorney (Participant 14), OTP, UN ICTR (Arusha, Tanzania, July 17, 2008) notes on file with author.
- Interview with Senior Defence Council (Participant 15), Defence, UN ICTR (Arusha, Tanzania, July 15, 2008) notes and recording on file with author.
- Interview with Senior Defence Council (Participant 16), Defence, UN ICTR (Arusha, Tanzania, July 15, 2008) notes and recording on file with author.
- Interview with Defence Investigator (Participant 17), Defence, UN ICTR (Arusha, Tanzania, September 12, 2008) notes on file with author.
- Interview with Legal Assistant (Participant 18), Defence, UN ICTR (Arusha, Tanzania, July 18, 2008) notes and recording on file with author.
- Interview with Associate Legal Officer (Participant 19), Chambers, UN ICTR (Arusha, Tanzania, July 17, 2008) notes on file with author.
- Interview with Senior Trial Attorney (Participant 20), OTP, UN ICTR (Arusha, Tanzania, July 24, 2008 and March 26, 2012) notes on file with author.
- Interview with Trial Chamber Judge (Participant 21), Chambers, UN ICTR (Arusha, Tanzania, July 25, 2008) notes and recording on file with author.
- Interview with Senior Trial Attorney (Participant 22), OTP, UN ICTR (Arusha, Tanzania, September 9, 2008 and March 26, 2012) notes on file with author.
- Interview with Trial Attorney (Participant 23), OTP, UN ICTR (Arusha, Tanzania, July 25, 2008) notes on file with author.
- Interview with Registry Staff (Participant 24), UN ICTR (Arusha, Tanzania, September 11, 2008) notes on file with author.
- Informal Discussion with a Trial Chamber Judge (Participant 25), Chambers, UN ICTR (Kigali, Rwanda, September 8, 2008) notes on file with author.
- Interview with Senior Trial Attorney (Participant 26), OTP, UN ICTR (Arusha, Tanzania, September 11, 2008) notes on file with author.
- Interview with Associate Legal Officer (Participant 27), Chambers, UN ICTR (Arusha, Tanzania, September 11, 2008) notes on file with author.
- Interview with Trial Chamber Judge (Participant 28), Chambers, UN ICTR (Arusha, Tanzania, September 12, 2008) notes on file with author.
- Interview with Defence Council (Participant 29), Defence, UN ICTR (Arusha, Tanzania, September 12, 2008) notes and recording on file with author.
- Interview with Trial Attorney (Participant 30), OTP, UN ICTR (Arusha, Tanzania, September 17, 2008) notes on file with author.
- Informal discussion with Defence Investigator (Participant 31), Defence, UN ICTR (Arusha, Tanzania, July 30, 2008) notes on file with author.
- Informal discussion with Associate Legal Officer (Participant 32), Chambers, UN ICTR (Arusha, Tanzania, July 17, 2008) notes on file with author.
- Interview with Legal Officer (Participant 33), Chambers, UN ICTR (Arusha, Tanzania, September 11, 2008) notes on file with author.
- Interview with Senior Trial Attorney (Participant 34) OTP, UN ICTR (Arusha, Tanzania, December 1, 2008) notes on file with author.

- Interview with Senior Defence Council (Participant 35), Defence, UN ICTR (Arusha, Tanzania, February 24, 2009) notes on file with author.
- Interview with Witnesses and Victims Support Staff (Participant 36) (Arusha, Tanzania, March 22, 2012) notes on file with author.
- Interview with Senior Trial Attorney (Participant 37) OTP, UN ICTR (Arusha, Tanzania, March 27, 2012) notes on file with author.
- Interview with Trial Chamber Judge (Participant 38) Chambers, UN ICTR (Arusha, Tanzania, March 27, 2012) notes on file with author.
- Interview with Senior Defence Council (Participant 39) Defence, UN ICTR (Arusha, Tanzania, March 27, 2012) notes on file with author.
- Interview with Senior Defence Council (Participant 40) Defence, UN ICTR (Arusha, Tanzania, March 27, 2012) notes on file with author.

INTERVIEWS AT THE RWANDAN NATIONAL COURTS

- Interview with National Court Administrator (Participant 1) Supreme Court (Kigali, Rwanda, August 5, 2008) interview conducted in conjunction with P. Clark, notes and recording on file with author.
- Interview with National Prosecutor (Participant 2), Parquet Général (Kigali, Rwanda, August 13, 2008) notes on file with author.
- Interview with National Court Judge (Participant 3) Supreme Court (Kigali, Rwanda, August 7, 2008) interview conducted in conjunction with P. Clark, notes and recording on file with author.
- Interview with National Prosecutor (Participant 4), Parquet Général (Kigali, Rwanda, August 13, 2008 and March 17, 2009) notes and recording on file with author.
- Interview with National Prosecutor (Participant 5) Parquet Général (Kigali, Rwanda, August 13, 2008) notes on file with author.
- Interview with Private Lawyer (Participant 6) (Regional, Rwanda, August 27, 2008) notes on file with author.
- Interview with former National Court Judge (Participant 7), Ministry of Justice (Kigali, Rwanda, September 3, 2008) interview conducted in conjunction with P. Clark, notes on file with author.
- Interview with National Prosecutor (Participant 8), Parquet Général (Kigali, Rwanda, August 14, 2008) notes on file with author.
- Interview with National Prosecutor (Participant 9), Parquet Général (Kigali, Rwanda, September 5, 2008) interview conducted with P. Clark, notes on file with author.
- Interview with Provincial Prosecutor (Participant 10), (Northern Province, Rwanda, August 27, 2008) interview conducted with P. Clark, notes on file with author.
- Interview with Private Lawyer (Participant 11) (Regional, Rwanda, August 27, 2008) interview conducted with P. Clark, notes on file with author.
- Interview with National Court Judge (Participant 12) High Court (Regional, Rwanda, August 27, 2008) interview conducted in conjunction with P. Clark, notes on file with author.
- Interview with Private Lawyer (Participant 13) Rwandan Bar (Regional, Rwanda, August 28, 2008) interview conducted with P. Clark, notes on file with author.
- Interview with National Prosecutor (Participant 14), Parquet Général (Kigali, Rwanda, March 17, 2009) notes on file with author.

- Interview with Provincial Prosecutor (Participant 15), (Western Province, Rwanda, April 17, 2009) interview conducted with P. Clark, notes on file with author.
- Interview with National Court Judge (Participant 16) High Court (Regional, Rwanda, April 23, 2009) interview conducted with P. Clark, notes on file with author.
- P. Clark, Interview with Private Lawyer (Participant 17) Rwandan Bar (Kigali, Rwanda, April 15, 2010).
- P. Clark, Interview with Private Lawyer (Participant 18) (Kigali, Rwanda, April 15, 2010).
- P. Clark, Interview with Private Lawyer (Participant 19) (Kigali, Rwanda, April 15, 2010).
- P. Clark, Interview with National Court Judge (Participant 20) High Court (Kigali, Rwanda, April 14, 2010), notes on file with author.
- P. Clark, Interview with Private Lawyer (Participant 21) Institute for Legal Practice (Kigali, Rwanda, April 14, 2010).
- P. Clark, Interview with National Court Judge (Participant 22) High Court (Kigali, Rwanda, April 14, 2010), notes on file with author.
- Interview with Witness Protection Staff Member (Participant 23), Parquet Général (Kigali, Rwanda, April 5, 2012) notes on file with author.
- Interview with Private Lawyer (Participant 24) Rwandan Bar Association (Kigali, Rwanda, April 9, 2012).

INTERVIEWS AT THE *GACACA* COURTS

- Interview with National Service for *Gacaca* Courts Personnel (Participant 1), (Kigali, Rwanda, August 14, 2008) interview conducted with P. Clark, recording and notes on file with author.
- Interview with Fatuma Ndangiza, Executive Secretary, National Unity and Reconciliation Commission (Participant 2) (Kigali, Rwanda, August 6, 2008).
- Interview conducted in conjunction with P. Clark, notes and recording on file with author.
- Interview with National Service for *Gacaca* Courts Personnel (Participant 3) (Kigali, Rwanda, August 7, 2008 and February 25, 2009) interview conducted with P. Clark, notes on file with author.
- Interview with Good Governance and Unity Director, Local Government (Participant 4) (Northern Province, August 28, 2008) interview conducted with P. Clark, notes on file with author.
- Interview with National Service for *Gacaca* Courts Personnel (Participant 5) (Rwanda, April 28, 2008) interview conducted in conjunction with P. Clark, notes on file with author.
- Interview with *Inyangamugayo* (Participant 6) (Rural District, Northern Province, Rwanda, August 29, 2008) interview conducted in conjunction with P. Clark, notes on file with author.
- Interview with *Inyangamugayo* (Participant 7) (Rural District, Northern Province, Rwanda, August 29, 2008) interview conducted in conjunction with P. Clark, notes on file with author.
- Interview with *Inyangamugayo* (Participant 8) (Rural District, Northern Province, Rwanda, September 2, 2008).
- Interview with *Inyangamugayo* (Participant 9) (Rural District, Northern Province, Rwanda, September 2, 2008).
- Interview with *Inyangamugayo* (Participant 10) (Rural District, Northern Province, Rwanda, September 2, 2009) notes on file with author.

- Interview with *Gacaca* participant (Participant 11) (Rural District, Northern Province, Rwanda, September 2, 2009) notes on file with author.
- Interview with *Inyangamugayo* (Participant 12) (Rural District, Northern Province, Rwanda, September 2, 2009) notes on file with author.
- Interview with *Inyangamugayo* (Participant 13) (Rural District, Northern Province, Rwanda, September 2, 2009) notes on file with author.
- Interview with National Service for *Gacaca* Courts Personnel (Participant 14) (Kigali, Rwanda, March 2, 2009) notes on file with author.
- Interview with *Inyangamugayo* (Participant 15) (Kigali, Rwanda, March 10, 2009) notes on file with author.
- Informal discussion with National Service for *Gacaca* Courts Legal Officer (Participant 16) (Kigali, Rwanda, February 27, 2009) notes on file with author.
- Informal discussion with National Service for *Gacaca* Courts Legal Officer (Participant 17) (Kigali, Rwanda, March 2–3, 2009) notes on file with author.
- Informal discussion with National Service for *Gacaca* Courts Legal Officer (Participant 18) (Kigali, Rwanda, March 4–5, 2009) notes on file with author.
- Informal discussion with National Service for *Gacaca* Courts Legal Officer (Participant 19) (Kigali, Rwanda, March 5, 2009) notes on file with author.
- Informal discussion with National Service for *Gacaca* Courts Legal Officer (Participant 20) (Kigali, Rwanda, March 9, 2009) notes on file with author.
- Informal discussion with National Service for *Gacaca* Courts Legal Officer (Participant 21) (Kigali, Rwanda, March 11, 2009) notes on file with author.
- Interview with National Service for *Gacaca* Courts Personnel (Participant 22) (Kigali, Rwanda, March 11, 2009) notes on file with author.
- Informal discussion with National Service for *Gacaca* Courts Legal Officer (Participant 23) (Kigali, Rwanda, March 16, 2009) notes on file with author.
- Informal discussion with National Service for *Gacaca* Courts Legal Officer (Participant 24) (Kigali, Rwanda, March 3, 2009) notes on file with author.
- Informal discussion with National Service for *Gacaca* Courts Legal Officer (Participant 25) (Kigali, Rwanda, March 16, 2009) notes on file with author.
- Interview with *Inyangamugayo* (Participant 26) (Rural District, Northern Province, Rwanda, March 20, 2009) notes on file with author.
- Interview with *Inyangamugayo* (Participant 27) (Rural District, Northern Province, Rwanda, March 20, 2009) notes on file with author.
- Interview with *Inyangamugayo* (Participant 28) (Rural District, Northern Province, Rwanda, March 20, 2009) notes on file with author.
- Interview with *Inyangamugayo* (Participant 29) (Rural District, Northern Province, Rwanda, March 20, 2009) notes on file with author.
- Interview with *Inyangamugayo* (Participant 30) (Rural District, Northern Province, Rwanda, March 20, 2009) notes on file with author.
- Interview with *Inyangamugayo* (Participant 31) (Rural District, Northern Province, Rwanda, March 20, 2009) notes on file with author.
- Interview with *Inyangamugayo* (Participant 32) (Rural District, Northern Province, Rwanda, March 20, 2009) notes on file with author.

- Interview with *Inyangamugayo* (Participant 33) (Rural District, Northern Province, Rwanda, March 20, 2009) notes on file with author.
- Interview with *Inyangamugayo* (Participant 34) (Rural District, Northern Province, Rwanda, March 21, 2009) notes on file with author.
- Interview with *Inyangamugayo* (Participant 35) (Rural District, Northern Province, Rwanda, March 21, 2009) notes on file with author.
- Interview with *Inyangamugayo* (Participant 36) (Rural District, Northern Province, Rwanda, March 21, 2009) notes on file with author.
- Interview with *Inyangamugayo* (Participant 37) (Rural District, Northern Province, Rwanda, March 21, 2009) notes on file with author.
- Interview with *Inyangamugayo* (Participant 38) (Kigali, Rwanda, March 21, 2009) notes on file with author.
- Interview with *Inyangamugayo* (Participant 39) (Kigali, Rwanda, March 26, 2009) notes on file with author.
- Interview with *Inyangamugayo* (Participant 40) (Kigali, Rwanda, March 26, 2009) notes on file with author.
- Interview with *Inyangamugayo* (Participant 41) (Rural District, Western Province, Rwanda, March 26, 2009) notes on file with author.
- Interview with *Inyangamugayo* (Participant 42) (Rural District, Western Province, Rwanda, March 26, 2009) notes on file with author.
- Interview with *Inyangamugayo* (Participant 43) (Rural District, Western Province, Rwanda, March 26, 2009) notes on file with author.
- Interview with *Inyangamugayo* (Participant 44) (Rural District, Western Province, Rwanda, March 26, 2009) notes on file with author.
- Interview with *Inyangamugayo* (Participant 45) (Rural District, Western Province, Rwanda, March 26, 2009) notes on file with author.
- Interview with *Inyangamugayo* (Participant 46) (Rural District, Western Province, Rwanda, March 26, 2009) notes on file with author.
- Interview with *Inyangamugayo* (Participant 47) (Rural District, Western Province, Rwanda, April 24, 2009) notes on file with author.
- Informal discussion with *Inyangamugayo* (Participant 48) (Rural District, Northern Province, Rwanda, April 15, 2009) notes on file with author.
- Focus group with *Inyangamugayo* (Rural District, Western Province, Rwanda, April 24, 2009) notes on file with author.
- Focus group with *Inyangamugayo* (Rural District, Northern Province, Rwanda, March 20, 2009) notes on file with author.
- Interview with *Inyangamugayo* (Participant 49) (Rural District, Southern Province, Rwanda, April 9, 2012) notes on file with author.
- Interview with *Inyangamugayo* (Participant 50) (Rural District, Southern Province, Rwanda, April 12, 2012) notes on file with author.

INTERVIEWS AT THE RWANDAN PRISONS

- Interview with Leopold (Participant 1) (Northern Province, Rwanda, September 5, 2009) notes on file with author.

- Interview with Ascel (Participant 2) (Northern Province, Rwanda, September 5, 2009) notes on file with author.
- Interview with Apollinaire (Participant 3) (Northern Province, Rwanda, September 5, 2008) notes on file with author.
- Interview with Michel (Participant 4) (Northern Province, Rwanda, September 5, 2008) notes on file with author.
- Interview with Victoire (Participant 5) (Northern Province, Rwanda, September 5, 2008) notes on file with author.
- Interview with Marie (Participant 6) (Kigali, Rwanda, April 16, 2009) notes on file with author.
- Interview with Céléstin (Participant 7) (Kigali, Rwanda, April 16, 2009) notes on file with author.
- Interview with André (Participant 8) (Kigali, Rwanda, April 20, 2009) notes on file with author.
- Interview with Alphonse (Participant 9) (Kigali, Rwanda, April 20, 2009) notes on file with author.
- Interview with Jean-Baptiste (Participant 10) (Kigali, Rwanda, April 20, 2009) notes on file with author.
- Interview with Aloys (Participant 11) (Kigali, Rwanda, April 20, 2009) notes on file with author.
- Interview with Evaliste (Participant 12) (Western Province, Rwanda, April 21, 2009) notes on file with author.
- Interview with Eugéne (Participant 13) (Western Province, Rwanda, April 21, 2009) notes on file with author.
- Interview with Silvestre (Participant 14) (Western Province, Rwanda, April 21, 2009) notes on file with author.
- Interview with Proper (Participant 15) (Western Province, Rwanda, April 21, 2009) notes on file with author.
- Interview with Athanase (Participant 16) (Western Province, Rwanda, April 21, 2009) notes on file with author.
- Interview with Ngabo (Participant 17) (Western Province, Rwanda, April 21, 2009) notes on file with author.

INTERVIEWS WITH GENERAL RWANDAN PARTICIPANTS

- Interview with *gacaca* participant (Participant 1) (Kigali, Rwanda, March 7, 2009) notes on file with author.
- Informal discussion with *gacaca* participant (Participant 2) (Kigali, Rwanda, March 14, 2009) notes on file with author.
- Informal discussion with *gacaca* participant (Participant 3) (Kigali, Rwanda, March 14, 2009) notes on file with author.
- Informal discussion with *gacaca* participant (Participant 4) (Kigali, Rwanda, March 14, 2009) notes on file with author.
- Informal discussion with *gacaca* participant (Participant 5) (Kigali, Rwanda, March 14, 2009) notes on file with author.

- Informal discussion with *gacaca* participant (Participant 6) (Rural District, Northern Province, Rwanda, April 1, 2009) notes on file with author.
- Informal discussion with *gacaca* participant and member of IBUKA (Participant 7) (Northern Province, Rwanda, April 1, 2009) notes on file with author.
- Informal discussion with *gacaca* participant and member of IBUKA (Participant 8) (Northern Province, Rwanda, April 1, 2009) notes on file with author.
- Informal discussion with *gacaca* participant (Participant 9) (Rural District, Northern Province, Rwanda, April 1, 2009) notes on file with author.
- Interview with *gacaca* participant (Participant 10) (Rural District, Northern Province, Rwanda, April 1, 2009) notes on file with author.
- Informal discussion with *gacaca* participant (Participant 11) (Rural District, Northern Province, Rwanda, April 1, 2009) notes on file with author.
- Informal discussion with *gacaca* participant (Participant 12) (Rural District, Northern Province, Rwanda, April 1, 2009) notes on file with author.
- Informal discussion with *gacaca* participant (Participant 13) (Rural District, Northern Province, Rwanda, April 1, 2009) notes on file with author.
- Interview with participant who declined to participate in *gacaca* (Participant 14) (Rural District, Northern Province, Rwanda, April 1, 2009) notes on file with author.
- Informal discussion with *gacaca* participant (Participant 15) (Rural District, Northern Province, Rwanda, April 15, 2009) notes on file with author.
- Interview with *gacaca* participant and member of IBUKA (Participant 16) (Kigali, Rwanda, March 19, 2009) notes on file with author.
- Informal discussion with *gacaca* participant (Participant 17) (Kigali, Rwanda, March 10, 2009) notes on file with author.
- Focus group with *gacaca* participants (Participants 18, 19, and 20) (Kigali, Rwanda, April 3, 2012) notes on file with author.
- Focus group with *gacaca* participants (Participants 21, 22, and 22) (Kigali, Rwanda, April 5, 2012) notes on file with author.
- Interview with *gacaca* participant (Participant 23) (Rural District, Huye District, April 9, 2012) notes on file with author.
- Interview with *gacaca* participant (Participant 24) (Rural District, Southern Province, April 10, 2012) notes on file with author.
- Interview with *gacaca* participant (Participant 25) (Rural District, Southern Province, April 10, 2012) notes on file with author.
- Interview with *gacaca* participant (Participant 26) (Rural District, Southern Province, April 10, 2012) notes on file with author.
- Interview with *gacaca* participant (Participant 27) (Rural District, Southern Province, April 10, 2012) notes on file with author.
- Interview with *gacaca* participant (Participant 28) (Rural District, Southern Province, April 10, 2012) notes on file with author.
- Interview with *gacaca* participant (Participant 29) (Rural District, Southern Province, April 10, 2012) notes on file with author.
- Interview with *gacaca* participant (Participant 30) (Rural District, Southern Province, April 10, 2012) notes on file with author.

- Focus group with *gacaca* participants (Participants 31, 32, 33, and 34) (Rural District, Southern Province, April 13, 2012) notes on file with author.
- Interview with *gacaca* participant (Participant 35) (Rural District, Southern Province, April 16, 2012) notes on file with author.
- Focus group with *gacaca* participants (Participants 36, 37, 38, 39, 40, 41, and 42) (Rural District, Southern Province, April 17, 2012) notes on file with author.
- Focus group with *gacaca* participants (Participants 43, 44, and 45) (Rural District, Southern Province, April 17, 2012) notes on file with author.

INFORMANT INTERVIEWS FOR CONTEXTUALIZING THE RESEARCH

- Interview with Karol Limondin, Head of Mission, The Danish Institute for Human Rights, (Kigali, Rwanda, August 20, 2008).
- Interview with Irenee Bugingo, Researcher, Institute for Research and Dialogue for Peace (Kigali, Rwanda, August 12 and 20, 2009).
- Interview with Apollinaire Mushinzimana, Researcher, Institute of Research and Dialogue for Peace (Kigali, Rwanda, August 20, 2008) interview conducted with P. Clark.
- Interview with Usta Kaitesi, Lecturer in Law, National University of Rwanda (Kigali, Rwanda, March 15, 2009).
- Interview with Appolinaire Mpumuro Kayitavu, Legal Aid Clinic Practitioner, Practice of Law, National University of Rwanda Date (Kigali, Rwanda, March 10, 2009).
- Interview with Elly Musafiri, Researcher, Centre for Conflict Management, National University of Rwanda (Kigali, Rwanda, March 10, 2009).

Glossary

BOURGMESTRE: mayor

CACHOTS COMMUNAUX: local prisons

CEKEKE: to hold your tongue; refers to people who refuse to speak at *gacaca* hearings

GACACA grass: refers to a community-level dispute resolution mechanism now implemented by the Rwandan government to hear genocide cases (pronounced ga-CHA-cha)

IBUKA: to remember; the word also refers to the largest organization of Rwanda genocide survivors

ICYITSO: accomplice

IMPUZAMUGAMBI: those with a single goal; refers to the youth militia of the CDR

INTERAHAMWE: those who work together; refers to the youth militia of the MRND and local killing groups

INYANGAMUGAYO: persons of integrity; refers to the laypersons who preside as judges over the *gacaca* hearings

INYENZI: cockroach; refers to the RPF during the civil war

KUBOHOZA: to free or liberate; refers to the practice of forcible recruitment into a political party

MWAMI: king

NYUMBAKUMI: head of ten households

UBUHAKE: form of voluntary vassalage

UMUHETO: an early practice by which individuals connected to the royal court would protect a kinship group's cattle in exchange for limited rights over the animals

UMUGANDA: community service

Bibliography

Akhavan P., "Beyond Impunity: Can International Criminal Justice Prevent Future Atrocities?" (2001) 95 The American Journal of International Law 7

Anderson B., *Imagined Communities: Reflections on the Origins and Spread of Nationalism* (Verso 1983)

Arendt H., *Eichmann in Jerusalem: A Report on the Banality of Evil* (Faber and Faber 1963)

Asmal K., "Truth, Reconciliation and Justice: The South African Experience in Perspective" (2000) 63 MLR 1

Barker R., *Legitimating Identities: The Self-Preservation of Rulers and Subjects* (Cambridge University Press 2001)

Beetham D., *The Legitimation of Power* (Jones P. and Weale A. eds, MacMillan 1991)

Berman P.S., "How Legal Pluralism Is and Is Not Distinct from Liberalism: A Response to Alexis Galán and Dennis Patterson" (2013) 11 International Journal of Constitutional Law 801

——, *Global Legal Pluralism: A Jurisprudence of Law beyond Borders* (Cambridge University Press 2014)

Betts A., "Should Approaches to Post-conflict Justice and Reconciliation Be Determined Globally, Nationally or Locally?" (2005) 17 The European Journal of Development Research 735

Bornkamm P.C., *Rwanda's* Gacaca *Courts: Between Retribution and Reparation* (Oxford University Press 2012)

Bosire L.K. and Lynch G., "Kenya's Search for Truth and Justice: The Role of Civil Society" (2014) 8 International Journal of Transitional Justice 256

Brown S. and Sriram C.L. "The Big Fish Won't Fry Themselves: Criminal Accountability for Post-election Violence in Kenya" (2014) 111 African Affairs

Burnet J.E., *Genocide Lives in Us* (The University of Wisconsin Press 2012)

——, "The Injustice of Local Justice: Truth, Reconciliation, and Revenge in Rwanda" (2014) 3 Genocide Studies and Prevention: An International Journal 173

Carothers T., "The End of the Transition Paradigm" (2002) 13 Journal of Democracy 5

Cassese A., *International Criminal Law* (Oxford University Press 2003)

Chakravarty A., "Navigating the Middle Ground: The Political Values of Ordinary Hutu in Post-Genocide Rwanda" (2014) 451 African Affairs 232

Clark P., "Hybridity, Holism, and 'Traditional' Justice: The Case of the *Gacaca* Courts in Post-genocide Rwanda" (2007) 39 The George Washington International Law Review 765

——, "Book Review: International Justice in Rwanda and the Balkans: Virtual Trials and the Struggle for State Cooperation" (2008) 22 Ethics and International Affairs 433

——, *The Gacaca Courts, Post-Genocide Justice and Reconciliation in Rwanda: Justice without Lawyers* (Cambridge University Press 2010)

Cobban H., "The Legacies of Collective Violence: The Rwandan Genocide and the Limits of Law" (2002) 27 Boston Review. http://new.bostonreview.net/BR27.2/cobban.html accessed November 26, 2014.

Corey A. and Joireman S.F., "Retributive Justice: The *Gacaca* Courts in Rwanda" (2004) 103 African Affairs 73

Crocker D.A., "Transitional Justice and International Civil Society: Toward a Normative Framework" (1998) 5 Constellations 492

Cruvellier T., *Court of Remorse: Inside the International Criminal Tribunal for Rwanda* (Voss C. tr, The University of Wisconsin Press 2010)

Cryer R. et al., *An Introduction to International Criminal Law and Procedure* (2nd edn, Cambridge University Press 2010)

Dallaire R., *Shake Hands with the Devil: The Failure of Humanity in Rwanda* (Carroll & Graf 2005)

de Lame D., "Mighty Secrets, Public Commensality, and the Crisis of Transparency: Rwanda through the Looking Glass" (2004) 38 Canadian Journal of African Studies

——, *A Hill Among a Thousand: Transformations and Ruptures in Rural Rwanda* (Arnold H. tr, University of Wisconsin Press 2005)

Des Forges A., "'The Drum Is Greater than the Shout': The 1912 Rebellion in Northern Rwanda" in Crummey D. (ed), *Banditry, Rebellion and Social Protest in Africa* (James Currey 1986)

——, *Leave None to Tell the Story: Genocide in Rwanda* (Human Rights Watch 1999)

Des Forges A. and Roth K. "Justice or Therapy?" (2002) 27 Boston Review. http://bostonreview.net/BR27.3/rothdesForges.html accessed March 10, 2011.

Drumbl M., "Rule of Law amid Lawlessness: Counselling the Accused in Rwanda's Domestic Genocide Trials" (1998) 29 Columbia Human Rights Law Review 545

——, *Atrocity, Punishment and International Law and Policy* (Cambridge University Press 2007)

Durrell L., *Balthazar (Alexandria Quartet)* (Penguin Books 1958)

Eltringham N., *Accounting for Horror: Post-Genocide Debates in Rwanda* (Pluto Press 2004)

Engle Merry S., "Legal Pluralism" (1988) 22 Law & Social Review 869

Falk Moore S., "Law and Social Change: The Semi-autonomous Social Field as an Appropriate Subject of Study" (1973) 7 Law and Society Review 70

Ferstman C., Goetz M., and Stephens A. (eds), *Reparations for Victims of Genocide, War Crimes and Crimes against Humanity* (Martinus Nijhoff Publishers 2009)

Fitzpatrick P., "Law and Societies" (1984) 22 Osgoode Hall Law Journal 115

Freeman M., *Truth Commissions and Procedural Fairness* (Cambridge University Press 2006)

Fujii L.A., *Killing Neighbors: Webs of Violence in Rwanda* (Cornell University Press 2009)

Gahima G., *Transitional Justice in Rwanda: Accountability for Atrocity* (Routledge 2013)

Galligan D.J., *Law in Modern Society* (Oxford University Press 2007)

Garland D., *Punishment and Modern Society: A Study in Social Theory* (Oxford University Press 1990)

Gasana J.K., "La Guerre, la paix et al Démocratie au Rwanda" in Guichaoua A. (ed), *Les Crises Politiques* (Karthala 1994)

Gasibirege S. and Babalola S., *Perceptions about the Gacaca Law in Rwanda: Evidence from a Multi-method Study* (Johns Hopkins University School of Public Health, Center for Communication Programs 2001)

Geertz C., "Thick Description: Toward an Interpretive Theory of Culture" in Geertz C. (ed), *The Interpretation of Cultures: Selected Essays* (Fontana Press 1993)

Glaser B.G. and Strauss A.L., *The Discovery of Grounded Theory: Strategies for Qualitative Research* (Aldine Pub 1967)

Gourevitch P., *We Wish to Inform You That Tomorrow We Will Be Killed with Our Families: Stories from Rwanda* (Farrar, Straus & Giroux 1998)

Hatzfeld J., *Into the Quick of Life: The Survivors Speak* (Feehily G. tr, Serpent's Tail 2005)

——, *The Strategy of Antelopes: Rwanda after the Genocide* (Serpent's Tail 2009)

Hayner P.B., *Unspeakable Truths: Facing the Challenge of Truth Commissions* (Routledge 2002)

Heller K.J., "A Sentenced-Based Theory of Complementarity" (2012) 53 Harvard International Law Journal 202

——, *The Nuremberg Military Tribunals and the Origins of International Criminal Law* (Oxford University Press 2011)

Hintjens H., "Reconstructing Political Identities in Rwanda" in Clark P. and Kaufman Z.D. (eds), *After Genocide: Transitional justice, Post-conflict Reconstruction and Reconciliation in Rwanda and Beyond* (Hurst 2008)

Huntington S.P., "The Third Wave: Democratization in the Late Twentieth Century" in Kritz N.J. (ed), *Transitional Justice: How Emerging Democracies Reckon with Former Regimes*, vol 1 (United States Institute of Peace 1991)

Iliff A.R., "Root and Branch: Discourses of 'Tradition' in Grassroots Transitional Justice" (2012) 6 International Journal of Transitional Justice 1

Ingelaere B., "Changing Lenses and Contextualizing the Rwandan (Post-) Genocide" in Reyntjens F. and Marysse S. (eds), *L'afrique Des Grands Lacs: Annuaire 2005–2006* (L'Harmattan 2006)

——, "'Does the Truth Pass across the Fire without Burning?' Transitional Justice and Its Discontents in Rwanda's Gacaca Courts" [2007] Institute for Development Policy and Management University of Antwerp Discussion Paper

——, "Living the Transition: A Bottom-Up Perspective on Rwanda's Political Transition" [2007] Institute for Development Policy and Management University of Antwerp Discussion Paper

——, "The Gacaca Courts in Rwanda" in Huyse L. and Salter M. (eds), *Traditional Justice and Reconciliation after Violent Conflict: Learning from African Experiences* (International Institute for Democracy and Electoral Assistance 2008)

——, "'Does the Truth Pass across the Fire without Burning?' Locating the Short Circuit in Rwanda's *Gacaca* courts" (2009) 47 Journal of Modern African Studies 507

——, *The Rise of Meta-conflict during Rwanda's* Gacaca *Process*, L'afrique Des Grands Lacs. Annuaire 2010–2011 (Reyntjens F., Marysse S. and Vandeginste S. eds, L'Harmattan 2011)

——, "Do We Understand Life after Genocide? Center and Periphery in the Construction of Knowledge in Postgenocide Rwanda" (2010) 53 African Studies Review 41

Jones B.D., *Peacemaking in Rwanda: The Dynamics of Failure* (Lynne Rienner 2001)

Jones N., *The Courts of Genocide: Politics and the Rule of Law in Rwanda and Arusha* (Routledge-Cavendish 2009)

Kagame A., *Le code des institutions politiques du Rwanda précolonial* (Belgian Royal Colonial Institute 1952)

Kamatali J.M., "The Challenge of Linking International Criminal Justice and National Reconciliation: The Case of the ICTR" (2003) 16 Leiden Journal of International Law 115

Karekezi U.A., Nshimiyimana A. and Mutamba B., "Localizing Justice: *Gacaca* Courts in Post-Genocide Rwanda" in Stover E. and Weinstein H.M. (eds), *My Neighbor, My Enemy: Justice and Community in the Aftermath of Mass Atrocity* (Cambridge University Press 2005)

Kaufman Z.D., "The United States Role in the Establishment of the United Nations International Criminal Tribunal for Rwanda" in Clark P. and Kaufman Z.D. (eds), *After Genocide: Transitional Justice, Post-conflict Reconstruction and Reconciliation in Rwanda and Beyond* (Hurst and Company 2008)

Kinzer S., *A Thousand Hills: Rwanda's Rebirth and the Man Who Dreamed It* (John Wiley 2008)

Kritz N.J., *Transitional Justice: How Emerging Democracies Reckon with Former Regimes* (United States Institute of Peace 1995)

Lemarchand R., *Rwanda and Burundi* (Pall Mall Press 1970)

——, "The Politics of Memory in Post-Genocide Rwanda" in Clark P. and Kaufman Z.D. (eds), *After Genocide: Transitional Justice, Post-conflict Reconstruction and Reconciliation in Rwanda and Beyond* (Hurst 2008)

Lessa F. and Payne L.A., *Amnesty in the Age of Human Rights Accountability* (Cambridge University Press 2012)

Loader I. and Mulcahy A., *Policing and the Condition of England: Memory, Politics and Culture* (Oxford University Press 2003)

Longman T., "Justice at the Grassroots? *Gacaca* Trials in Rwanda" in Roht-Arriaza N. and Mariezcurrena J. (eds), *Transitional Justice in the Twenty-First Century* (Cambridge University Press 2006)

——, "An Assessment of Rwanda's *Gacaca* Courts" (2009) 21 Peace Review: A Journal of Social Justice 304

Lutz E. and Sikkink K., "The Justice Cascade: The Evolution and Impact of Foreign Human Rights Trials in Latin America" (2001) 2 Chicago Journal of International Law 1

Mallinder L. and McEvoy K., "Rethinking Amnesties: Atrocity, Accountability and Impunity in Post-conflict Societies" (2011) 6 Contemporary Social Science: Journal of the Academy of Social Science 107

Mamdani M., *When Victims Become Killers: Colonialism, Nativism and the Genocide in Rwanda* (James Curry 2001)

Maquet J.J., *The Premise of Inequality in Ruanda* (Oxford University Press 1961)

McEvoy K., "Beyond Legalism: Towards a Thicker Understanding of Transitional Justice" (2007) 34 Journal of Law and Society 411

——, "A Commentary on Locality and Legitimacy" in Palmer N., Clark P. and Granville D. (eds), *Critical Perspectives in Transitional Justice* (Intersentia 2012)

McEvoy K. and Eriksson A., "Restorative Justice in Transition: Ownership, Leadership and 'Bottom-Up' Human Rights" in Sullivan D. and Tifft L. (eds), *Handbook of Restorative Justice: A Global Perspective* (Routledge 2006)

McEvoy K. and McGregor L., "Transitional Justice from Below: An Agenda for Research, Policy and Praxis" in McEvoy K. and McGregor L. (eds), *Transitional Justice from Below: Grassroots Activism and the Struggle for Change* (Hart Publishing 2008)

Melvern L., *Conspiracy to Murder: The Rwandan Genocide* (Verso 2004)

Mendez J.E., "Accountability for Past Abuses" (1997) 2 Human Rights Quarterly 255

Meyerstein A., "Between Law and Culture: Rwanda's *Gacaca* and Postcolonial Legality" (2007) 32 Law & Social Inquiry 467

Morris M.H., "The Trials of Concurrent Jurisdiction: The Case of Rwanda" (1996) 7 Duke Journal of Comparative and International Law 349

Morris V. and Scharf M.P., *The International Criminal Tribunal for Rwanda*, vol 1 (Transnational Publishers 1998)

Møse E., "Main Achievements of the ICTR" (2005) 3 Journal of International Criminal Justice 920

Nelken D., "Using the Concept of Legal Culture" (2004) 29 Australian Journal of Legal Philosophy 1

Newbury C., *The Cohesion of Oppression* (Columbia University Press 1988)

Newbury C. and Newbury D., "A Catholic Mass in Kigali: Contested Views of the Genocide and Ethnicity in Rwanda" (1999) 33 Canadian Journal of African Studies 292

Newbury D., "The Clans of Rwanda: An Historical Hypothesis" (1980) 50 Africa 389

——, "Precolonial Burundi and Rwanda: Local Loyalties, Regional Royalities" (2001) 34 International Journal of African Historical Studies 255

Newbury D. and Newbury C. "Bringing the Peasants Back In: Agrarian Themes in the Construction and Corrosion of Statist Historiography in Rwanda" (2000) 105 The American History Review 832

Ní Aoláin F. and Campbell C., "The Paradox of Transition in Conflicted Democracies" (2005) 27 Human Rights Quarterly 172

Nino C.S., "The Duty to Punish Past Abuses of Human Rights Put into Context: The Case of Argentina" (1991) 100 The Yale Law Journal 2619

Nouwen S.M.H., *Complementarity in the Line of Fire: The Catalysing Effect of the International Criminal Court in Uganda and Sudan* (Cambridge University Press 2013)

Nsanzuwera F.-X., "The ICTR's Contribution to National Reconciliation" (2005) 3 Journal of International Criminal Justice 944

Ntampaka C., "Le Gacaca Devenu une Justice aux Mains des Victimes" [1999] Umubano

Olsen T.D., Payne L.A., and Reiter A.G., *Transitional Justice in Balance: Comparing Processes, Weighing Efficiency* (U.S. Institute of Peace Press 2010)

Orentlicher D.F., "Settling Accounts: The Duty to Prosecute Human Rights Violations of a Prior Regime" (1991) 100 The Yale Law Journal 2537

Osiel M., *Mass Atrocity, Collective Memory and the Law* (Transaction Publishers 1997)

Palmer N., "Book Reviews: The Nuremberg Military Tribunals and the Origins of International Criminal Law" [2012] European Human Rights Law Review 246

——, "Transfer or Transformation?: A Review of the Rule 11 *bis* Decisions of the International Criminal Tribunal for Rwanda" (2012) 20 The African Journal of International and Comparative Law 1

Peskin V., "Courting Rwanda: The Promises and Pitfalls of the ICTR Outreach Programme" (2005) 3 Journal of International Criminal Justice 950

——, *International Justice in Rwanda and the Balkans: Virtual Trials and the Struggle for State Cooperation* (Cambridge University Press 2008)

Pillay N., "The Rwanda Tribunal and Its Relationship to National Trials in Rwanda" (1998) 13 American University International Law Review 1469

Polman L., *We Did Nothing: Why the Truth Doesn't Always Come Out When the UN Goes In* (Viking 2003)

Pozen J., Neugebauery R., and Ntaganira J., "Assessing the Rwanda Experiment: Popular Perceptions of *Gacaca* in Its Final Phase" (2014) 8 International Journal for Transitional Justice 22

Prunier G., *The Rwanda Crisis 1959–1994: History of the Genocide* (Hurst 1995)

——, "Opération Turquoise: A Humanitarian Escape from a Political Dead End" in Adelman H. and Suhrke A. (eds), *The Path of a Genocide: The Rwanda Crisis from Uganda to Zaire* (Transaction Publishers 1999)

——, *From Genocide to Continental War: The "Congolese" Conflict and the Crisis of Contemporary Africa* (Hurst Publishers 2009)

Rettig M., "*Gacaca*: Truth, Justice, and Reconciliation in Postconflict Rwanda?" (2008) 51 African Studies Review 25

Reydams L., "The ICTR Ten Years On: Back to the Nuremberg Paradigm?" (2005) 3 Journal of International Criminal Justice 977

Reyntjens F., "Le Gacaca ou la Justice du Gazon au Rwanda" [1990] Politique Africaine 31

——, *Rwanda: Trois jours qui ont fait basculer l'histoire* (Centre d'Etudes et de Documentation africaines 1995)

——, "Constitution-Making in Situations of Extreme Crisis: The Case of Rwanda and Burundi" (1996) 40 Journal of African Law 234

——, "Rwanda, Ten Years On: From Genocide to Dictatorship" (2004) 103 African Affairs 177

——, "Constructing the Truth, Dealing with Dissent, Domesticating the World: Governance in Post-Genocide Rwanda" (2011) 110 African Affairs 1

Rhodes R. and Bevir M., "Defending Interpretation" (2006) 5 European Political Science 69

Rimé B., Kanyangara P., Yzerbyt V., and Paez D., "The Impact of *Gacaca* Tribunals in Rwanda: Psychosocial Effects of Participation in a Truth and Reconciliation Process after a Genocide" (2011) 41 European Journal of Social Psychology 695

Roberts P. and McMillan N., "For Criminology in International Criminal Justice" (2003) 1 Journal of International Criminal Justice 315

Robinson D., "The Identity Crisis of International Criminal Law" (2008) 21 Leiden Journal of International Law 925

——, "Three Theories of Complementarity: Charge, Sentence, or Process" (2012) 53 Harvard International Law Journal 166

Rosen L., *Law as Culture: An Invitation* (Princeton University Press 2006)

Rudasingwa T., "The Rwanda Tribunal and Its Relationship to National Trials in Rwanda" (1998) 13 American University International Law Review 1484

Sarkin J., "The Tension between Justice and Reconciliation in Rwanda: Politics, Human Rights, Due Process and the Role of the *Gacaca* Courts in Dealing with the Genocide" (2001) 45 Journal of African Law 143

Sarkin J. and Daly E., "Too Many Questions, Too Few Answers: Reconciliation in Transitional Societies" (2004) 35 Columbia Human Rights Law Review 661

Schabas W., "Justice, Democracy, and Impunity in Post-Genocide Rwanda: Searching for Solutions to Impossible Problems" (1996) 7 Criminal Law Forum 523

——, *An Introduction to the International Criminal Court* (3rd edn, Cambridge University Press 2007)

——, "Post-Genocide Justice in Rwanda: A Spectrum of Opinions" in Clark P. and Kaufman Z.D. (eds), *After Genocide: Transitional Justice, Post-conflict Reconstruction and Reconciliation in Rwanda and Beyond* (Hurst and Company 2008)

Scharf M.P., "Responding to Rwanda: Accountability Mechanisms in the Aftermath of Genocide" (1999) 52 Journal of International Affairs 621

Schotsmans M., "'Blow Your Mind and Cool Your Heart': Can Tradition-Based Justice Fill the Transitional Justice Gap in Sierra Leone?" in Palmer N., Clark P., and Granville D. (eds), *Critical Perspectives in Transitional Justice* (Intersentia 2012)

Seligman C.G., *Races of Africa* (Thornton Butterworth 1930)

Shaw R., Waldorf L., and Hazan P., *Localizing Transitional Justice: Interventions and Priorities after Mass Violence* (Stanford University Press 2010)

Sikkink K., *The Justice Cascade: How Human Rights Prosecutions Are Changing World Politics* (Politics NSoW ed, WW Norton and Company 2011)

Sluiter G., "The ICTR and the Protection of Witnesses" (2005) 3 Journal of International Criminal Justice 962

Snyder J. and Vinjamuri L., "Trial and Error: Principle and Pragmatism in Strategies of International Justice" (2003) 28 International Security 5

Stahn C. and El Zeidy M.M., *The International Criminal Court and Complementarity: From Theory to Practice* (Cambridge University Press 2011)

Straus S., *The Order of Genocide: Race. Power, and War in Rwanda* (Cornell University Press 2006)

Straus S. and Waldorf L., "Introduction: Seeing Like a Post-conflict State" in Straus S. and Waldorf L. (eds), *Remaking Rwanda: State Building and Human Rights after Mass Violence* (University of Wisconsin Press 2011)

Teitel R.G., *Transitional Justice* (Oxford University Press 2000)

——, "Transitional Justice Genealogy" (2003) 16 Harvard Human Rights Journal 26

——, "The Law and Politics of Contemporary Transitional Justice" (2005) 38 Cornell International Law Journal 26

Thomson S.M., "'That Is Not What We Authorised You to Do . . .': Access and Government Interference in Highly Politicised Research Environments" in Sriram C.L. et al. (eds), *Surviving Field Research: Working in Violent and Difficult Situations* (Routledge 2009)

——, "Whispering Truth to Power: The Everyday Resistance of Rwandan Peasants to Post-Genocide Reconciliation" [2011] African Affairs 1

Thomson S.M. and Nagy R., "Law, Power and Justice: What Legalism Fails to Address in the Functioning of Rwanda's Gacaca Courts" (2011) 5 The International Journal of Transitional Justice 11

Tiemessen A.E., "After Arusha: *Gacaca* Justice in Post-Genocide Rwanda" (2004) 8 African Studies Quarterly 57

Uvin P. and Mironko C., "Western and Local Approaches to Justice in Rwanda" (2003) Global Governance 219

Vansina J., *Antecedents to Modern Rwanda: The Nyiginya Kingdom* (author Tbt tr, James Curry 2004)

Villa-Vicencio C., "Transitional Justice, Restoration, and Prosecution" in Sullivan D. and Tifft L. (eds), *Handbook of Restorative Justice: A Global Perspective* (Routledge 2006)

Wagner M., "All the Bourgmestre's Men: Making Sense of Genocide in Rwanda" (45)1 Africa Today 25

Waldorf L., "Mass Justice for Mass Atrocity: Rethinking Local Justice as Transitional Justice" (2006) 79 Temple Law Review 88

Wibabara C., Gacaca *Courts versus the International Criminal Tribunal for Rwanda and National Courts* (Nomos 2014)

Wilson R.A., "Judging History: The Historical Record of the International Criminal Tribunal for the Former Yugoslavia" (2005) 27 Human Rights Quarterly 908

——, *Writing History in International Criminal Trials* (Cambridge University Press 2011)

Zacklin R., "The Failings of Ad Hoc International Tribunals" (2004) 2 Journal of International Criminal Justice 541

Zalaquett J., "Confronting Human Rights Violations Committed by Former Governments: Principles Applicable and Political Constraints" in Kritz N.J. (ed), *Transitional Justice: How Emerging Democracies Reckon with Former Regimes* vol 1 (United States Institute of Peace 1995)

Zedner L., "Comparative Research in Criminal Justice" in Noaks L., Maguire M., and Levi M. (eds), *Contemporary Issues in Criminology* (University of Wales Press 1995)

TREATIES AND UNITED NATIONS RESOLUTIONS

African Charter on Human and Peoples' Rights (adopted June 27, 1981, entered into force October 21, 1986) 21 ILM 58 (ACHPR)

Convention on the Non-applicability of Statutory Limitations to War Crimes and Crimes against Humanity (adopted November 26, 1968, entered into force November 11, 1970) 754 UNTS 73

Convention for the Prevention and Punishment of the Crime of Genocide (adopted December 9, 1948, entered into force January 12, 1951) 78 UNTS 277

Geneva Convention Relative to the Protection of Civilian Persons in Time of War (adopted August 12, 1949, entered into force October 21, 1950) 75 UNTS 287 (Geneva Convention IV)

International Covenant on Civil and Political Rights (adopted December 16, 1966, entered into force March 23, 1976) 999 UNTS 171 (ICCPR)

Letter from the Permanent Representative of Rwanda Addressed to the President of the Security Council (September 28, 1994) UN Doc S/1994/1115

Protocol Additional to the Geneva Conventions of 12 August 1949, and Relating to the Protection of Victims of International Armed Conflicts (adopted June 8, 1977, entered into force December 7, 1978) 1125 UNTS 3

United Nations Security Council Resolution 912 (21 April 1994) UN Doc S/RES/912.

United Nations Security Council Resolution 955 (8 November 1994) Statute of the International Criminal Tribunal for Rwanda UN Doc S/INF/50

United Nations Security Council Resolution 1503 (28 August 2003) UN Doc. S/RES/1503.

ORGANIZATIONAL REPORTS

Amnesty International, "Rwanda—Unfair Trials: Justice Denied" (Report) (April 8, 1997) AI-Index AFR 47/08/197

Amnesty International, "Rwanda—The Troubled Course of Justice" (Report) (April 2000) AI-Index AFR 47/10/00

Amnesty International, "*Gacaca*: A Question of Justice" (Report) (December 2002) AI-Index AFR 47/007/2002

Avocats Sans Frontières, "Monitoring of the *Gacaca* Courts—Judgment Phase" (Analytical Report 3) October 2006–April 2007

International Crisis Group, "Five Years after the Genocide in Rwanda: Justice in question" (Report) (April 7, 1999)

M. Moussalli, "Report on the Situation of Human Rights in Rwanda" (Report) (February 25, 2000) Economic and Social Council E/CN.4/2000/41.

Penal Reform International, "*Gacaca* Jurisdictions and Its Preparations" (Research on Gacaca Report 1) (July–December 2001)

Penal Reform International, "The Guilty Plea Procedure, Cornerstone of the Rwandan Justice System" (Integrated Report on Gacaca Research and Monitoring Report 4) (January 2003)

Penal Reform International, "Pilot Phase" (Integrated Report on Gacaca Research and Monitoring Report 2) (December 2005)

Penal Reform International, "Eight Years On . . . A Record of *Gacaca* Monitoring in Rwanda" (Final Research and Monitoring Summary) (March 31, 2010)

Redress, "Report on Universal Jurisdictional Developments" (January 2006–May 2009) http://www.redress.org accessed October 1, 2009

Redress, "Testifying to Genocide: Victim and Witness Protection in Rwanda" Redress (October 2012) with P. Clark and N. Palmer http://www.redress.org/africa/rwanda accessed August 28, 2014.

Republic of Rwanda Office of the President, "Report on the Reflection Meetings Held in the Office of the President of the Republic from May 1998 to March 1999" (August 1999)

United Nations Office of the High Commission for Human Rights, "Report of the Mapping Exercise Documenting the Most Serious Human Rights and International Humanitarian Law Committed within the Territory of the Democratic Republic of the Congo between March 1993 and June 2003" (Report) (August 2010)

United States Department of State. "Rwanda Country Report on Human Rights Practices for 1998" (Report) (February 26, 1999)

WEBSITES AND PRINT JOURNALISM

Avocats Sans Frontières, Vade-Mecum: Le Crime de Genocide et les Crimes Contre L'Humanite devant les Juridictions Ordinaires du Rwanda [The Crime of Genocide and Crimes against Humanity in Rwanda's Courts] (2004) available at http://www.asf.be/fr/publication accessed January 13, 2011

Heller K.J., "The PTC's Erroneous Decision regarding the Surrender of Al-Senussi" http://opiniojuris.org/2013/06/15/the-ptcs-terrible-decision-regarding-the-surrender-of-al-senussi/ accessed August 31, 2014

International Centre for Transitional Justice (Vision and Mission Statement) http://ictj.org/about/vision-and-mission, accessed July 11, 2011

Jallow H., "Letter in Response to Kenneth Roth, Executive Director of Human Rights Watch" (22 June 2009 OTP/2009/P/084') http://www.hrw.org/sites/default/files/related_material/2009_06_Rwanda_Jallow_Response.pdf accessed August 31, 2009

Kinzer S., "Kagame's Authoritarian Turns Risk Rwanda's Future" Guardian (London 27 January 2011) http://www.guardian.co.uk/commentisfree/cifamerica/2011/jan/27/rwanda-freedom-of-speech accessed January 28, 2011

"Mpanga, a Stronghold for the UN in Rwanda" International Justice Tribune (5 May 2008) http://www.rnw.nl/international-justice/article/mpanga-stronghold-un-rwanda accessed July 10, 2011

Official website of the International Criminal Court http://www.icc-cpi.int/Menus/ASP/states + parties/ accessed October 12, 2010

Official website of the International Criminal Tribunal for Rwanda http://www.unicrt.org accessed April 1, 2011

Rice X., "Rwanda Election Set to Return Kagame as President" The Guardian (London 9 August) http://www.guardian.co.uk/world/2010/aug/09/rwanda-election-kagame-president accessed February 14, 2011.

Roth K., "Letter to the Prosecutor of the International Criminal Tribunal for Rwanda regarding the Prosecution of RPF Crimes" (May 26, 2009) http://www.hrw.org/node/83536 accessed August 31, 2009

"Rwandan Military Court Acquits Two Officers and Sentences Two Others (24 October 2008) http://www.hirondellenews.com/content/view/11594/291/ accessed March 7, 2011

"The Politics of Violence and Accountability in Kenya" (Oxford Transitional Justice Research Working Paper Series) <http://otjr.crim.ox.ac.uk/index.php/working-papers/current-debates/44-the-politics-of-violence-and-accountability-in-kenya.html> accessed 11 July 2011

"Uganda's First War Crimes Trial of LRA Commanders Opens" BBC World News (11 July 2011) http://www.bbc.co.uk/news/world-africa-14106941 accessed July 11, 2011

Table of Cases

Table of Statutes

Index

www.ingramcontent.com/pod-product-compliance
Ingram Content Group UK Ltd.
Pitfield, Milton Keynes, MK11 3LW, UK
UKHW012141150926
473393UK00012B/245

9 780190 941895